CULTIVATING CONFIDENCE
Verification, Monitoring, and Enforcement for a World Free of Nuclear Weapons

The NUCLEAR THREAT INITIATIVE
gratefully acknowledges
the following foundations
for their generous support of the
Nuclear Security Project and this book:

THE CARNEGIE CORPORATION OF NEW YORK
THE JOHN D. AND CATHERINE T. MACARTHUR FOUNDATION

CULTIVATING CONFIDENCE
Verification, Monitoring, and Enforcement for a World Free of Nuclear Weapons

EDITED BY

Corey Hinderstein

a publication of the
NUCLEAR THREAT INITIATIVE
Washington, D.C.

The Nuclear Threat Initiative (NTI) is a non-profit organization with a mission to strengthen global security by reducing the risk of use and preventing the spread of nuclear, biological, and chemical weapons, and to work to build the trust, transparency, and security which are preconditions to the ultimate fulfillment of the Non-Proliferation Treaty's goals and ambitions.

www.nti.org

A publication of the Nuclear Threat Initiative through the agency of the Hoover Institution Press.

Hoover Institution Press Publication No. 596
Hoover Institution at Leland Stanford Junior University,
Stanford, California, 94305-6010

First printing 2010
17 16 15 14 13 12 11 10   9 8 7 6 5 4 3 2 1

Manufactured in the United States of America

Library of Congress Cataloging-in-Publication Data
    Cultivating confidence : verification, monitoring, and enforcement for a world free of nuclear weapons / edited by Corey Hinderstein.
        p.   cm. — (Hoover Institution Press publication ; no. 596)
    Includes index.
    "A publication of the Nuclear Threat Initiative,"
    ISBN 978-0-8179-1205-5 (pbk. : alk. paper) —
    ISBN 978-0-8179-1206-2 (e-book)
    1. Nuclear nonproliferation. 2. Nuclear arms control. I. Hinderstein, Corey.
II. Nuclear Threat Initiative.
    JZ5675.C85 2010
    327.1'747—dc22   2010031849

Contents

Acknowledgments

The editor would like to express gratitude to the many people who provided support for this volume, offered comments on its contents, and assisted in its editing, proofreading, and design.

I would like to thank George Shultz, William Perry, Henry Kissinger, and Sam Nunn for providing leadership and guidance to the Nuclear Security Project, a project of the Nuclear Threat Initiative (NTI) in cooperation with the Hoover Institution. Very special thanks are due to the leadership of NTI, past and present, including President Joan Rohlfing, President Emeritus Charles B. Curtis, and Executive Vice President Deborah Rosenblum. I also would like to recognize Jayne Brady, Matthew Dupuis, Cathy Gwin, Laura Holgate, Carmen MacDougall, Lynn Rusten, Bryan Wilkes, and Isabelle Williams, all of whom in their different capacities at NTI supported the production of this volume and the work that served as its foundation.

I would also like to acknowledge the project consultants and paper reviewers who took the time to assess the technical and substantive content of the papers and help the authors improve them. These include David Albright, Trevor Findlay, Richard Hooper, Sally Horn, Ray Juzaitis, Peter Sawczak, and Lawrence Scheinman.

Very special thanks are offered to James W. Tape who provided guidance, review, and input throughout the development of the project and provided significant new thinking that is included and acknowledged in the introduction of this book.

Special thanks are also offered to Jennifer Presley and her colleagues at Hoover Institution Press and Michael Bass and his team at Michael Bass Associates who produced the final version of the book.

Finally, I would like to acknowledge the support of the John D. and Catherine T. MacArthur Foundation and the Carnegie Corporation of New York for their support of the Nuclear Security Project and this book.

Introduction

COREY HINDERSTEIN

In 2007, former secretaries of state George Shultz and Henry Kissinger, along with former secretary of defense William Perry and former senator Sam Nunn launched the Nuclear Security Project (NSP), a major initiative to galvanize global action on urgent nuclear issues. The NSP, through a broad range of activities, including analytic studies, builds on the January 4, 2007, *Wall Street Journal* op-ed coauthored by the four senior statesmen, linking the vision of a world free of nuclear weapons with concrete threat reduction steps that can and should be taken to reduce urgent nuclear dangers and build support for reducing reliance on nuclear weapons, ultimately ending them as a threat to the world. Over the past several years, the work of the four statesmen has reframed global debate on nuclear issues and garnered international support and promising cooperation. The Nuclear Threat Initiative (NTI), in cooperation with the Hoover Institution, coordinates the work of the Nuclear Security Project along with that of its four principals.

As part of its work, the NSP seeks to add to existing analytic work defining major mileposts on the path to disarmament by addressing gaps in both conceptual frameworks and technical details. This work in turn can be provided to government leaders as a blueprint for action on policymaking, arms control, and diplomacy to reduce nuclear dangers. Verification, the subject of this book, is one such area where meaningful work needs to be done. Notably, the study identifies key technical, political, and diplomatic challenges associated with the verification, monitoring, and enforcement of a world free of nuclear weapons and provides potential solutions to these challenges.

This volume comprises nine chapters written in 2009, each addressing specific topics within the area of verification, monitoring, and enforcement. Unifying themes, common to all subjects, include principal challenges or stumbling blocks; current technical limitations on what can be done and, in light of these, how best to inform decisions regarding further investments in research and technical analysis; the technical constraints on developing the kind of system required ultimately to achieve a world free of nuclear weapons; and, finally, developing the architecture for a verification system. This study is not intended to be comprehensive; rather, it discusses many of the key issues that will need to be understood and managed in order to move along the path toward a world free of nuclear weapons.

As a final note of introduction, this study has defined *verification* as the process of determining whether parties to an agreement are in compliance with their obligations; *monitoring* as the function of collecting, analyzing, and reporting data on the activities of the parties to an agreement; and *enforcement* as the ability of the international community, collectively or individually, to impose negative consequences on a violator of international norms or commitments. One of the reasons for these distinctions is that verification systems cannot be evaluated separately from the measures that they are meant to verify. A system of verification is meant to give confidence to interested parties that a particular set of commitments is being upheld. Because of this, it is always necessary to separate the verification, monitoring, and enforcement goals and to recall the sometimes disparate purposes that they serve.

Positive Findings

Perhaps the greatest reason for optimism on the challenge of verifying, monitoring, and enforcing a world free of nuclear weapons is, as we discovered through this study, that the international community already knows how to do much of what we anticipate will be needed to verify a world free of nuclear weapons.

So often, "verifiability" is the hook on which people who disagree with the end goal of a world free of nuclear weapons hang their objections. There are still many issues left to be addressed for which an appropriate research agenda will need to be developed and completed. It is gratifying, however, to note that the work over the last several decades within the scientific and technical community, as well as at the International Atomic Energy Agency (IAEA) and in other national and multilateral bodies, and implementation of existing arms control agreements have resulted in significant accomplishments. These achievements, in turn, bear directly on our ability to envision and scope a credible verification regime on the path to, and ultimately in, a world free of nuclear weapons.

Review of the chapters reveals a number of common elements. Focusing on a few of these elements helps us demonstrate why the current debate about verification produces new and different discussions than those held in previous years.

The first element is the "stakeholders" who will need to be defined during any discussion of verification regimes. Traditionally, the technical problems of arms control verification have been within the jurisdiction of technical experts in the nuclear weapon states as part of the implementation of arms control treaties. Decisions about acceptable risk were made by policymakers in those same states. In a world where states commit to a joint enterprise to work toward a world free of nuclear weapons, we recognize that *all states*, both nuclear and non–nuclear weapon states, have equities and responsibilities in the progress of disarmament efforts.

A second element is the classified nature of information and the implementation of information security. With respect to nuclear technology and nuclear weapons, the standards by which information is deemed to be classified may rest on potentially outdated assumptions about the unique value of the information and how it is shared. It may ultimately be more practical to share certain previously classified information than to develop complicated procedures designed to protect information no longer deemed sensitive. This is not to say that there is not an appropriate role for the protection of classified information, but rather to carefully review the underlying assumptions if sharing the information would be critical to the success of a future verification regime. The topic of why information is classified should not be an off-limits question, even if, in many cases, judgments on classification may remain the same.

A third element is determining compliance or noncompliance with new norms, legal obligations, or commitments. The papers do not discuss in depth the issue of determining noncompliance. In recent years, the agency responsible for detecting and reporting violations of nuclear safeguards agreements, the IAEA, has made some judgments related to the intent of violators in a way that may prejudice the consequences for the violator. This development has been encouraged by some and criticized by others. But it highlights the fact that compliance and noncompliance judgments are not always black-and-white. In the case of a world free of nuclear weapons, a noncompliance issue could range from the suspicion that a state is conducting nuclear weapons or fissile material research secretly to a case where a state suddenly brandishes one or more nuclear weapons, which would clearly constitute a failure of the system. In this way, the issue of how a system makes a finding of compliance is different from verification or enforcement questions and is worth further exploration.[1]

A fourth element is a systems-based approach to verification. A theme throughout this volume is the need to conceive of verification as a system of different political and technical approaches that has political acceptance informed by an acknowledgment of the defined risk. No individual verification measure is infallible, and there is not a technical solution to all problems. Rather, by constructing a "system of systems," we maximize the opportunity for the weakness of one measure to be compensated by another. An effort to structure a system that leverages all tools available, including technical approaches, legal and political commitments, the roles of the public and insiders, incentives for compliance, deterrence of noncompliance, and an honest qualitative and quantitative acceptance of risk is the only appropriate way to determine if the system makes sense for each state. Such an approach has been described as "Swiss cheese": every slice has holes, but we have to do our best to make sure all the slices do not have holes in the same places. This system-based analysis for verification is the only way to build lasting confidence in our ability to detect and respond to potential violations.

Finally, we have been struck by the creativity of people thinking about verification, monitoring, and enforcement and the value of considering nontraditional approaches as part of a verification system. Parties such as nongovernmental organizations, independent scientists, and other nonstate actors have resources and expertise to contribute to the development of verification strategies. Some of the newer ideas include the concept of societal verification—what role those with no legal obligation to find or report violations can play—and the model of public-private partnerships to take advantage of information that may be held by particular segments of society, such as industry. These kinds of approaches require more rigorous analysis to determine their real marginal value in a state-driven verification system. We believe, from the outset, however, that they show promise and encourage us that there is room for new ideas.

The Challenge of Establishing Confidence in the Baseline[2]

Ensuring security in a world with few or zero nuclear weapons will, *inter alia*, require confidence in the accuracy of global inventories of nuclear materials, nuclear materials production capabilities, numbers of nuclear weapons, and possibly nuclear weapon delivery systems. Each of these major components of a nuclear weapons enterprise presents different challenges for monitoring; however, in all cases the items or activities to be monitored are likely to be declared by the owning party and made available for technical monitoring measures that support bilateral, multilateral, and/or international verification of such agreements.

The biggest challenge to the overall verification and monitoring agenda may be that posed by uncertainties regarding the quantities of existing stocks of fissile material. This will also be true, but to a lesser extent, for quantities of nuclear weapons. This challenge looms large because of the difficulty of detecting small, but significant, quantities of hidden material and the associated hesitancy of most parties to move forward toward a world free of nuclear weapons without confidence in our ability to do so. We must develop strategies to reduce the residual uncertainties regarding completeness of initial declarations as all declared weapons-related inventories go to zero. This will be instrumental in managing the risk that "country X" hedged its bets by hiding nuclear materials, weapons components, weapons, and delivery systems prior to committing to deep cut agreements. Establishing this confidence in countries' initial baseline declarations will likely be a key point in all states' decisions to move to very low numbers, much less zero.

A second challenge is to maintain confidence that the growing inventories of nuclear materials in civil applications and the spread of nuclear capabilities to previously nonnuclear regions of the world remain in peaceful use. Although there are baseline issues associated with civil programs in nuclear weapons states and non-NPT (Non-Proliferation Treaty) states, the dominant feature of civil nuclear materials inventories may be their growth and distribution globally. How to deal with growing civil inventories and capabilities is well understood conceptually and technically, but managing that growth will require significantly evolving the IAEA safeguards system and other instruments designed to appropriately manage the spread of sensitive nuclear technology. This will require increased IAEA resources as well as new institutional measures and mechanisms.

Implications of Time

Time is a fundamental parameter to consider when addressing these questions and can be broken down into two concepts: the time to successful breakout from an agreement, and possible changes in the baseline inventory uncertainty as a function of the passage of time. For example, breakout based on reprocessing spent power reactor fuel and fabricating recovered reactor-grade plutonium into nuclear weapons will take longer and have more signatures available for detection by a monitoring system than will breakout with a secret cache of nuclear weapons that were never declared. And, as time passes, progress will continue to be made in improving the effectiveness and efficiency of the international safeguards system for the civil fuel cycle, making the reprocessing breakout scenario less likely.[3] What about the secret cache of weapons as time passes? How likely is it that they will remain functional and/or secret for 20 years? Fifty years? Would the absence of indicators of such a secret inventory over many years increase confidence that it never existed?

Risk acceptance, confidence building, and trust are also functions of time that are important considerations in thinking about uncertainties in the completeness of declarations. Changes in the political and security environment over time are likely to have a major impact on the perceptions of the risks associated with baseline inventory uncertainties. Furthermore, monitoring activities carried out over time and continually improved will provide additional information that can be assessed to reduce the residual uncertainties in the baseline.

Generally, establishing confidence in the baseline—the completeness of initial declarations—will involve ongoing analysis of all information available about the inventory in question, including the history of the activity. Given all that is known about a program, is the declared inventory reasonable? Is the range of uncertainty militarily significant at a particular stage of reductions? Would increased cooperation and transparency, the provision of additional information,[4] and an evolving political context improve confidence with time? It seems likely that with significant cooperation and analytical effort that the residual uncertainties could be tolerable at weapon levels above zero and would have to be carefully evaluated at zero.

The ability to establish confidence in the baseline is central to progress in deep reductions in nuclear arms, and it would be easy to conclude that the problem is too difficult or that optimists are engaging in wishful thinking. However, a step-by-step approach to reducing the residual uncertainties in each category of inventory, taking account of technical monitoring measures and all-source information analysis carried out over many years, seems likely to improve the confidence in initial declarations.

A key question is, what steps can be taken now to reduce baseline inventory uncertainties? Experience in the United States suggests that all states with nuclear weapons could be investing in extensive research into the history of their nuclear programs and developing information to support initial declarations of nuclear materials production; warhead production, deployment, retirement, and disposition; nuclear materials production capabilities; and delivery systems inventories. They could also be preparing their civil nuclear enterprise to accept full-scope safeguards. At the same time, it would be expected that investments in intelligence analysis of nuclear weapons programs and civil nuclear activities of other states would need to increase. These activities are not trivial in effort or time, but they would in any event be prudent home-work for all states with nuclear materials or weapons.

Future Research Agenda and Next Steps

While much important work has been done to date on verification, monitoring, and enforcement in a world free of nuclear weapons, the following chapters raise a number of areas requiring additional work, research, and study before one would have confidence in any given system or system of systems. We highlight several areas here but do not intend the lists to be exhaustive. We have divided the issues into technical and policy development challenges and hope they spur development of a forward-looking agenda.

Technical Considerations

Technical tasks include those that require new or renewed lines of scientific and practical investigation by experts. Often these activities will be well suited for investigation by the national laboratories or by independent scientists.

With regard to fissile materials, many questions will need to be addressed if there is to be significant progress in negotiating and implementing a verifiable fissile material cutoff treaty (FMCT). The following are additional challenges that go beyond the presumed scope of an FMCT:

- Examining how best to address verification requirements at complex, operational facilities not designed for such measures. Approaches may include trial investigations at the actual facilities or at similar facilities, in the nuclear-armed states or elsewhere.
- Seeking better methods to detect and characterize fissile materials, at high resolution, in remote and nonintrusive ways
- Developing verification techniques for fissile material used for nonexplosive military applications (such as for highly enriched

uranium [HEU] in naval reactors) or exploring how and where HEU can be eliminated from these applications, thereby obviating the need for the same level of verification
- Utilizing environmental sampling for detecting undeclared fissile material production in non–nuclear weapon states. Modified equipment and procedures as well as research may be needed to use environmental sampling for nuclear disarmament, including detecting clandestine centrifuge enrichment.
- Investigating the usefulness of techniques such as isotope ratio methods to confirm historical plutonium production as a means to improve confidence in the final stages of reductions.

A number of challenges are related to the dismantlement of nuclear weapons, including:

- Developing a common approach among all states for designing a process for converting classified forms of fissile material (such as the plutonium triggers or HEU "secondary" components of a nuclear weapon) by removing their classified properties
- Refining the criteria for determining whether data are classified in order to enable greater transparency and facilitate verification
- Certifying completed warhead dismantlement prototype systems through vulnerability testing by responsible authorities in each state to confirm that their use would not divulge classified information, as well as by the verifying entity to assure that the results obtained were authentic
- Developing and certifying "chain of custody" technology for verifying the process of removing warheads from weapon delivery systems
- Performing architectural studies to design warhead dismantling facilities that could be built in each nuclear-armed state, incorporating design features to facilitate verification, and allowing occasional managed access into the dismantling areas
- Refining attribute verification capabilities to verify receipts of warheads at dismantlement

- Creating techniques for identifying a given model for a nuclear weapon pit or secondary, and thereby confirming the demounting, storage, dismantling, or conversion of specific weapon systems without divulging classified information.

We also need to develop new ideas to sustain a cadre of technically competent nuclear weapons scientists, engineers, and production workers when, in the future, the stockpiles of the major nuclear powers may become relatively small, causing scientists and engineers to assess that there is little challenging design or production work for the key technical personnel to do. The "road to zero" and the challenge of protecting the world from nuclear terror involves technical challenges that call for the same skills as needed for the enterprise of nuclear weapon development and production, but oriented along a different national mission. Some of the technical questions just listed, and others discussed in the chapters, could provide appropriate work for these experts in the short and medium term.

Policy Considerations: Individual State Efforts

In support of greater security as the world works toward the elimination of nuclear weapons, individual states could begin immediately by increasing the transparency of their nuclear activities. This could include working to develop full baseline inventories of holdings of nuclear weapons and fissile materials, whether they are disclosed or not. The goal would be to begin to build confidence and develop an accurate baseline from which reductions could be measured. Such actions would likely need to be an iterative process. The United States, United Kingdom, and France, which have traditionally been open about their forces and plans, could take the lead, gradually encouraging other states to follow.

It is also possible to work on models for creating win-win situations in the field of information sharing between industry and governments. Through public-private partnerships, verification might be improved with information that industry and technology holders glean from export activities. These relationships could also be guided by a set of to-be-developed rules designed to build confidence around shared information.

Policy Considerations: Multinational and International Efforts

International organizations and bodies, such as the IAEA, the United Nations Security Council, and regional groups, have an important role to play in supporting the disarmament agenda. Some tasks for these bodies are listed here. It is important to note that in most cases, the international organs are functions of the policies of state parties and thus are not independent actors. Therefore, one cannot "call on" a body to do something without first building consensus among the states-parties for the common agenda, which could include the following actions:

- Creating a "culture of compliance"—"zero tolerance" toward noncompliance with arms control agreements. Countries could be reminded in a timely fashion of their obligations, and failures to comply would be publicized—a form of "name and shame." If a country needed advice or assistance in meeting its obligations, which likely would be the case for many countries, it could request it, and the means to do so would be developed by members of the international community.
- Developing an International Satellite Verification Agency (ISVA) and beginning to train an international cadre of experts in imagery analysis to increase international knowledge about, and stakes in, monitoring and verification. This idea was originally proposed by France in the 1970s but was rejected by both the United States and then the USSR. This agency would use commercial imagery now widely available and could even develop its own satellite capability.
- Motivating still abstaining states to adopt the IAEA Additional Protocol. As part of this initiative, efforts would be made to refine and strengthen its measures, and to demonstrate increased transparency.

Some measures will likely need to be undertaken by specific groups of states or "coalitions of the willing." Examples may include the following:

- Conducting a U.S-Russian or multilateral pilot program on monitoring and verifying reductions and the ultimate elimination of nuclear weapons through the verified dismantlement of warheads
- Reaching consensus among non–nuclear weapon states on which attributes must be verified, with sufficient confidence and without breaching the NPT, regarding the presence of a nuclear weapon subject to dismantlement, or weapons-grade fissile materials subject to monitored storage or destruction
- Discussing the concept of "trusted agents," or non–nuclear weapon states that could be proxy for the others in disarmament verification activities. In any disarmament verification process, inspectors from a small group of "trusted agent states" should be present to act on behalf of the broader group of non–nuclear weapon states.
- Discussing, among all the nuclear weapons states, relevant monitoring and verification issues. Talks could be started soon among any subset of nuclear armed states willing to participate in the process.
- Developing further the concept of a Fissile Material Control Initiative. In this voluntary endeavor, states would collaborate in order to increase security, transparency, and control over fissile material stocks worldwide, to prevent their theft or diversion to nonstate actors or additional states, and to move fissile materials verifiably and irreversibly out of nuclear weapons and into forms unusable for nuclear weapons. Working on the challenges of the FMCI and FMCT should pave the way for the challenge of fully verifying fissile materials.

Conclusion

Not surprisingly, verifying, monitoring, and enforcing agreements on the path toward a world free of nuclear weapons will be complex and challenging. In some cases, negotiation of future agreements between the United States and Russia may be both a driver to better refine future verification regimes as well as the product of progress on verification. Similarly, during the NPT review process and other international discussions verification and enforcement of current agreements may serve as a point of departure for cooperation and progress but also as a roadblock to further action if confidence in such measures is low. In all cases, progress on both unilateral and cooperative efforts on verification, monitoring, and enforcement could positively influence the ongoing nonproliferation and disarmament agenda.

The chapters that follow are the work of the authors alone and do not necessarily reflect the views of the Nuclear Security Project principals or NTI. We do, however, think that each chapter makes a substantial new contribution to the discussion of verification, monitoring, and enforcement for a world free of nuclear weapons. We hope that this volume informs and inspires technical and policy work on the vital questions that remain to be answered before we can fulfill the vision and make significant progress on some of the steps called for by George Shultz, William Perry, Henry Kissinger, and Sam Nunn and echoed by so many around the world.

Notes

1. A special thank you to Trevor Findlay for his contribution to our thinking on the issue of compliance.

2. This discussion is drawn directly from work done by James W. Tape in his role as a consultant to the Nuclear Security Project.

3. Breakout by abrogating safeguards agreements is detected immediately. A more challenging scenario is undeclared reprocessing and weapons manufacturing with a goal of having weapons before detection.

4. Although weapons designs and other proliferation-sensitive information will remain classified, much of what has been protected in the past could be shared, at least on a limited basis, such as total numbers of weapons, inventories of nuclear materials held for weapons, naval propulsion inventories, and so forth. The inventory declarations could resemble international safeguards declarations provided by non–nuclear weapon states to the IAEA.

1. Political Dimensions of Determining "Effective" Verification

EDWARD IFFT

There is general, though not universal, agreement among political leaders that the current levels of nuclear weapons in the world are much too high for any rational purpose.

Commitment to significant reductions in the levels of nuclear weapons will be very important for nonproliferation goals—in particular, at the 2010 Non-Proliferation Treaty (NPT) Review Conference.

Reductions to about 1,000 deployed strategic nuclear weapons each for the United States and the Russian Federation could be carried out bilaterally using existing and proven verification techniques.

Reductions to fewer than about 1,000 deployed strategic nuclear weapons would entail increasingly difficult political and technical decisions. These would include how to involve all states with nuclear weapons in the process, how to structure smaller forces, how to maintain deterrence (including extended deterrence), targeting issues, the role of antiballistic missile (ABM) defenses, and, perhaps above all, verification issues. In addition, at this level, we could not continue to ignore tactical and nondeployed nuclear weapons.

At levels below about 50 to 100 nuclear weapons, verification issues would be even more crucial and difficult. Although many arms control verification regimes are in place and operating effectively, these, as they stand today, would not be adequate for providing confidence at very low levels.

If we wish to move toward a world free of nuclear weapons, we must begin now to devise more effective and intrusive verification and transparency regimes. These will obviously apply to the current nuclear weapon states (NWS) and other states with nuclear weapons, but non–nuclear weapon states (NNWS) will also have to accept some such measures. Scientific research to this end should be stepped up. We also need to begin to change the political culture surrounding nuclear weapons; in particular, we need to continue to decrease the roles and legitimacy of nuclear weapons.

Some additional important decisions will come into play as we approach zero. While it is useful to begin to think about these, such decisions need not be made now. Among these would be the question of hedging capabilities and who should control the last few nuclear weapons. In addition, the role of conventional weapons and the concern that the reduction/elimination of nuclear weapons must not make the world safe for conventional war must be addressed. It is important that the debate not be allowed to focus on these endgame issues now. Interesting as they are, their detailed solutions will not be needed and are probably not foreseeable for many years. Becoming obsessed with how to eliminate the last 10 nuclear weapons should not be allowed to delay the important next steps that are relatively easily and safely available now.

It would be naive to assume that there will not be strong opposition to deep reductions and that there will not be compliance problems. Therefore, we will need more vigorous and effective implementation and compliance mechanisms than exist today. Although arms control agreements are generally operating effectively, international efforts to deal with compliance issues to date have been cumbersome, inconsistent, and uneven. We may need new compliance and enforcement bodies to assure confidence in all states that agreements are operating as intended. We will also need to improve our use and understanding of terms like *monitoring*, *verification*, and *confidence-building measures*. Part of this process should be gaining a deeper understanding of nations' perception and tolerance of risk. This should include education of publics about what is possible and what is important in the world of verification and compliance.

Recognizing that moving toward a world free of nuclear weapons would be seen by some as a radical and dangerous move, careful attention to creating a favorable political climate and meeting the legitimate concerns of skeptics, especially in the areas of verification and compliance, will be absolutely essential. Serious problems in these areas, whether real or perceived, could bring the entire process to a halt rather quickly.

Background

Based on official statements in the UN First Committee, the Conference on Disarmament, Review Conferences of the NPT, as well as in many other sources, it is clear that the vast majority of world leaders believe that the level of nuclear weapons in the world is far too high. They frequently cite Article VI of the NPT as requiring deep reductions in and eventual elimination of nuclear weapons. There is a renewed drive for fulfilling this commitment, inspired by the well-known efforts of George Shultz, William Perry, Henry Kissinger, Sam Nunn, and others. The British government has also been very active. President Barack Obama has stated, "I state clearly and with conviction America's committment to seek the peace and security of a world without nuclear weapons."[1] UN secretary-general Ban Ki-moon has recently spoken in similar terms, urging "deep and verifiable reductions" in U.S. and Russian nuclear arsenals.[2] A recent article in *Foreign Affairs* laid out a comprehensive rationale for going to zero and urged "airtight verification," though without specifying what this means or how it could be achieved.[3]

This new effort brings the issue of verification, always a key component of arms control, to the fore. Verification is one of the most commonly used concepts in arms control and nonproliferation. The word comes from the Latin *verificare*—"to prove to be true by demonstration, evidence, or testimony." In the U.S. government, the concept is actually divided into two parts. *Monitoring* is used to denote the collection of data relevant to an obligation in an agreement. This could be from satellites or other national technical means (NTM),[4] inspectors on the ground, or other sources, including human sources and open sources. *Verification* is used to denote a judgment, made at the political level (a government or international body), as to whether a party is in compliance with its obligations. In popular usage in the United States and elsewhere, however, *verification* is commonly used to include both functions.

Verification is a neutral concept and says nothing about its effectiveness. In general, it is not useful, beyond a bumper-sticker mentality, to ask whether an agreement is "verifiable" or "not verifiable." Any agreement may be monitored/verified with some degree of confidence. Whether this is "good enough" or not is a somewhat subjective decision that must be made on a case-by-case basis. Inputs to this decision would include the difficulty of cheating, the consequences of undetected cheating, the compliance history of the party in question, what options are being given up in the agreement, and so forth. In the Nixon, Ford, and Carter administrations, the standard for good enough with respect to agreements on nuclear weapons was "adequate verification." The Reagan administration, wishing to place greater stress on verification, ridiculed this standard and replaced it with "effective verification." However, when the new standard was finally defined, it proved to be virtually identical to the earlier one—that is, the ability to detect any significant violations that could change the strategic balance in time to take corrective action. While establishing changing the strategic balance as the standard was appropriate in the context of U.S.-Soviet competition during the Cold War, a better criterion for effective verification now might be to refer to the timely detection of actions that would have a significant military or political impact. A further standard mentioned by Secretary James Baker in connection with the START treaty is the desirability of being able to detect a pattern of small violations. Such a pattern, even if it were not significant substantively, could have a negative political impact, especially if it appeared to be deliberate.

As we move to lower levels, any uncertainty about compliance may assume greater prominence. Therefore, it will be important to be precise in the use of terms like *monitoring, verification,* and *confidence-building measures,* which can carry political weight. Educating the public should be a key part of this effort. However, regardless of how carefully we explain to the public what is possible, and what is and what is not important, it is clear that considerable subjectivity will remain, and different conclusions regarding what is "effective" will be reached by different people and in different contexts. In the context of this discussion, it is obvious that the ability to detect 10 illegal nuclear weapons would be far more important in a world in which only a handful are allowed than in a world in which thousands are allowed. In any case, the concept of "effective verification" has become widely used throughout the world and, properly understood, is a useful shorthand for a complicated issue.[5]

It is clear that 100 percent confidence in monitoring/verification will not be possible or necessary in most cases. There are, of course, important cases in which 100 percent confidence is possible. This was true, for example, when Intermediate-Range Nuclear Forces Treaty (INF) missile systems were blown up, crushed, or launched to destruction in the presence of U.S. and Soviet inspectors. The same should be true for the dismantlement of nuclear weapons under the circumstances foreseen in this study. Where 100 percent confidence is not possible is in assuring that no additional missiles or nuclear weapons are hidden elsewhere. This dilemma is illustrated by the experience of United Nations Special Commission (UNSCOM), UN Monitoring, Verification, and Inspection Commission (UNMOVIC), and the International Atomic Energy Agency (IAEA in Iraq). They could not conclusively prove the negative—the absence of weapons of mass destruction (WMDs). However, they could and did provide compelling evidence that was not given sufficient consideration by the international community and, given more time, could have made a more convincing case for the absence of WMDs.

It has long been known that a major benefit from a system of effective verification is deterrence. The fact and perception that violations are likely to be detected and punished can deter potential violators from attempting violations in the first place. An interesting example of this is that Saddam Hussein's perception of the capabilities of the UNSCOM and IAEA inspectors was evidently a key factor in his decision not to pursue Iraq's WMD programs after the first Gulf War.

To be politically acceptable, verification must strike a balance between the rights of both the monitoring and monitored parties. On the one hand, the *monitoring* party (perhaps an international organization) must have sufficient access to information to be able to gain a reasonable assurance that obligations are being complied with. On the other hand, the *monitored* party must be protected from unwarranted intelligence gathering or unreasonable interference with its normal activities. In some cases, this may involve the need to protect proprietary information. Striking this balance has been a major issue in negotiating virtually all modern arms control agreements, especially those involving on-site inspection. The fact that these agreements are generally operating successfully shows that the negotiators have been able to strike a good balance between these competing interests. Moving toward zero nuclear weapons will almost certainly require moving the balance more toward greater access and transparency. Indeed, the Congressional Commission on the Strategic Posture of the United States judges in its "Interim Report" that it will require "a fundamental transformation of the world political order."[6]

Experience with Existing Arms Control Agreements

A significant number of arms control agreements are operating successfully today, and much can be learned from experiences with them. They govern nuclear, chemical, biological, and conventional weapons. They have quantitative, qualitative, and operational constraints, along with many types of inspections and requirements for data exchanges. Most have some sort of implementation body. Some have encountered compliance issues. The precedents set by these agreements should facilitate the political and technical decisions and compromises that will be needed to reach a world free of nuclear weapons. The most relevant agreements are discussed briefly in the following sections.[7]

Nuclear Non-Proliferation Treaty (NPT)

It is curious that something as important as the NPT has no organization responsible for overall implementation. The IAEA is responsible primarily for safeguards. These are designed to detect the diversion of a "significant quantity" of fissile material (defined as 8 kilograms of plutonium or

25 kilograms of highly enriched uranium [HEU]) from peaceful applications. The IAEA is capable of detecting microscopic amounts of fissile material but, of course, must know where to look. Weaknesses in the system, which involved inspecting only *declared* sites, were exposed by the illegal activities of Iraq and are being addressed by the Additional Protocol. With some 500 inspectors conducting some 2,000 inspections per year, plus the work of its Action Team in Iraq, the IAEA has vast experience and should be a valuable source of expertise and advice for the tasks posed by this study. Its overall annual budget is just under 300 million euros, of which about 117 million is devoted to nuclear verification. The Board of Governors has the power to report/refer compliance issues to the United Nations Security Council (UNSC) and has done so with both North Korea and Iran. The IAEA received the Nobel Peace Prize in 2005.

SALT I Agreements

Neither the Interim Agreement on Strategic Offensive Arms nor the ABM Treaty remains in force. The former achieved its goals with minimal compliance problems. The ABM Treaty, however, was a source of controversy until the United States withdrew in 2002. One major problem was a radar the Soviet Union constructed in Siberia, which was not permitted by the treaty. After years of controversy, the Soviets admitted their violation and dismantled it. Another major controversy concerned the U.S. switch, during the Reagan administration, from the "traditional" interpretation of what activities were allowed to the more permissive "broad" interpretation. This was hotly disputed by the Soviets, along with many experts in the United States, until the United States returned to the traditional interpretation during the Carter administration.

INF Treaty

The INF Treaty successfully eliminated all ground-launched U.S. and Soviet ballistic and cruise missiles (almost 2,700 in all) with ranges between 500 and 5,500 kilometers. It provided the model for most arms control on-site inspections (OSIs) and contained five types of inspections, including perimeter and portal continuous monitoring (PPCM) of one key facility on each side. The latter experience should be quite useful in designing monitoring systems for deep reductions in nuclear weapons. During the 13 years of inspections, which ended in 2001, 851 were conducted. These were carried out at 130 sites in Russia, Ukraine, Belarus, and Kazakhstan, and at 31 sites in the United States, United Kingdom, Germany, Belgium, the Netherlands, and Italy. The treaty remains in force.

START Treaty

The START Treaty achieved its ambitious reductions in deployed strategic offensive nuclear weapons systems by 2001. START has 12 different types of OSIs, plus PPCM. Through the 2009 expiration of the treaty, the United States conducted 659 START inspections and Russia 481.[8] The cost to the United States of conducting a START inspection in Siberia or the Russian Far East was roughly $250,000. The treaty provided for special access visits (a kind of challenge inspection), but this was never used, since suspicions of undeclared illegal facilities never arose. A massive data exchange of over 100 pages was updated every six months with data on the numbers, locations, and technical characteristics of specified systems. Between these updates, an extensive system of notifications, using the Nuclear Risk Reduction Centers of the sides, maintained an up-to-date database of the numbers and locations of all relevant systems.

The treaty generally operated very successfully. Issues generally involved differing interpretations of treaty language or circumstances not foreseen by the negotiators. The Joint Compliance and Inspection Commission (JCIC) met at least twice a year in Geneva and issued over 100 agreements and joint statements to improve the treaty's viability and effectiveness.

Moscow Treaty (SORT)

The Moscow Treaty represents a radical departure from the general trend in verification, which has been toward more intrusive monitoring and greater transparency. Although it usefully requires significant reductions in deployed strategic nuclear warheads, it contains no definitions, no counting rules, no agreed procedures for dismantling systems, no provision for verification, and it expires on the same day that the reductions take effect (December 31, 2012). It thus goes against the widely held view that reductions should be "irreversible" and "effectively verifiable." The crucial importance for verification of having agreed counting rules is illustrated by the fact that the difference in the number of strategic nuclear warheads deployed by the United States as determined by the agreed START rules and the (not agreed) U.S. SORT rule is huge— about 3,000 warheads.[9] This treaty is the product of the view of the Bush administration (reluctantly accepted by the Russians) that the new era of cooperation and openness between the United States and Russia makes traditional monitoring and verification unnecessary. It does not seem to provide a useful model for the issues posed in this book.[10]

Chemical Weapons Convention (CWC)

The CWC is administered by the Organization for the Prevention of Chemical Weapons (OPCW) in The Hague. It is responsible for the destruction of the 71,000 metric tons of chemical weapons declared, the overwhelming majority of which are in the United States and Russia. About 60 percent of these have been destroyed to date. It appears that the agreed deadlines for completing the process will not be met, but the fact that good-faith efforts to that end continue in both countries is encouraging.

The OPCW has conducted about 4,000 inspections of various types worldwide at over 1,000 sites and spends about 74.5 million euros per year. There are suspicions that some countries are in violation of the CWC, and the United States has accused some specific countries (Iran, Russia) of violations, while others are accused of maintaining a "capability."[11] However, no state-party has thus far made use of the option of a challenge inspection, which is provided for in the CWC.

Biological Weapons Convention (BWC)

The BWC is somewhat unique in that it has no verification regime and no implementing body. The 2006 Review Conference did, however, establish three full-time staff positions in the UN Department of Disarmament Affairs, at least until 2011, to deal with BWC implementation. A 1992 Trilateral Agreement among the United States, United Kingdom, and Russia attempted to deal with the problem and did lead to some visits to relevant facilities, but results were disappointing. Extensive efforts to establish a verification regime were abandoned in 2001, at the insistence of the United States. Meetings of experts, however, are making some progress at devising confidence-building measures, such as codes of conduct for scientists and greater awareness of biosecurity. A major problem is the protection of proprietary information in the pharmaceutical and biotech industries, which would likely be the subject of any inspection regime. As in the case of the CWC, the United States believes that some countries (Iran, North Korea, Russia) are violating the convention.[12] Little action has been taken to clarify or respond to these suspicions.

Conventional Forces in Europe Treaty (CFE)

The CFE Treaty, called "the cornerstone of European security," successfully eliminated over 80,000 items of military equipment in five categories. Serious definitional issues involving Soviet coastal defense forces and naval infantry arose soon after signature, but they were resolved quickly at a high level. Large numbers of inspections have been conducted among the 30 states-parties, and these are unique in the use of multilateral teams. Remarkable agility and goodwill were shown by the states-parties when they were able to adapt what was basically a NATO–Warsaw Pact Treaty into a treaty more appropriate to post–Cold War realities. However, major problems have erupted because of Russia's "suspension" of its participation. At issue are the ratification of the Adapted Treaty and the continuing presence of Russian troops in Moldova and Georgia, further complicated by the Russia-Georgia conflict in 2008. The implementing body for CFE is the Joint Consultative Group (JCG), based in Vienna.

Open Skies Treaty

The Open Skies Treaty was originally envisioned as part of the CFE monitoring regime, but it has become essentially a confidence-building tool. There are 34 states-parties, and they have the right to overfly each other's territory without restriction, acquiring images with specified optical, infrared, and radar sensors. The information is shared among the states-parties at nominal cost, regardless of whether they actually participated in the flight. This can be a useful benefit, especially for countries without access to their own satellite imagery. The United States has conducted about 47 quota missions and escorted 12. In addition, over 100 Joint Trial Flights were conducted before entry into force. The idea that countries need not wait for an agreement to enter into force to practice monitoring techniques is a very useful one, which was also used in the START Treaty. It can help build confidence and enables the negotiators to fine-tune proposed equipment and procedures based on real experience. One can envision that a modified version of Open Skies might play a role in monitoring the agreements in this study. The Open Skies Consultative Commission is based in Vienna.

Comprehensive Test Ban Treaty (CTBT)

The CTBT, while not yet in force, is a very instructive study in monitoring. It has by far the most ambitious monitoring system ever devised, based on four technologies: seismic, radionuclide, hydroacoustic, and infrasound. The worldwide international monitoring system (IMS) will consist of 337 facilities in 89 countries and is about two-thirds complete. An International Data Center (IDC) in Vienna receives the authenticated data from these facilities and performs analyses. The treaty also provides for an intrusive challenge OSI regime. The OSI capabilities are being thoroughly tested, most recently at the 2008 Integrated Field Exercise at the former Soviet nuclear test site in Kazakhstan (IFE08). Satellite data and information gathered by other forms of NTM are admissible evidence in calling for an OSI.

It is interesting that the capabilities of the IMS were not specified in advance during the negotiations, although individual countries may have had certain goals in mind. Rather, the system the countries were willing to build and host on their territories was judged effective enough. However, one of the objections made by the U.S. Senate in refusing to give its consent to ratification by a 48–51–1 vote in 1999 was that the

IMS and OSI regimes did not provide "effective verification." This may well be revisited by the Obama administration. The capabilities of the CTBT verification regime are proving to be better than was expected in 1999. The CTBTO Preparatory Commission in Vienna has an annual budget of about $100 million.

Ottawa Convention (Landmine Convention)

The Ottawa Convention is basically a coalition of over 150 countries that pledge to eliminate antipersonnel landmines. On-site inspections are possible, but there is no implementing body. There are no obvious compliance issues, but the absence of major players (United States, Russia, China) from the convention limits its effectiveness. One interesting aspect of the convention is the monitoring role played by civil society. A network of NGOs, called Landmine Monitor, monitors compliance and produces an annual report.[13]

Other Agreements

Other less prominent agreements, some of which are on the borderline between arms control and peacekeeping, have interesting features that could be relevant. For example, the creation of the Multinational Force and Observers (MLO) essentially turned monitoring of the 1979 peace treaty between Egypt and Israel over to 11 third countries (as diverse as the United States, Hungary, and Fiji). Their unique operations have helped keep the Sinai peaceful. The Decommissioning in Northern Ireland created a commission, also composed entirely of foreigners, which used creative techniques to put weapons "verifiably beyond use." The Dayton Peace Accords used a variety of agreements and inspection, observation, and monitoring to help implement these agreements. The experience gained in these and other efforts should be studied and built upon as appropriate.

Lessons Learned

This brief survey leads to certain conclusions. We have a great deal of experience with constraining and eliminating military items. Much of this experience involves on-site inspections, which have been taken to a high level of expertise. In the United States, the Defense Threat Reduction Agency (DTRA) has about 600 people in its Inspection Directorate, with an annual budget of about $35 million. Other states involved in OSI have similar organizations, but not on the scale of the DTRA effort. At the political level, all the NWSs, with the possible exception of China, seem comfortable with the idea that intrusive inspections can be effective, while protecting their legitimate national security interests. At the same time, countries with less experience in arms control, or serious regional security concerns, may still be uneasy about the degree of openness that will be required to eliminate nuclear weapons. They may also be uneasy about a possible loss of the stability that they believe has been provided by a nuclear umbrella.

Other than the informal initiatives of Presidents Bush, Gorbachev, and Yeltsin in the early 1990s, the world has not yet dealt with *tactical* nuclear weapons. This must be done soon if we are to move to much deeper reductions in *strategic* nuclear weapons, and details are dealt with elsewhere in this volume. Negotiations on these systems may be difficult, and these weapons are, of course, smaller and more mobile than those already dealt with, but, in principle, the monitoring problems they pose are not fundamentally different than those we have already solved. From a verification point of view, the distinctions between strategic and tactical nuclear weapons look increasingly irrelevant as levels are reduced.

A more difficult challenge will be dealing with *nondeployed nuclear warheads*, which has never been attempted. Effective verification of the disposition of these items will require a more intrusive system of tags, seals, chain of custody, monitoring of the provenance of fissile materials, and so on, than has been politically acceptable thus far. Again, in principle, this can be done, but the political and legal barriers may be more formidable than the technical ones. In this connection, the Trilateral Initiative among the United States, Russia, and the IAEA was established to develop procedures for dismantling U.S. and Russian nuclear warheads and accounting for their fissile material. It seemed to be making good progress on these problems until it was suspended.[14] It is important that this work be revived and pursued vigorously. Such work need not be seen now as a commitment to eliminate all nuclear weapons, but it is important to have solutions in our toolbox in order to have options in the future and to allow time for political leaders to become comfortable with the solutions developed by scientists and engineers.

The problem of judging intent is a particularly difficult one. In general, having the intent to violate an agreement, while relevant in a political sense, is not legally a violation of the agreement. Under the CTBT, *preparations* to conduct a nuclear explosion are not a violation—only the actual *conduct* of an explosion itself would violate the treaty. However, some agreements require judgments regarding intent or purpose to be made. For example, both the CWC and BWC contain a distinction between "offensive" and "defensive" purposes and between "peaceful" and "hostile" intent. Thus, work on a disease could be to develop a vaccine (legal) or to develop biological weapons (illegal). Likewise, the same chemicals can be used to produce insecticides or chemical weapons. A similar problem of intent and dual-use materials and technologies arises between nuclear weapons and peaceful nuclear applications. This problem will become even more relevant as the use of nuclear power spreads. Intent is, of course, at the heart of the controversy over Iran's nuclear activities.

Another problem more in the political sphere is the world's rather unsatisfactory record in dealing with compliance problems. The ongoing issues regarding the nuclear activities of Iran and North Korea are the most obvious, but there are others, as noted earlier. In the agreements between the United States and the former Soviet Union, most compliance disputes have involved technical issues. Most have been resolved, but some have been allowed to fester for years. The implementing bodies for these agreements conduct their work in private, which has been a considerable advantage in that the playing to the public galleries that plagues other forums can be avoided. In the multilateral forums, right up to the UNSC, the record of dealing with compliance disputes is not encouraging. It may be that a harder or softer approach would be appropriate in individual cases, but the lack of consensus and resulting paralysis that often occurs undermines the integrity of the process and encourages a cavalier attitude toward compliance in general. The world may be able to afford this at levels of thousands of nuclear weapons—it cannot do so when disputes arise at very low levels.

The possibility of monitoring of an agreement by civil society is generally ignored in arms control discussions, apart from the occasional casual mention that a defector might reveal an illegal activity. The surprising effectiveness of Helsinki Watch groups in monitoring the implementation of the provisions of the Helsinki Final Act in the former Soviet Union, along with the Landmine Monitor, are instructive. It may be that a network of "Disarmament Watch" groups in many countries might be a useful instrument in the toolbox for the current task and could make up for the inevitable shortcomings of technical means of monitoring as the world tries to rid itself of nuclear weapons.

As noted, the standard of "effective verification" is a somewhat elastic and subjective one. In the United States, the intelligence community is generally required to analyze the verifiability of any new arms control agreement. This is an input to the political net judgment made by the executive and legislative branches regarding whether the agreement is in the overall best interest of the country. Verification generally plays a prominent role in any opposition to an agreement. In the case of the BWC, the countries that negotiated it in 1972 decided that an effective monitoring/verification regime was neither necessary nor possible. Although many countries have since changed their minds in response to terrorism and advances in biotechnology, the Bush administration in 2001 basically reaffirmed the original decision. An additional important factor is that the option being given up in the agreement—creation and potential use of biological weapons—is not one that the country wished to have in any case. It is important to note that the lack of such a formal negotiated regime in this or any other agreement itself does not mean there is no monitoring at all. Countries still have at their disposal NTM, human sources, and open sources. Similar observations could be made about the Outer Space Treaty and the Seabed Treaty.

Experience with many agreements has shown that, regardless of how clever the negotiators might be, technical developments and unforeseen changes (e.g., new technologies, breakup of the USSR) are likely to occur. Therefore, it is essential that agreements provide a mechanism for changes to improve the "viability and effectiveness" of the agreement, without having to resort to the very cumbersome and difficult amendment procedure. Liberal use of the phrase "unless otherwise agreed" in an agreement has saved the day on more than one occasion. This will be particularly relevant in an agreement as long-term and as fraught with unknowns as one moving toward a world free of nuclear weapons. It would also be wise to build in some flexibility to adjust levels and reductions schedules as appropriate to meet changing conditions.

In addition to technical issues, great importance should be assigned to creating a favorable political atmosphere for moving toward a world free of nuclear weapons. Effective verification and compliance mechanisms are obviously essential. However, the *perception* that these exist and are functioning properly can also be crucial. The CTBT ratification debacle during the Clinton administration showed how years of good scientific work can be overwhelmed by the failure to mount an effective education campaign for the public and Congress. It is interesting that this occurred in spite of overwhelming support for the treaty in public opinion, which is one reason proponents were so caught off-guard by the negative vote. This indicates that meeting the concerns of members of Congress and their staffs may be even more important than relying on polls to gauge support. The fierce opposition to the U.S.-India nuclear deal in the Indian Parliament and the problems Boris Yeltsin had in dealing with the Russian Duma over ratification of the START II treaty show that conflict between the executive and legislative branches over international security issues is not just an American phenomenon.

The possible role of politically binding arrangements, as opposed to formal treaties, must also be considered. The former approach got a major boost when it was applied to the problem of long-range, nuclear-armed, sea-launched cruise missiles (SLCMs) in the START I Treaty, and it became the preferred method of dealing with nuclear weapons issues in the George W. Bush administration, It amounts to a good-faith promise to do, or not do, something, but without a formal legal commitment. Another notable example was the reciprocal, unilateral steps taken by the United States and Russia in 1991–1992 with respect to shorter-range nuclear weapons. Such arrangements are considered easier to negotiate, avoid bruising ratification battles, provide flexibility to change one's mind later, and generally involve less precision. In the case of the Presidential Nuclear Initiatives, there have been questions raised, precisely because of the lack of verification arrangements. The default position, for matters as weighty as the ones discussed here, should be that commitments should be precise and legally binding. However, it is possible that certain confidence-building measures might be best expressed in politically binding form. Examples might be commitments to greater transparency, agreements to publish certain data periodically, budgetary commitments, and so on. In a strict legal sense, the term *violation* is not appropriate for politically binding arrangements—an important distinction likely to be lost on many observers.

The agreements in question should have clear procedures for consultation and clarification regarding compliance issues. These are well developed in the CTBT. Careful thought must also be given to the procedures (and possible penalties) for withdrawal. States will insist on the right to withdraw, but doing so could be an extremely serious event. Discussions now under way regarding strengthening the criteria and penalties for withdrawal from the NPT could provide a useful guide.

Serious problems in the areas of verification and compliance, whether real or perceived, could bring the entire process to a halt rather quickly. Dealing with legitimate doubts regarding whether radical nuclear disarmament will work—and even if it does, whether it is a good idea—will require extraordinary leadership.

Issues[15]

Will states that have consistently advocated disarmament continue to maintain that position when they must begin to give up their own weapons and accept strict monitoring and transparency measures?

India comes to mind here. While a long-term leader in advocating disarmament by the NWS, India showed great reluctance to accept monitoring of its own nuclear facilities in connection with the U.S.-India nuclear deal. A number of NNWS may well be assuming that nuclear disarmament will involve no cost or inconvenience to them. This will clearly not be the case, at least at very low levels.

Will some states insist that deep reductions in nuclear weapons be accompanied by new constraints on conventional weapons?

We are already seeing the view that the elimination of nuclear weapons (which are not useable) will give an unfair advantage to states with powerful conventional weapons (which are useable). Although this is a legitimate point, and it is true that many of the roles previously assigned to nuclear weapons can today be carried out by precision conventional weapons, this view amounts to moving the goal posts. This sort of linkage could well make progress impossible, since it is very difficult to see how the world could solve both problems simultaneously. The solution may be to put more effort into strengthening regional alliances and solving regional security problems.[16]

In addition, some of the political and security concerns of the NNWS regarding a shrinking nuclear umbrella and the growing importance of conventional weapons could be met by strengthening positive security assurances (PSAs), and especially negative security assurances (NSAs). In 1995, in connection with the indefinite extension of the NPT, the NWS provided rather comprehensive NSAs to the NNWS. This was welcomed by the UNSC in Resolution 984. Since then, however, all the NWS except China appear to have softened and made less clear these assurances, which has alarmed many NNWS. The NWS could restate and clarify their NSA, perhaps recast somewhat to take account of the threat of WMD terrorism. These assurances could also be made legally binding, which has not been the case up to now. This was recommended by the Blix WMD Commission.[17]

How great will nations' tolerance of risk be as reductions proceed?

This is a key question that is unknowable at present. Much will depend on the overall security environment and whether serious problems arise as reductions proceed. Risk has both technical and psychological components. The willingness of the Bush administration to accept the risk of not even attempting to devise a verification regime for the BWC, FMCT, and Moscow Treaty (SORT) provides an interesting example of a recent risk versus benefit analysis. Sharp contrast to this is provided by world reactions to the possibility that Iran might acquire a few nuclear weapons, at a time when the United States and Russia each have thousands. States with less experience with intrusive monitoring, or with serious regional security concerns (e.g., Israel, India, Pakistan, China), may have a view of risk that causes them to be reluctant to accept verification measures others believe are essential. A patient process of demonstrations, trials, and consistent successes will be necessary. As noted, demonstrations of proposed equipment and procedures while an agreement is still being negotiated can provide reassurance to skeptical states.

The United States and Russia could bilaterally reduce to about 1,000 deployed nuclear weapons without changing anything really fundamental; the Triad, deterrence, and superiority to third countries would still be in place much as they are today. It has been reported that Russia has already proposed reductions to this level.[18] As levels get lower, the pace may need to slow down, and patience and a lower tolerance for compliance problems will be needed. In terms of verification, several pauses or plateaus in the reductions process may be needed to assess how well the verification system is functioning and to make course corrections as necessary.

In addition to nuclear weapons themselves, are there other items that should be constrained for verification reasons?

In addition to nuclear weapons themselves, a close look will need to be taken at their delivery systems. The START treaty constrains delivery systems (strategic ballistic missiles and their launchers and heavy bombers). It also constrains the numbers of nuclear warheads that can be deployed, but not the disposition of warheads removed from deployed systems. The Moscow Treaty constrains the numbers of deployed nuclear warheads, but not their delivery systems. Most descriptions of deep reductions refer to nuclear weapons but do not mention delivery systems. This confusion obviously must be cleared up. At least at low levels, one cannot allow large numbers of uncounted ICBMs and SLBMs without warheads, or launchers without missiles, to remain deployed (or perhaps even in storage) because of the considerable risk of breakout this would pose.

In addition, at least some reductions will be achieved through "downloading," in which missiles and bombers will be deployed with less than their maximum loadings. Again, this must be controlled to prevent an excessive risk of cheating or breakout. A further complication is that, in some cases, nuclear warheads may be replaced by conventional warheads, a change already proposed in the United States. This should be acceptable in principle, but verification issues must be worked out so that countries can have some assurance regarding the numbers and types of warheads being deployed.

A further issue concerns the fissile material recovered from dismantled nuclear weapons, which is discussed in detail later in this book. One fundamental problem with regard to monitoring both nuclear weapons and fissile material concerns the detection of HEU. While weapons-grade plutonium can be detected under reasonable conditions, the detection of HEU remains very difficult, especially if shielding is employed. The physics behind this situation will not change. Active interrogation of suspicious objects with neutron beams is one possible solution, but this approach involves health and safety issues.

What definitional problems must be solved for effective verification to be possible?

During the reductions process, there must be clear counting rules and clear agreed-on procedures for removing nuclear weapons and their delivery systems from the count. These are present in the START treaty, but not in the Moscow Treaty. There is some latitude for what the details of these definitions and rules may be, but they must be clear and agreed. In addition, nuclear weapons consist of many components, and, especially at low levels, there must also be a clear understanding of what constitutes a nuclear weapon. A similar problem was encountered, and solved, in the START treaty on the question of what constitutes an ICBM or SLBM for counting purposes. Because of different practices, different definitions were applied to U.S. and Soviet missiles, and this was perfectly satisfactory and effectively verifiable. Later, however, issues arose that related to interpretations of language, which provides a cautionary note for the care with which such matters must be negotiated.

Should the goal be the total elimination of nuclear weapons, or should a small residue be retained?

This is an interesting question, but not one that needs to be answered now. When the world eliminated smallpox, some samples were retained "just in case." A similar model could apply to nuclear weapons. On the one hand, for purely verification purposes, complete elimination would be preferable. On the other hand, a few nuclear weapons, if securely maintained by a reliable and trusted international organization or state, could reduce fears of cheating or massive aggression using non–nuclear weapons. One possible approach would be to aim for the second approach, but to move to total elimination only once confidence and trust had reached a level that made it acceptable.

When compliance disputes arise, who decides guilt or innocence?

This is a thorny political issue that needs urgent attention. The consistent U.S. position has been that such decisions are the responsibility of the individual states-parties, not of an implementing organization, such as an executive council or its secretariat. Agreements have generally been drafted to reflect this approach, but not always in an unambiguous fashion. The United States and other highly developed countries have access to NTM and have vast analytical and diplomatic capabilities that enable them to make such decisions on their own. Smaller countries, however, lack these advantages, and many want the implementing organizations to make these difficult compliance decisions for them, or at least provide advice. An interesting compromise is found in the CTBT. Although the organization in Vienna will not be empowered to make decisions on guilt or innocence, the International Data Center will conduct relevant analyses at no cost in response to requests from states-parties to help them make their individual compliance decisions.

A related point illustrating the distinction between monitoring and compliance is that inspectors under the START treaty can identify "ambiguities" but not "violations." In other cases, they may report that they are "unable to confirm" something. A judgment regarding whether a *violation* has occurred is wisely reserved to the political level where all relevant information is available, not just what was seen at a particular place and time.

A further issue is how, assuming decisions regarding compliance are made by individual states-parties, these are turned into an overall verdict of the international community. The UNSC, of course, is the supreme authority, but it does not seem reasonable that all compliance issues must rise to that level for resolution. Finally, there is the problem of whether whatever body is given the authority to make these decisions can only issue a guilty verdict, or whether it can also proclaim an accused state innocent. Here one again encounters the problem of proving the negative, which was so troublesome in Iraq. This arises in particular if the accusation is broad (this country is hiding nuclear warheads somewhere) rather than specific (this batch of warheads was not dismantled according to agreed procedures). If there is no definitive mechanism for closing out an issue, it will fester for years and undermine the entire process. These are legal issues that are certainly solvable, but we must find something better than the ad hoc processes that now exist.

What can be done to improve the resolution of compliance disputes?

As already noted, the overall record is not encouraging. Violations could be divided into minor or technical violations (failure to meet deadlines, inadvertent mistakes by local commanders, submission of incomplete or incorrect data, etc.) and "material breach." The latter is defined by the Vienna Convention on the Law of Treaties as the unsanctioned repudiation of the treaty or "the violation of a provision essential to the accomplishment of the object or purpose of the treaty." The latter entitles other states-parties to withdraw completely or suspend their compliance with portions of the treaty.[19]

There is general agreement that compliance and enforcement need to be improved, but there is no consensus on how to achieve this. Even in existing agreements, there is little consistency in the mechanisms for handling compliance issues. Most, but not all, have some sort of implementation/compliance body, and some have an executive council. Some agreements specify possible penalties for bad behavior (fines, loss of vote, etc.), and some do not. Some (NPT, CWC, BWC) make explicit mention of resorting to the UN General Assembly or Security Council. The CWC explicitly mentions the possibility of seeking an advisory opinion from the International Court of Justice. The supreme authority with the power to impose serious penalties, such as economic/political sanctions or military action, is, of course, the UNSC. The difficulties of achieving consensus in the UNSC in the cases of Iraq, Iran, and North

Korea are well-known. These result from differing national perspectives and the veto power. One factor in the reluctance of these bodies to take decisive action is the justifiable fear of making the situation worse. Another is the perception that there is a double standard in judging compliance and in what constitutes "a threat to international peace and security," thus justifying a Chapter VII resolution.

One can imagine a nightmare situation in which bloggers are constantly setting compliance brush fires, which spread rapidly through the Internet and are followed by charges of cover-ups before responsible intelligence judgments can be made. It may prove easier in theory than in practice to ignore such problems. The solution must be a system to separate the wheat from the chaff and to resolve compliance issues fairly and within a reasonable period of time. It is difficult to imagine that any such system could be effective if any state could exercise a veto over its operations and conclusions.

These issues are discussed in more detail later in this book. One possibility would be a new body specifically established to deal with compliance issues. It would have wide representation and make decisions by majority or supermajority vote, without any veto rights. A further issue, beyond the scope of this chapter, would be how to implement remedial actions and punishments as appropriate following a guilty verdict.

Who should pay for monitoring and verification?

This will probably be a contentious issue. Based on our experience with other agreements, the cost of an effective monitoring system, together with a mechanism for making and enforcing compliance decisions, will be substantial. However, the costs will surely be less than the cost to individual countries of maintaining nuclear weapon forces. For example, it is estimated that the United States spent more than $50 billion on activities related to nuclear weapons in FY 2008.[20] During negotiation of the CTBT, the substantial cost of developing the IMS and OSI regimes was controversial. Some states believed that the state with nuclear weapons should bear the entire cost, since they had "caused the problem." The P-5 objected to this, pointing out the benefits of the CTBT to the entire world and noting that it had been vigorously sought for decades by the G-77 and other NNWS. It was finally agreed that all states-parties would contribute, based on the UN scale of assessments. A possible compromise could also follow the CWC model and have each country bear the cost of dismantling its own nuclear weapons systems, with all states sharing in the cost of the common monitoring tasks.

Another approach would be to continue to rely on the NPT/IAEA monitoring system, suitably strengthened and adapted to a world with few nuclear weapons, to keep the NNWS free of nuclear weapons. The NWS (all states with nuclear weapons, not just the five states defined in the NPT) then would accept a separate system devised specifically for them. This could be run by the IAEA or by the NWS themselves. There would presumably need to be two separate types of inspections for the NWS. The first would be those that monitor the dismantling of nuclear devices and the disposition of their fissile material. The second would be those that inspect facilities formerly (or currently, during reductions) associated with nuclear weapons. The latter would need to include any challenge inspections. One of many issues to be solved would be what access, if any, inspectors from NNWS should have to sensitive technology in the NWS.

It may well be that some states will require technical and economic assistance in the reductions process, which should be provided as appropriate. The United States (through its Cooperative Threat Reduction Program) and other states have been quite generous in assisting the states of the former Soviet Union to deal with obligations regarding their WMDs, as well as in improving the security of the remaining nuclear weapons. This could serve as a good model for the future.

How would hedging affect verification?

It is difficult to foresee today what sort of hedging or safeguards programs might be permitted and pursued at very low or zero levels. One would expect the United States and Russia, and perhaps others, to maintain some capability to resume production/deployment of nuclear weapons in the event of serious cheating, breakout, or other dire threats to national security. Under the current testing moratorium (and presumably under the CTBT after it enters into force), the United States maintains the capability to resume nuclear testing within a certain period of time. France is the only NWS that has completely closed its nuclear test site. Some sort of safeguards program would almost certainly be a requirement for ratification in the United States and perhaps other countries. Again, the closer a state is to acquiring or reacquiring nuclear weapons, the more tenuous verification becomes. Safeguards programs, perhaps under international supervision, could make states less nervous about the consequences of cheating or breakout. There is little more one can say about this topic at this early stage, except that any such programs should be transparent and, of course, legal.

Will these problems be simply too difficult to solve?

There needs to be a happy medium between the 1,000 pages of the START treaty, which took nine years to negotiate, and the 2 pages of the Moscow Treaty (SORT), which took a few hours. U.S. defense secretary Robert Gates has supported a new post-START/SORT agreement with further reductions, noting that one would not wish to repeat the complexity and negotiating effort of START. He urged an agreement that is "shorter, simpler and easier to adjust to real-world conditions" than current agreements. That is a sentiment shared by many, but whether it is compatible with effective verification, at least as it has been understood up to now, is problematic. Of course, Secretary Gates was addressing the next big step in nuclear arms control, not the problem of getting to zero.[21] This illustrates that, while it is important to reaffirm the overall commitment in the NPT, it would be best not to think of one cosmic agreement but a series of agreements over many years, each building upon the lessons of the previous ones.

Options

The preceding discussion leads to several possible options in the field of verification. Note that the options listed here are simply ideas, not necessarily recommendations. Some of these possible options are not needed today, but they would show seriousness of purpose and begin to create the international political climate that will be needed to achieve reasonably effective verification.

- States should recommit themselves to the goal of Article VI of the NPT. They should reaffirm the relevant portions of the "13 Steps" agreed at the 2000 Review Conference—such as an "unequivocal undertaking" to eliminate nuclear arsenals, and a commitment that this process should be "irreversible," "under effective international control," and accompanied by "verification capabilities necessary to ensuring compliance." This step should be accompanied by a strengthening of the NPT in general, including the commitments in Articles I and II, and should be a centerpiece of the 2010 Review Conference.
- States could lay out a notional schedule (time-bound framework) for achieving the NPT goals.
- States could begin intensive research and development on the verification tools necessary for effective verification in moving toward a world free of nuclear weapons. British initiatives in this regard should be pursued.[22] In particular, the work started under the Trilateral Initiative should be revived and pursued vigorously.
- Talks could be started soon among all the NWS on the relevant monitoring and verification issues.
- Talks could be started soon among the P-5, plus India, Pakistan, and Israel, on the relevant monitoring and verification issues.
- Talks could be started soon in the Conference on Disarmament on general issues related to nuclear disarmament.
- States could begin to "get tough" on compliance issues under all existing arms control agreements.
- States could begin to develop a "zero tolerance" attitude toward noncompliance with arms control agreements. This would include relevant UNSC resolutions, such as 1540. This approach of not tolerating even minor crimes, such as graffiti and broken windows, has improved the environment in certain urban areas. This would not mean meting out punishments for "minor" offenses, such as failure to submit required declarations. It would, however, mean that no arms control compliance issues would go unnoticed. Countries would be reminded in a timely fashion of their obligations and failures to comply would

be publicized—a form of "name and shame." When a country needs advice or assistance in meeting its obligations, which sometimes seems to be the case for smaller countries, such help should be asked for and provided.

- States could begin to increase the transparency of their nuclear activities. This would include working toward full declarations of holdings of nuclear weapons, including nondeployed weapons, and fissile materials by all states. At least initially, there would be no regime to monitor these voluntary declarations. The goal would be to begin to build confidence and develop an accurate baseline from which reductions could be measured. This would clearly be a gradual and iterative process. The United States, United Kingdom, and France, which have traditionally been open about their forces and plans, should take the lead, gradually encouraging Russia, China, India, and Pakistan to follow. At the other end of the spectrum, one would need to understand that Israel could not, and probably should not, make dramatic revelations about its nuclear potential at this time.

- States could study the lessons learned from the work of UNSCOM, UNMOVIC, and the IAEA Action team in Iraq and consider how to apply these to future monitoring and verification problems.

- States could create an International Satellite Verification Agency (ISVA) and begin to train an international cadre of experts in imagery analysis to increase international knowledge about, and stakes in, monitoring and verification. This idea was originally proposed by France in the 1970s but was rejected by both the United States and the USSR. This agency would use commercial imagery now widely available and could even develop its own satellite capability.

- The UN could create an independent international monitoring capability with special expertise in nuclear matters. This could be modeled on UNMOVIC, which was recently disbanded. Such a body could be given overall responsibility for monitoring nuclear disarmament, or it could be used as a rapid reaction team, under the control of the UN secretary-general to investigate compliance problems. Ad hoc on-site investigations have been conducted by the UN in the past (e.g., to investigate yellow rain, alleged use of chemical weapons, etc.), but the use of ad hoc pickup teams would not be adequate to this task. Of course, care would need to be taken to harmonize the responsibilities of such a body with those of existing monitoring organizations, such as the IAEA, OPCW, CTBTO, and U.S.-Russia bilateral bodies.[23]

Consequences

The consequences of attempting to eliminate nuclear weapons but failing to establish an effective and trusted system of monitoring/verification/compliance could be very serious. Such a failure might make actual cheating more likely. Even more probable would be continuous disputes, charges, and countercharges. Especially at low levels, international security and stability could be at risk, with a greater risk of both conventional and nuclear war. More probably, the reduction process would not get very far, because lack of confidence in the process would make it politically impossible to continue. Even if the verification process worked perfectly, if it were not accompanied by effective mechanisms for enforcement and redress, the results would be similar.

It must be recognized that there will almost certainly be significant opposition, both in the United States and abroad, to the actions contemplated in this volume.[24] The arguments against will be along two principal lines, which parallel those used against the CTBT: that giving up nuclear weapons would decrease national security, and that the verification system would not be effective enough to guarantee the compliance of others. The verification issue will be whipped up by allegations of cheating (which may or may not have some foundation). We saw this during the Cold War when some saw nuclear explosions in earthquakes, attempts to blind satellites in pipeline fires, and so forth. There was also twisting of treaty language and provocative claims regarding the intent and character of the other side's leaders. Some charges will be made out of genuine concern, while others may be attempts to derail the process or to discredit other states-parties. The Internet is likely to fan suspicions of violations and subsequent cover-ups.

Recognition of these consequences leads to the conclusion that an effective verification system, whose details are discussed elsewhere in this book, is essential. This system will almost certainly have unprecedented requirements for intrusive inspections and transparency. This feature will encounter opposition, in the United States and other countries, on the grounds of defending national sovereignty and proprietary information. All these legitimate concerns can be met through a patient program of education, demonstrations of equipment and techniques, and, above all, an unblemished record of success as reductions proceed. This does not mean that no problems will occur—they almost certainly will. It means that such problems must be dealt with promptly and fairly, so that publics and elites in all countries acquire confidence that the system works.

The *positive* consequences of establishing a successful monitoring/ verification/compliance system are also obvious and need not be elaborated here. There are also possible secondary benefits. The technical nature of the CTBT IMS/OSI systems has brought together scientists from many countries in cooperative efforts and produced benefits beyond the narrow goals of monitoring the CTBT—better understanding of geophysics and earthquakes, tsunami warning, monitoring of radiation hazards, and more. Similar spin-off benefits from international cooperation in nuclear disarmament could result from our present efforts. Thus, the mechanisms and possible new bodies created by our efforts could, if successful, find additional roles in resolution of disputes, regional security problems, and other international challenges that have eluded solution.

Honesty compels us to admit that we cannot see today the details of the monitoring and verification systems that will be needed to get the world safely to zero nuclear weapons. To see that clearly today would require an accurate understanding of the degree of openness, trust, and conflict that will exist in the world years into the future. The greatest ingenuity will be needed near the end of the process. Academics and think tanks can usefully begin to occupy themselves with these issues. Governments, in contrast, should not allow the debate to focus on these endgame issues, which will span many administrations and whose solutions are not needed now. Their priority should be on the near-term task of negotiating the follow-on agreements to the START and SORT treaties.[25] This should include further reductions and confidence-building measures, which, though not simple, are well within our present knowledge and ability. They should also set in motion the research and development that will be needed further down the road to achieving one of humanity's greatest and most urgent goals.

Notes

The views and characterizations expressed are those of the author and do not necessarily reflect the policies of the U.S. government or Georgetown University.

1. President Barack Obama, speech in Prague, Czech Republic, April 5, 2009.

2. "UN Chief Outlines Five-Point Nuclear Disarmament Plan," Agence France Presse, October 24, 2008.

3. Ivo Daalder and Jan Lodal, "The Logic of Zero: Toward a World without Nuclear Weapons," *Foreign Affairs*, November/December 2008.

4. It has been suggested that "National Technical Means" be replaced by "National Means and Methods" to emphasize that even states without sophisticated technical assets can play a role in monitoring. This formulation has not been widely accepted internationally, but it was used in the draft agreement on a Fissionable Material Cutoff Treaty tabled by the United States at the Conference on Disarmament in 2006.

5. A useful recent discussion of effective verification is found in David Hafemeister, "The Comprehensive Test Ban Treaty: Effectively Verifiable," *Arms Control Today*, October 2008.

6. "Interim Report of the Congressional Commission on the Strategic Posture of the United States," December 15, 2008, p. 9.

7. For a more detailed discussion of experience with compliance issues, see Masahiko Asada, Ola Dahlman, Edward Ifft, Nicholas Kyriakopoulos, Jenifer Mackby, Bernard Massinon, Arend Meerburg, and Bernard Sitt, *Assessing Compliance with Arms Control Treaties* (Geneva: Geneva Centre for Security Policy; Paris: Centre d'Études de Securité Internationale et de Maitrise des Armements, 2007. See also Edward Ifft, "Witness for the

Prosecution: International Organizations and Arms Control Verification," *Arms Control Today*, November 2005.

8. Defense Threat Reduction Agency, http://dtirp.dtra.mil/TIC/synopses/start.cfm, confirmed May 18, 2010.

9. Amy F. Woolf, "Strategic Arms Control after START: Issues and Options," Congressional Research Service, December 23, 2008, p. 23.

10. On April 8, 2010, after this chapter was completed, Presidents Obama and Medvedev signed the New START Treaty. Upon entry into force, it will replace both START and SORT. It incorporates many features of the START verification regime, generally in simplified form.

11. U.S. Department of State, "Adherence to and Compliance with Arms Control, Nonproliferation and Disarmament Agreements." The most recent report covers the period from January 2002 to January 2004.

12. See ibid.

13. United Nations Institute for Disarmament Research (UNIDIR) and the Verification Research, Training and Information Centre (VERTIC), *Coming to Terms with Security: A Handbook on Verification and Compliance* (Geneva and London: Authors, 2003), chap. 4.

14. A good discussion of some of the techniques studied in the Trilateral Initiative is contained in *Monitoring Nuclear Weapons and Nuclear-Explosive Materials*, U.S. National Academy of Sciences, 2005. See also Thomas E. Shea, "The Trilateral Initiative: A Model for the Future?" *Arms Control Today*, May 2008.

15. The landmark study inspired by the *Wall Street Journal* articles is *Reykjavik Revisited: Steps toward a World Free of Nuclear Weapons*, ed. George P. Shultz, Sidney D. Drell, and James E. Goodby (Stanford, CA: Hoover Institution and Nuclear Threat Initiative, 2008). For a further comprehensive analysis of the issues and options involved in deep reductions, see George Perkovich and James M. Acton, *Abolishing Nuclear Weapons*, Adelphi Paper 396 (London: International Institute for Strategic Studies, 2008). See also Sidney D. Drell and James E. Goodby, *What Are Nuclear Weapons For?* (Washington, DC: Arms Control Association, October 2007), and Alexei Arbatov and Vladimir Dvorkin, *Beyond Nuclear Deterrence* (Washington, DC: Carnegie Endowment for International Peace, 2006).

16. For a further discussion of nuclear deterrence by the author, see Edward Ifft, "Deterrence, Blackmail, Friendly Persuasion," in *Defence & Security Analysis* (London: Routledge, 2007), 237–256.

17. Hans Blix et al., *Weapons of Terror: Freeing the World of Nuclear, Biological and Chemical Arms*, Report of the WMD Commission (Stockholm: Fritzes & WoltersKluwer-foretag, 2006), 73.

18. Lev D. Ryabev, "Fundamental Principles of Russian-U.S. Cooperation in the Nuclear Arena: A Review of Opportunities and Threats," in *Future of the Nuclear Security Environment in 2015* (Washington, DC: U.S. National Academy of Sciences, 2009), 16.

19. Vienna Convention on the Law of Treaties, Art. 60, para. 3.

20. Stephen I. Schwartz and Deepti Choubey, "Nuclear Security Spending: Assessing Costs, Examining Priorities" (Washington, DC: Carnegie Endowment for International Peace, January 2009).

21. Robert Gates, "Nuclear Weapons and Deterrence in the 21st Century," address and Q & A at the Carnegie Endowment for International Peace, October 28, 2008.

22. See, for example, David Miliband, "A World without Nuclear Weapons," *The Guardian*, December 8, 2008. A further exposition of British views is contained in "David Miliband Sets Out Six-Point Plan to Rid World of Nuclear Weapons," *The Guardian*, February 4, 2009.

23. A more detailed discussion of this idea is contained in Trevor Findlay, "A Standing United Nations Verification Body: Necessary and Feasible," in *Compliance Chronicles* (Ottawa: Canadian Centre for Treaty Compliance, December 2005).

24. A responsible case against nuclear disarmament was given by Harold Brown and John Deutch in "The Nuclear Disarmament Fantasy," *Wall Street Journal*, November 19, 2007. See also Michael May, "The Trouble with Disarmament," *Bulletin of the Atomic Scientists*, November/December 2008.

25. A recent proposal for this is found in Alexei Arbatov and Rose Gottemoeller, "New Presidents, New Agreements?" *Arms Control Today*, July/August 2008. See also Alexei Arbatov, "Russia and the United States—Time to End the Strategic Deadlock," *Carnegie Moscow Center Briefing* 10, no. 3 (June 2008).

2. Enforcement of the Rules in a Nuclear Weapon–Free World

HARALD MÜLLER

To date, enforcement policies in the context of the Nuclear Non-Proliferation Treaty (NPT)—the model closest to the conditions of a nuclear weapon–free world—have a very mixed record. In particular, the United Nations Security Council (UNSC) has not acted in a determined fashion to enforce the NPT. National interests by one or more of the P-5 have stood in the way of effective enforcement. In a nuclear weapon–free world, former nuclear weapon states might not condone violations of the rules by their clients, as nuclear deterrence would not be a cheap option to fall back on for preserving their security. Collective enforcement may thus be more promising in that environment.

The UNSC, while legally the enforcer of the nonproliferation regime, is confronted with a lack of legitimacy because of missing representation and because the nuclear weapon states are called upon to enforce the non–nuclear weapons status of others. In a nuclear weapon–free world, the latter shortcoming would be eliminated along with the difference in status, and the former shortcoming might count less for the same reason or might be mitigated by UNSC reform.

Decisions on enforcement must be based on reliable forensics. The IAEA is already in a good position to grant the necessary fusing of information from state reports, inspections, intelligence provided by member states, "societal verification," and open sources. The International Atomic Energy Agency (IAEA) needs additional expertise in weapon technology that could be drawn from P-5 nuclear weapons laboratory staff acquired by the IAEA and put in a special department. To create a reliable and impartial procedure for establishing evidence, the IAEA should be the only authoritative voice determining compliance and non-compliance with the rules of a nuclear weapon–free world.

There are several ways to move from a determination of noncompliance to an international response. One would be to declare a situation in which the IAEA found a state in violation of its undertakings and assessed the time to achieve a nuclear weapons capability at less than 18 months as justifying self-defense of all members of the United Nations under Article 51 of the UN Charter. While the legitimization would be given by a neutral international organization, the decision to respond would be left to the individual states without the threat of a veto in the UNSC. In parallel to this legitimization, the UNSC could still determine an appropriate response, compelled by the possibility that otherwise a member state might act on its own and still be within the bounds of international law. Alternatively, the veto could be suspended by agreement for all cases in which a state violated the rules of the nuclear abolition treaty, or the United Nations General Assembly could legitimize action under the "Uniting for Peace" procedure.

In a world of virtual arsenals[1] rather than true abolition, falling back on nuclear deterrence after the reconstitution of nuclear weapons would appear easy, but it would undo the whole project of a nuclear weapon–free world. Envisaging this very possibility, states might take preparations that would undermine mutual trust, lead to a dangerous and unstable rush for the bomb, and result in more states with nuclear weapons than exist today. A conventional military response would be the alternative, though not pleasant, possibility both against smaller and bigger perpetrators. If conventional arms control accompanies nuclear disarmament, conventional forces, including ballistic missiles, could be reconfigured in a way as to facilitate such collective action. Missile defenses, if thoroughly limited and configured, might serve as reassurance against breakout. To facilitate the process toward nuclear disarmament, missile defenses should be strictly limited right away.

A nuclear weapon–free world has the best prospects for coming into being, for credible enforcement procedures, and for sustainability, if the great powers follow the rules of the classical "Concert" that relied on mutual respect, recognition of vital interests, close consultation, and the renunciation of the unilateral use of force. These conditions appear to be challenging, but by no means impossible, steps on the way toward the final vision.

Background

Enforcement is the Achilles' heel of the vision of a nuclear weapon–free world in a double sense. States possessing nuclear weapons (and their allies covered by extended deterrence) will take the last step from a low-number posture to true abolition only if there is a convincing answer to the crucial "what if" question: What will happen if a country party to the abolition covenant cheats on its undertakings and tries clandestinely to procure nuclear weapons, and there are strong indications of such a breach of the rules? In a nuclear weapon–free world, the single country that will possess—if for an interim period only—a nuclear weapon monopoly might be perceived to enjoy an extraordinary sway over its peers.[2] Since the monopoly would have been acquired on the basis of ill will, as one would probably conclude from cheating and rule break-ing, it augurs badly for the security of all others. For this reason, how to bring the rule breaker back to terms is a, if not *the*, key issue on the path toward complete nuclear disarmament.

Enforcement, so far, has not been the strength either of the nuclear nonproliferation regime or of the UN Security Council, which is not only the supreme authority on global security but also the ultimate guar-antor of the integrity of the NPT. The record so far is sobering: In 1991, the Security Council acted on a violation of the NPT in an incidental manner, as the consequence of a military intervention it had authorized for quite a different reason—namely, in response to Iraq's invasion of Kuwait against international law. Creatively, the Security Council installed a new instrument, the United Nations Special Commission on Iraq, via SC Resolutions 687 and 715, to enforce the disarmament of Saddam Hussein's state. While the first few years witnessed strong sup-port for UNSCOM activities by the UNSC, this support evaporated as some council members appeared willing to use the imposed sanctions for the objective of dethroning the dictator and effecting regime change, while other council members wanted to return to normalcy. UNSCOM was caught between a rock and a hard place, and no UNSC response ensued when Iraq effectively stopped its collaboration. The air operation Desert Fox in 1998 was conducted by the United States and the United Kingdom on their own authority and without the support of the UNSC as a whole. That Iraq did not admit UN inspectors after the air attack evoked no unified UNSC response. In addition to the disagreements among the P-5, the suspected abuse of UNSCOM by some members who seconded intelligence personal to UNSCOM and had those individuals reporting back to their home headquarters information, including information useful for targeting, discredited UNSCOM in the eyes of the Iraqis and other countries.[3] Nonetheless, in the main result—the complete disarmament of Iraq's WMD programs—the commission's activities were quite successful.[4]

In 1992, the UNSC imposed far-reaching sanctions on Libya in retaliation for the terror attack against a civilian airliner at Lockerbie, Scotland, with the aim of coercing Libya to admit its responsibility and pay compensation to the families of the victims. As a side effect, these sanctions convinced Libya that, to overcome its increasingly damaging isolation from the international community, it had to get rid of its weapons of mass destruction programs. In 2003, the Libyan government finally did so, again not as a consequence of a specific disarmament policy by the UNSC but as a side effect of policies targeted otherwise, and the intense diplomatic efforts of the United Kingdom and the United States.[5]

In the case of North Korea, the compliance procedures of the NPT worked initially as prescribed. The IAEA Secretariat found North Korea in violation of its NPT safeguards agreement, and after several IAEA attempts to remedy the situation by diplomatic means the agency's board of governors referred the case to the UNSC. The UNSC, in turn, was prevented from taking determined action by the cautiousness of China, North Korea's patron. It thus delegated the matter to bilateral negotiations between Washington and Pyongyang that led to the Framework Agreement of 1994; this agreement appeared to settle the issue. However, in 2002, the problem popped up again. The UNSC, once more, reacted with great caution on China's behest and left the problem to regional negotiations. It reacted to the nuclear weapon test North Korea conducted in 2006 with resolution 1718, imposing limited targeted sanctions, but did not go further. Nevertheless, the regional negotiations may still bear fruit.[6]

The case of Iran progressed at first along the path prescribed by regime procedures. The IAEA secretariat followed the lead provided by an Iranian opposition group and found the regime in violation of its safeguards agreement with the agency pursuant to the NPT. It reported the case to the board of governors, which tried at first to resolve the matter directly with Iran. When Iranian cooperation proved insufficient, the case was referred to the Security Council, according to the IAEA statute, after lengthy deliberations. The UNSC took notice of the issue and delegated further efforts to a group encompassing three major EU countries that had been negotiating with Iran on their own initiative, plus the rest of the P-5. After the negotiators found Iran intransigent, a first round of sanctions was enacted in 2006 and were tightened slightly one year later. The UNSC could not agree on farther-reaching sanctions in the light of continued Iranian noncompliance with its resolutions and continued dissatisfaction at IAEA headquarters concerning Iranian cooperation. Russia and China opposed harsher sanctions that the Western permanent UNSC members were demanding. In general, the procedures worked as they should, but P-5 unity is lacking, and the outcome is highly unpredictable at the time of this writing.[7]

Finally, there is the case of Iraq in 2002–2003. After a latent period of four years, the UNSC took up the matter of Iraq's WMD programs again in summer 2002 on the initiative of the United States and in the context of the military buildup in the Persian Gulf by the United States and the United Kingdom. The UNSC created a new instrument, UNMOVIC, with broader authority than UNSCOM, and—in contrast to UNSCOM—staff that did not remain on the parent state's payroll but were fully employed by the UN. The system worked very well. The UNSC kept a degree of unity toward Iraq well into February 2003. The cooperation between UNSC-IAEA and UNMOVIC was excellent (despite misgivings by the United States and the United Kingdom that the reports by the two organizations were not harsh enough). The military pressure brought Saddam Hussein to terms. Cooperation by Iraq was improving, and the agencies found little evidence for an ongoing weapons program, a conclusion that has stood the scrutiny of time and was not revised by the Iraq Survey Group that the United States sent to Iraq after the war in the hope of finding the weapons or weapons programs that UNMOVIC and IAEA were not capable of uncovering. Indeed, the international agencies had, like UNSCOM and the IAEA in the nineties, done a superb job. The UNSC worked well in another respect as it denied the war-willing parties a mandate. The majority of members assessed correctly that there was no legitimate reason to enact military enforcement as there was no case for it. Contrary to the allegations of the American and British leadership at this time, the UN had not failed in this case; it was the war-willing members of the UNSC who had engaged in a game of reality denial.[8]

Altogether, the record of the enforcement system is very much mixed. The UNSC was relatively successful in terminating nuclear weapons programs, or contributing to such termination, in the context of addressing a larger issue (e.g., Iraq's aggression against Kuwait, Libya's involvement in terrorist acts, or—to cast the net still wider—South Africa's apartheid policies). Sanctions (Libya, South Africa) or military action (Iraq 1991) had the side effect of terminating WMD programs. Acute proliferation crises are hard to handle; military action is often on the table, given the severity of the matter. But there is no guarantee for success, and military action risks unexpected and unintended consequences. That the UNSC has outsourced diplomatic efforts to other groups (as in the cases of North Korea and Iran) is not condemnable. This might be a sensible route to test the possibility of a diplomatic solution. As long as the UNSC preserves the supervision of the process, there is no real problem. But that it is virtually incapable of strong action when other approaches don't bear fruit is a disturbing finding.

Issues

The preceding analysis of past experiences shows the dilemmas and difficulties of the challenge of responding to breaches of the rules. In the present world, nuclear weapon states and their allies can fall back on deterrence; however, even now there are doubts whether deterrence will work under all circumstances and against all possible enemies. The debate about the deterrability of "rogue states"—relevant in the light of the irresponsible and irrational utterances against the existence of Israel by Iranian president Mahmoud Ahmadinedjad—illustrates this dilemma. Before we enter a more detailed discussion of the issues, we must realize that most analysts of the issue have concluded that the advantages conferred to a rule breaker by what would be necessarily a relatively small nuclear arsenal are small, while the risks and costs are high. Sanctions of some form would certainly ensue, the risk of one's nuclear assets being attacked would be very high, and the potential strength of the sanctioning parties—practically the whole world minus the perpetrator—would in any event surpass his own. (The exception to this rule would, at present, seem to be the United States. Unequal growth rates, as in the past decades, over the next decades, however, would make it highly unlikely that the United States could keep its share of world military expenditures and the ensuing relative strength of its armed forces.). The probability of being caught in the act of developing and producing nuclear weapons would be high in a well-devised verification system, and even the possibility for a former nuclear weapon state that had stored away a few warheads to be exposed by internal "whistle-blowers" would be distinct, notably if incentives for blowing the whistle would be part and parcel of the non-nuclear security regime.[9]

In a nuclear weapon–free world, nuclear deterrence against a perpetrator is not an option; at a minimum, it would require reconstitution of a nuclear-deterrent force. Reconstitution would be proportionally easier if "zero nukes" means "virtual arsenals" rather than a completely erased nuclear weapon complex—meaning the complete destruction of the conventional components of the weapons, and the transfer of the fissile and fusionable materials of the "physics package" to civilian uses (or transmutation). The first question, then, is to inquire whether virtual arsenals would facilitate reactions to cheating and thereby contribute to security in a nuclear weapon–free world. It must be recognized, however, that this would mean replacing "enforcement" with "nuclear deterrence," which is counterintuitive and requires further debate: The breach of the non-nuclear rule would be countered by the return to nuclear armed multipolarity. The trade-off has to be thoroughly evaluated.

The second issue, then, is how to determine whether there is a need to enforce—that is, whether a breach of the rules occurred. This is the question of the methods and quality of verification, and in whom to entrust the highly delicate task of weighing the evidence provided by the verification organization.

The third issue is *who* is to take, in what institutions and under what procedures, the eventual enforcement decision. Can one use existing institutions, notably the veto-ridden UNSC? Is it necessary to change the existing decision-making rules and to establish something new? Is multilateral enforcement preferable to unilateral enforcement under all circumstances, or could they complement each other? In this context, the lessons of past compliance politics, as analyzed in the last section, must be taken into account. There are three impediments in the way of effective enforcement:[10]

- First, the executors of nonproliferation are the erstwhile sinners. The central role of the P-5 in NPT enforcement is seen by many as objectionable, yet without their participation, initiative and leadership enforcement would just not happen. Fortunately, in a world of progressing disarmament or the final stage of abolition, this problem would cease to exist as the inequality in the system would be abolished together with the weapons.
- Second, diverging geostrategic as well as economic national interests of the P-5 stand in the way of a determined response to rule breaking. Such interests may be legitimate in an overall pursuit of national grand strategy in a competitive international environment, but they are counterproductive for nonprolifera- tion and, consequently, for disarmament, which both require a cooperative if not collective approach to security. If it comes to upholding a nuclear weapon–free world, individual national interests could be fatal; they have to be overcome if this final objective is to be achieved.
- Third, if it comes to sanctions—notably military ones— the lack of global representation in the Security Council is

a serious handicap as it could undermine the legitimacy of a decision that needs the support of many. Sanctions, military ones in particular, must enjoy broad global support if they are to be effective.

In addition to these three barriers, there are issues connected to enforcement on which well-minded and honest people might simply disagree: whether cheating is in fact under way or intended, how serious is the matter and how urgent is enforcement action, which means of enforcement are appropriate, and whether enforcement is more likely to be successful or counterproductive.[11]

Throughout the following deliberations, we must distinguish between two different possibilities: the rule breaker could be a former nuclear weapon state and a great power, or an ambitious novice with much less clout. It is self-evident that the international community would face a different challenge if the perpetrator were, say, China, the United States, Russia, or India, than if it were Switzerland, Serbia, Syria, or Vietnam. If renuclearization is pursued by a state in possession of all other power resources, one would need different remedies than in a situation where nuclear weapons were meant to substitute for otherwise lacking instruments of power.

How shall one evaluate the various options to deal with these three weighty issues? The first criteria is a *reality check*: how likely is it that they are politically feasible? This standard for evaluation can be further differentiated into the "political will" factor and the possibility of institutional evolution: First, are incentives in a nuclear weapon–free world distributed in such a way as to make it probable that major actors will feel compelled to do the "right thing"? Second, is the institutional setup needed to produce the needed policies likely (or at least possible) to evolve between now and then? The second criteria is expected *effectiveness*: how likely is it that they may do the job of dealing with serious cases of noncompliance? The third criteria is whether the option would *stabilize* rather than destabilize the basis for maintaining a nuclear weapon–free world. One has to be careful to devise the remedies in such a way as to not create incentives to turn back to nuclear weapons.

Options

Forensics

To devise appropriate verification procedures for the assessment of breakout that would—or could—trigger enforcement measures is one of the most tricky and difficult issues in the whole discussion about the possibility of a nuclear-free world. The assessment must be solidly based on technical evidence. It is, however, inevitable that the assessment itself would have a political component, as it would serve as the basis for a highly charged political decision. This connection of the technical and the political makes it advisable to try to keep politics away from the technicalities to as great an extent and for as long as is possible.

This initial consideration counsels strongly to keep the IAEA, notably its secretariat, in the center of technical assessment, as far as nuclear weapons materials and, eventually, nuclear weapons themselves, are concerned. On nuclear testing, the Commission for the Comprehensive Nuclear-Test-Ban Treaty Organization (CTBTO) would clearly be the institution to turn to; while on delivery capabilities and missile defenses, other procedures or institutions would have to be chosen or created. (This issue is not further addressed in this chapter.)

The way the IAEA has functioned in diverse crises—provided the member states and the UNSC, notably the P-5, have permitted it to utilize all its assets—is remarkable. Today, the IAEA is in a position to rely on cutting-edge technology to integrate the checking of country reports for their coherence, consistency, and credibility; the results of its own inspections; public source information; and intelligence data provided by member states into a comprehensive analysis, and to draw conclusions from this mixture of quantitative and qualitative information of varying degrees of reliability. How this is technically done is not the subject of this chapter, as this is very much a matter of the verification system itself and the technical criteria inherent in it which would count as indicators of noncompliance. It is also a matter of the verification system at which level inside the agency this determination should be first made. Once this stage of decision making is reached, it is up to the director-general to take the issue up and to represent the secretariat's position.

It is notably in the realm of intelligence data and of information supplied by nonstate sources (e.g., journals, newspapers, and opposition groups) that independent and neutral expertise is absolutely crucial to walk the tightrope between complacency and false alarms, to discern the plausible from the nonsensical or the malevolent, and to derive conclusions that are convincing and reliable. The credibility of this process is the very basis of all enforcement policy. The significant loss of credibility of country-supplied intelligence information that the United States and Britain caused in the run-up to the Iraq war makes the intervention of a neutral agency indispensable for any viable enforcement system. This is one more reason to build the forensic aspect of the enforcement procedure into the IAEA. The technical capability that the IAEA would be required to possess would inevitably include knowledge about weapons design and engineering. Initially, this would have to be supplied from the weapons laboratory and factory staff of the nuclear weapons possessors whom the IAEA would have to hire. The IAEA then would have to establish procedures to regularly check the integrity of this staff; they should be, or at least should become, increasingly independent from their home countries and must be categorically prohibited from reporting back to former headquarters. Only this sort of *incommunicado* status can preserve the IAEA's credibility.

At a later stage, it might be considered whether there could be in-house training to transfer weapons knowledge to novices who may be recruited just for their talent and without regard to their country of origin. At that time, weapons knowledge would slowly fade away in former nuclear weapon states, and Articles I and II of the NPT might be replaced by stipulations that would allow the IAEA to attract good people and to transfer sensitive knowledge to a small and distinguished group of them, on the understanding that precautions would be taken so that these persons would not return to their countries and start weapons programs there. Life-long supervision, as sad as this might sound, would certainly be in order to ensure the integrity of such a system.

The alternative option to this central role of the IAEA would be a technical assessment center ("special inspectorate") at the United Nations.[12]

The rationale for this would be to have a strong technical advisory capacity as close to the Security Council, the General Assembly, and the secretariat as possible. In practice, that would mean that assessments by the IAEA on the state of compliance by a suspected state, and the seriousness of any violations, would be scrutinized by what could be called a "second technical chamber." Both false alarms and complacency might be less likely if two competent authorities, rather than one, would screen the same evidence. On the other hand, the unique competence of the IAEA results from its permanent involvement in safeguarding practice, laboratory activities, self-critical reflection about its own practices, the results, shortcomings in the system, and new technical possibilities. It is hard to see how this competence could be matched by a body remote from practice. Even if the members of such a UN-based assessment center would be recruited from the IAEA inspectorate, they would lose their close contact to practice. The risk would arise, then, that the technical competence of this second assessment actor would be weaker than that of the first one, the IAEA. At the same time, the proximity to the UNSC might create the danger of immersing politics into this last stage of technical assessment and thus undo the very purpose of the whole consideration of this section: how to create an assessment process that is as little politicized as possible. The last thing one would wish is a quarrel between competing agencies defending their turf when clarity is most needed. For these reasons, it appears more sensible to leave technical assessment of noncompliance, including its seriousness (i.e., closeness to weapon status and quantities involved) to the IAEA and focus the deliberations at the UN on the appropriate response. Technical advice at UN headquarters should be limited to liaison officers seconded by the IAEA.[13]

Evaluation

Major powers might be inclined to agree on the IAEA as the assessment center for a couple of reasons. Institutional design would be cheap; freedom of action would be constrained, but not absolutely; and the risk of unilateralism—which one might fear from other great powers—would be satisfactorily curbed. The requirements for institutional change would be minimal in the case of the "liaison" option but greater for a full-fledged UN technical assessment unit that, as a duplication of what we have got already in the nuclear field, would probably meet opposition on grounds of cost.

Effectiveness can be expected to be high and would probably improve with the IAEA's improvement in forensic technology and additional experience with cases of suspected noncompliance. The double-checking by the IAEA and a new assessment unit at UN headquarters risks contradictory and thus less effective outcomes of assessment procedures. With high reliability of the IAEA, there would be no visible incentives, at this stage of the enforcement process, to retain a nuclear option or to return to nuclear weaponry.

Decision Making

The process of determining the appropriate response to a violation could be constructed one of several ways. It could be a generalized license for individual countries to react to an alarming IAEA assessment; it could be the normal UNSC procedure, possibly with a referral to the UN General Assembly (UNGA) if the veto blocks a necessary response; it could be an extraordinary UNSC procedure with a treaty-regulated suspension of the veto; or it could be the collective decision of all states-parties to the nuclear abolition treaty.

Green Light Procedure: IAEA Secretariat Decision as Trigger Mechanism

The simplest procedure would be a "green light" arrangement: If and when the IAEA secretariat finds a state in serious noncompliance with its undertakings under a nuclear abolition treaty, it would state that it had reason to believe that the state had embarked on a nuclear weapons program, report a lack of cooperation by the state to clarify the situation and to remedy its noncompliance, and indicate that it could not guarantee that the said state could not produce nuclear weapons within a time frame of less than 18 months. This would then give other states the right to apply appropriate measures of self-help under Article 51 of the UN Charter. The stipulation might be included in the abolition treaty, and it might be confirmed or not by a UNSC resolution to the same effect.[14]

The procedure avoids the problems with automatic sanctions that oblige states to act in a certain way if such a finding is made. States would probably prefer to define their own assessment of a particular situation and thereby object to automaticity.[15] If the response to such a finding, however, is left to the choice of individual governments, the likelihood that one or the other would act is clearly above zero, which would serve as a useful deterrent in the deliberation of any government to defy the abolition treaty, while the misgivings connected to automaticity would be avoided. At the same time, the flaws and risks of nonlegitimized unilateral action would be avoided, as the authoritative statement by the IAEA secretariat would be needed to make military action legal.

Such a right of preventive defense against a future nuclear threat might entail the enhancement of the meaning of "self-defence" in Article 51 of the UN Charter; this could create concern that this authorization of unilateral action could undermine international security.[16] However, to make the right contingent on the assessment of an impartial international agency should go a long way to mitigate this concern.

One may object that the IAEA secretariat is a technical entity only, installed to serve the interests of the member states of that organization, and thus not in a position to take a decision of such political weight and impact. On the other hand, the contents of the IAEA report are, indeed, purely technical, even though they have grave political implications. One could argue that this is the very advantage of this particular procedure: without much politicking, the switch would be flipped. For a state considering noncompliance in a world free of nuclear weapons, the risk would be considerable to be caught red-handed (provided the verification system is well designed, an issue that is not the subject of this chapter); being caught red-handed, then, would mean that the incriminated state would automatically run the risk of becoming the victim of legal and legitimate preventive attack; since legitimacy and legality would no longer be a concern by the state considering a military response, the threshold to enact forceful action would be considerably lowered, and the deterrence value of the arrangement against moves of noncompliance would be considerable. While governments now entitled to respond might still be under constraints such as pacifist public opinion, the perpetrator could not count on the effectiveness of such constraints.

This considerable strengthening of the position of the secretariat is recommended to avoid the problems of possible politicking that arise already in the IAEA board of governors, not only in the UNSC. To give a finding by the secretariat a "trigger function" has thus the big advantage to make the whole system more reliable. If the pure technicality of this procedure would be considered unsatisfactory, one might consider having the IAEA board confirm the report of the secretariat. The board is undoubtedly a political body, but it is authorized to take its decision with majority (even though it strives to avoid voting). Since no veto applies, a noncompliant actor could not undermine another state's claim of a legal right to respond militarily by objecting to an IAEA board decision.

UN Security Council

The second option is a procedure prescribed by the NPT that could be transferred to a nuclear abolition treaty: Following the finding by the IAEA inspectorate and an ensuing report by the IAEA director-general on a case of grave noncompliance, the board of governors would report the matter to the UNSC without this action having the automatic invocation of the right to self-defense as in the option just discussed. The UNSC would then inquire into the matter with a view to determine whether the danger arising from this case of noncompliance was grave enough to justify a collective mandate for preventive action. Such a mandate would presumably, following past precedents, authorize "UN member states in a position to do so to apply all necessary means to remedy the situation." Whether the UNSC would go further in prescribing specific action and in obliging member states to participate is an additional question that needs no further elaboration here. One can only speculate that the gravity of a breach of an abolition treaty in a nuclear weapon–free world would motivate the UNSC to ensure that collective, rather than individual, action would be appropriate—but this is a matter that can be left to the circumstances prevailing at the time.

The UNSC would be, of course, hampered by the veto if the perpetrator was either one of the veto-endowed permanent members or a close ally that the member state would not like to be in harm's way even if the suspicion of nuclear weapons ambitions looms large. It would appear, though, that the latter scenario lacks persuasive power in a nuclear weapon–free world. Once the P-5 have effectively disarmed, the move to the contrary by anybody, including their own clients, might be seen as such a risk to their own national interest that they would be inclined to sanction even a close friend. At best, the patron might seek to offer alternative ways of addressing the motivations that induced this state to embark on the nuclear weapons road in the first place, such as reliable security guarantees. Eventually, they might consent even to military sanctions, since the precedence of someone succeeding with nuclear rearmament is just too great a risk.[17] This objection, though, provides little assurance against a P-5 state invoking its veto when it is *itself* the perpetrator.

To address this possibility, three paths appear possible:

- The first one would return to the classical "Uniting for Peace" procedure whereby the UNGA takes the driver's seat on security matters once the UNSC is stalled by a veto. The International Court of Justice (ICJ) ruled in the 1960s that the UNGA cannot replace the UNSC in mandating forceful action in a Chapter VII mode. However, rules like this are bound to change by state practice. If an "all but one decision" is taken by the UNSC and confirmed by a two-thirds majority in the UNGA (the quorum required by the Uniting for Peace procedure), it would be extremely hard to argue that forceful action to rid the world of the risk of a new nuclear arms race (if not of the risk of nuclear war) would not enjoy legitimacy or even legality.[18]
- The second alternative would be a change in the UN Charter that the veto would be suspended on matters concerning noncompliance with the abolition treaty. Such a resolution would of course, presume that all veto powers would enter the abolition treaty in good faith; otherwise they would not vote for a resolution that would deprive them of their veto once they cheat. This might well be the case; P-5 governments might be convinced that their security is best served in a nuclear weapon–free world, but future leaders (or new elites that might

come to power after a political earthquake in one of the P-5) might reconsider the renunciation of nuclear weapons. It might also be considered to install this exemption of veto power by a simple resolution of the UNSC rather than by a change in the Charter, but lawyers may object that a resolution cannot change a substantial provision of the Charter. Since the consent of all P-5 would be needed both for a resolution and for the change of the Charter, it might be advisable for legal reasons to go for the legally safer step.

- The third option would be for the states-parties to the abolition treaty to establish a collective defense agreement among themselves. If one among them would cheat on its basic obligations, the rest would be entitled, individually and collectively, to take remedial action. This would also apply for a state that were to withdraw from the treaty.

There are two sensitive issues here. First, to deny the right to withdrawal notwithstanding a *rebus sic stantibus* change would be a revolution in international law.[19] The Vienna Convention on the Law of Treaties as well as customary international law permit a state to withdraw from a given legal undertaking if the circumstances prevailing at the time of ratification, and which are related to the subject matter of the treaty, change profoundly. However, to preserve the necessary security assurance that renouncing nuclear weapons, and to abolish one's existing arsenals, would not compromise national security in the long run, all states must be permanently bound by the obligation to stay non–nuclear. Withdrawal must thus be prohibited.[20]

The second sensitive issue concerns the possibility that states-parties may wish to take action against a nonparty to the treaty. While the agreement to apply military sanctions inside the treaty may already be seen as problematic because it intrudes into the prerogative of the UNSC, extending the application of sanctions to countries that have never bound themselves to the obligations of the abolition treaty might be seen as strictly extralegal. States might decide not to accede to this treaty at all or states that emerge from the dissolution of a larger state might declare themselves not bound by undertakings the "mother country" had entered (as the Baltic states did not want to be parties to the CFE Treaty that had been ratified by the Soviet Union). To create a "bias" in favor of membership by stipulating that all states—existing or in the future—shall be bound by the abolition treaty after it enters into force unless they declare explicitly their nonmembership[21] alleviates the situation without solving the problem for good.

Several remedies can deal with this situation:

- First, the conditions steering entry into force of the abolition treaty may require universality. This is probably not desirable, as one would wish its obligations to apply once all nuclear weapons possessors and states with a nuclear technological capability have ratified, and one would not wish to have the treaty going out of force if a new state renounces its membership. However, since the NPT would still bind the other states to non-nuclear status, there would be no damage. In that situation, the NPT might be amended so that it would become identical to the abolition treaty.
- The second remedy would be to declare the stipulations of the treaty, early on, customary international law (by various declarations of the UNGA, the UNSC, and individual states).
- The third remedy would be for the UNSC to adopt a resolution making the obligations from the abolition treaty universal, as it has done in UNSCR 1378 (covering the fight against the financing of terrorism) and 1540 (concerning measures to curb the access on nonstate actors to WMD weapons and materials). The UNSC must play its potential role as universal legislator with great humility and moderation. But the cause of nuclear disarmament would probably attract applause to such a move rather than misgivings and criticism.

Evaluation of the Different Options

Transferring the fateful decision about noncompliance (with an automatic authorization for self-defense) to the IAEA might make the P-5 hesitate. On second thought, however, they might be inclined to agree.

Each of them could be confronted by a rule breaker who is the friend of a peer, and each of them might be confronted with a peer who is himself the rule breaker. Being entitled to fall back on Article 51 in a flawlessly legal and legitimate way and thereby to preserve freedom of action in a situation of potential national emergency might be attractive enough to elicit consent. If—as for Article 51 in general—the UNSC retains the right to take over the matter in the case of P-5 agreement, the loss of status of the P-5 would be minimal, and the gain in prospective security considerable. The institutional change needed is not very large, it appears, and could be managed through a careful wording of the abolition treaty and, optimally, a confirming resolution by the UNSC. In general, it is assumed here that the privileged position of the P-5 will remain unchanged; it is hard to believe that, as they give up their nuclear weapons for good, they would surrender their pivotal power in international decision making at the same time.

Referring cases to the UNGA under Uniting for Peace might be much more controversial. It could, nevertheless, happen if the vast majority of non-nuclear weapon states, except for a few states not represented as permanent members (e.g., India, Brazil, Japan, or Germany) would take the lead. Facing this risk—which would indeed present a major loss of status—the P-5 may then be inclined to make the UNSC work. Herein lies a strong incentive against the frivolous use of the veto.

The least feasible option, in terms of the "reality check," is entrusting the change to the abolition treaty. Presenting a heroic challenge anyway, the institutional change implied here would possibly overtax the capabilities of the negotiators to move toward consensus. This could be a showstopper that should not burden the disarmament endgame.

Concerning effectiveness, the combination of the "green light" procedure, combined with the option of the UNSC to take up the issue after the IAEA has spoken, and of the UNGA to move once the UNSC proves incapable to strike a deal, presents a nice cascade of possibilities that make the likelihood of some determined response on one of these levels highly probable. This multistage system would serve as a powerful deterrent against rule-breaking, and as a good tool to create trust in the enforcement system.

This, in turn, suggests that the multilayered decision-making process augurs well for stability, too. Incentives to pursue a policy of "hedging"—that is, readiness to return to nuclear capabilities in a short time frame—will be all the higher the more unlikely a determined (conventional) response to rule-breaking appears. With the solid probability that such a response will emerge from one of the layers, these incentives will remain rather low.

Therefore, the three major options do not appear completely incompatible. It might be wise to combine the first one—the "green light" authorization to take defensive preventive action based on an IAEA secretariat finding of serious noncompliance—and the second and/or third one—some determination by either the UN or the abolition treaty community representing (nearly) universal membership. Pending collective action, individual states would be entitled to remedy the situation which the rule-breaker has caused; at the same time, the international community would apply due process to devise a collective counteraction against the rule-breaker as quickly and as effectively as possible. It can be surmised that the prospect that, sooner or later, a powerful state would take action on its own might serve as a mighty incentive for Security Council members to do business; the loss of authority, and therefore of the status, of the nonacting council members might motivate them to put aside more narrow considerations of national interest and help make the UNSC a more effective body.

Response

In the following sections, military sanctions against an emerging nuclear weapons program are discussed. The reason is straightforward. In the present world, the balance of incentives and disincentives for "going nuclear" is very much different from the one in a world of nuclear abolition. In this very different environment, embarking on a nuclear weapons road requires much stronger motivations than today. In our world, emulating the nuclear weapon states might look quite attractive and justified to would-be proliferators. In a nuclear weapon–free world, the non-nuclear norm would be so unequivocally entrenched that much stronger motivations must be suspected to drive the rush for the bomb.

Either the security situation of a country must look completely desperate to induce a government to defy the whole world, or a megalomaniac personality or elite with world-hegemonic dreams must govern in a country and view nuclear weapons as the safest way to preponderance. Either constellation would not emerge overnight and would thus give the rest of the world advance strategic warning, helping focus inspection efforts, intelligence, diplomatic approaches, and contingency military planning on these "breakout candidates."

Diplomacy and Security Guarantees

The use of force will always be considered as a last resort after all alternatives have been unsuccessfully exhausted. Even in a legal environment where a finding by the IAEA Secretariat of noncompliance would provide the license for self-defense, states in a position to take military action would still wish to explore whether other options could work. On the condition that some time was still left before the point of no return, prompt and intense diplomatic efforts would ensue. They could take several forms; given the urgency of the matter, the UNSG could be mandated by the UNSC to conduct the diplomatic campaign aimed at persuading the perpetrator to return to a state of good standing regarding its undertakings. Well-targeted sanctions might be part of this campaign or not, depending on the specific circumstances. All the while, countries determined to do so would probably prepare the necessary capabilities to take military action in case negotiations failed. This would be the equivalent of the Iraqi situation in 2002–2003 before and after resolution 1441 was adopted. As we recall, this was not a bad environment to bring a rule-breaker to terms.

If the desire of the accused state to acquire nuclear weapons was rooted in deep concern about a perceived security threat, the remedy would be to remove the threat and/or offer alternative ways to ensure national security—such as a "great power guarantee"—provided that the nuclear weapons program would be brought promptly to an end under international verification. It is essential that the diplomatic approaches be quick, intense (no long pauses between negotiation rounds), well coordinated, and conducted with determination and without wavering.

Unity within the UNSC, and among the P-5 in particular, would be indispensible; the experiences discussed in the "Background" section prove this requirement unambiguously. If one of the P-5 was itself the target of the effort—a very unlikely, but not completely impossible, scenario—the motivation was probably the perceived threat coming from another P-5 member (or another very large and powerful state). Efforts must then be taken to have the behavior of the perceived threat maker changed in a way that would convince the perpetrator that nuclear weapons were not needed for assuring national security. If, in the run-up to abolition, the major powers strive to establish a "concert" among themselves (discussed later), the latter constellation would be virtually excluded.

Return to Nuclear Deterrence in a Virtual Arsenal Situation

Nuclear deterrence would be a cheap fallback option in a world where "zero nukes" would mean virtual arsenals. If verification were extensive and effective, a nuclear program or significant reconstitution activity would be discovered early on, and former nuclear weapon states would be in a position to return to a nuclear weapons posture before a new-comer could finalize its first weapon. However, if the cheater was one of their peers, it would probably be a hard race, but the perpetrator could never be sure that the peers would not be equally fast or even faster, and it could certainly not ensure that he could mount a posture good enough to disarm in a first strike all competitors even if he would be the one to have a complete nuclear weapon first.

However, from the perspective of an orderly enforcement regime and the supreme goal of ensuring the continuation of a nuclear weapon–free world, the option of quickly returning to nuclear deterrence would be counterproductive. States would have no incentive to build down from a virtual arsenal posture and, to the contrary, ample incentive to get as close to the last turn of the screw as possible. Every actor considering the quick return to nuclear deterrence as the panacea against breakout would know that all its peers would probably think and act along the same lines. As a consequence, not only the singular event of a "rogue" breakout would figure as standard scenario to which one would have to react, but also the simultaneous stampede of all those close enough to the bomb. The race for early preparedness would no doubt feed mutual distrust among all actors in that position. Even worse, states that are by now far from a virtual capability would have all incentives to move toward one, in order to be as well prepared for a future breakout as everybody else. Since it would be utterly hard in a non-nuclear environment to find any good argument—and even less so a willing audience—for continued technical privileges accruing to former nuclear weapon states, we would have to expect a great number of countries with weapons-usable fissile material and probably all the other preparations for quick weaponization "just in case." It thus appears that relying on the intrinsic response capability of virtual arsenals carries the risk of preventing one of the most important preconditions for a zero-nuclear world from emerging, namely a robust framework of trust among the largest possible number of actors. Rather than relying on collective action, actors would be completely and unambiguously thrown back to their self-help devices. Predictably, this constellation would have the strong propensity to turn actors back to nuclear armament, this time—in contrast to today's situation—in much greater numbers and—because of the probable rush forward—in a most unstable process.[22] Once this happens, the chances for a nuclear weapon–free world would disappear for a long, long time.

Conventional Military Response

In a non-nuclear world, military response to "cheating" would have to be achieved by conventional means.[23] There is a trade-off between keeping open the option of unilateral action (as in the "green light" procedure described earlier) and the possibility of creating the necessary motivation among the major powers to abolish their arsenals completely. Conventional response requires, at a minimum, destroying the facilities designed to produce weapons material, the weapons themselves, and, possibly, the delivery systems. It is assumed here that verification and intelligence enables the outside world to locate the related sites. Successful prevention of an attempt at cheating, then, presupposes the availability of long-range, precise power projection capabilities with a reliable destructive potential by ballistic missiles, air forces, or cruise missiles launched from forward-deployed naval or air platforms; even space-based weaponry might appear useful for that mission. Today, the United States possesses such capabilities (with the exception of space-based strike assets).

However, the extensive availability of such power projection capabilities in *national* hands might be a serious barrier to achieve nuclear abolition, notably if they remain as asymmetrically distributed as they are today. Unilateral capabilities of this kind might create exactly the anxiety of being helplessly subjected to conventional aggression that might caution governments against giving up a minimum deterrence nuclear posture.[24] Curbing offensive potentials (e.g., prohibiting, or minimizing the number of, long-range ballistic missiles[25]) would help with these anxieties but, at the same time, curb the capability of the more powerful states, the United States in particular, to act promptly and successfully against a would-be violator of the abolition treaty.

If there were trust enough in effective collective action, national conventional capabilities could be shaped in such a way as to permit no state to take offensive action alone, but only in combination with other states. This would require having, in parallel with nuclear disarmament, a well-designed conventional arms control process. Ideally, security cooperation among major powers could reach a quality in the evolution of nuclear disarmament that such an agreement, today unthinkable, could be seriously considered.[26] From today's vantage point, though, it is an open question whether major states would muster the will to embark on either path simultaneously; maintaining strong conventional capabilities might be seen as the indispensible compensation for relinquishing nuclear arms.

There might be a compromise line to devise conventional structures that are capable to destroy promptly a limited number of targets but not fit to serve a large-scale offensive to conquer and subdue a major enemy. This could be good enough to take out the key installations of a nuclear weapons program but not good enough to create fears of a total conventional onslaught that only a nuclear deterrent could probably prevent. In any event, this is a critical question that should be noted and revisited repeatedly throughout the process of nuclear disarmament in order to consider new solutions that might become possible as the character of world politics undergoes fundamental change. It should be noted in passing that, if a few nuclear weapons were built and actually used, the major powers would dispose of the conventional capabilities to retaliate in a devastating way.[27]

The Role of Missile Defenses

Missile defenses in a denuclearized world would engender quite different consequences than today. Under present circumstances, they enhance the fear by numerically and/or technologically inferior nuclear weapon states that their deterrent might be compromised. The construction of nation-wide missile defenses by one state thus triggers almost automatically a response by other states of enhancing offensive capabilities (numbers or penetration technology, or both) of strategic nuclear forces. National missile defenses thus have a destabilizing and arms race–driving effect.[28]

In a nuclear weapon–free world, national missile defenses would look less threatening.[29] It would not look threatening at all if ballistic missiles were prohibited altogether, as in President Reagan's classical vision.[30] Missile defenses would then only represent a precaution against breakout from this prohibition. If holding limited numbers of ballistic missiles were permitted to bolster an offensive preventive option for the international community against breakout from the nuclear abolition treaty, national missile defenses might look suspicious as a possible preparation for such a breakout. Two options would mitigate this effect.

- The first one would be an international agreement to keep missile defenses numerically substantially inferior to the combined ballistic missile capabilities of the international community that could be mustered to conduct the legal preventive action; the missile defense system then could be easily saturated and the preventive option would still be possible (provided antiballistic missile production capability was also limited, so that surge production was not possible).
- The second option would be a truly global system whose national components could be deactivated if a quorum of system members would enter a certain code. A perpetrator, thus, would have

to face a situation where everybody else would enjoy missile defenses while he would not. On the other hand, a mischievous state, or a very small group thereof, could not collude to take the missile defense of an enemy out of action. The technicalities of such a complex system would be challenging. But 30 or 40 years down the road, they should not be insurmountable.

Ballistic missile defenses as well as limits on the number of ballistic missiles would not only reduce the incentive for breakout but would also serve as a hedge against any threat by a perpetrator to retaliate against military efforts aimed at preventing him from completing nuclear weapons development or, if nuclear weapons were already available, at removing these nuclear assets.[31] It goes without saying, though, that the problem of unconventional delivery in such a situation cannot be addressed by missile defenses. In any case, for the time being, strict limits on national missile deployments should be agreed in a kind of multilateral Anti-Ballistic Missile (ABM) Treaty treaty in order to eliminate incentives to build up, rather than down, nuclear arsenals, and to make possible the reduction of strategic nuclear forces.[32]

Evaluation

Since a diplomatic approach would be the first line of defense of a non–nuclear world against a breach of the rules, no particular evaluation is needed other than the self-explanatory statement that this would work all the better the more united the negotiating nations stand, and that unity would be achieved best if rivalries and conflicts among the major players were being managed in a reasonable and cooperative way.

Virtual arsenals as springboards for reconstituting nuclear deterrence would probably be acceptable, if not desirable, from the perspective of the current nuclear weapon states and notably their nuclear establishments, to whom such a posture would give a breath of prolonged life. The institutional requirements would be at least as demanding as for a truly disarmed world, as the boundaries between the permitted and the prohibited would involve difficult and complex technical judgments and thus probably be hard to verify. Also, it is unlikely that institutional precautions could be taken to obviate the obvious incentives for present non-nuclear weapon states to creep toward a robust virtual posture.

Virtual arsenals enabling reconstitution of nuclear deterrence would probably be an effective counter to rule breaking under two assumptions: That reconstitution would be achieved without the reconstitution race ending in mutual attempts at preemption, and that the perpetrator would be deterrable. Since one of the two motivations for striving for nuclear weapons in a non-nuclear world is the rather lunatic quest for domination, neither condition could be assumed with ultimate certainty.

Virtual arsenals as an option to grant security in a non-nuclear world are thus most vulnerable under the stability criterion. They create a precarious interim position between a nuclear weapons posture and a truly non-nuclear world. They motivate retaining rather sizable technical, bureaucratic, and military establishments for preparedness purposes whose thinking will be directed toward driving the spiral upward. The activities of these bodies will be a constant source of distrust in the strategic communities elsewhere. The risk for misperception leading to the start of a multilateral reconstitution race is high. At the same time, the knowledge that reconstitution would be the first answer to a breach of the rules may lead to the neglect of other (conventional) options to deal with it. Once reconstitution occurs—in a highly charged and thus dangerous politico-military climate—a ratchet effect is to be expected that would prevent the return to nuclear disarmament for a long while.

Conventional options to take out nuclear assets are being developed anyway. They appear realistic, feasible, and thus effective, assuming good intelligence is available. The motivation to employ them against a rule breaker would be high, and higher indeed if the reconstitution option is not available in the desired time frame. It is the institutional issue that is of concern: Will it be possible to frame a conventional arms control agreement guiding the offensive, high-tech conventional posture of the major players in a way that would grant a fair chance of destroying the perpetrator's nuclear assets while being nonthreatening against each other? The connection between nuclear disarmament and conventional arms control, which is already placed in Article VI of the NPT (while in the slightly exaggerated notion of a "treaty on complete disarmament") makes a lot of sense here. To strike a balance between the understandable desire of nation-states to have a ready response to nuclear proliferation, and the equally understandable interest of granting no overwhelming conventional power to any single actor presents a considerable challenge to arms control negotiators. Such challenges can be met, as the intricate construction of the Treaty on Conventional Armed Forces in Europe (CFE) at the end of the Cold War showed. If they are, the stability problem will be solved. But it remains an "if," and the answer is contingent on prudent state practice in the decades to come. Once more, a solution would be tremendously facilitated if great power relations would move toward viable and sustainable security cooperation in the process of disarmament.

Missile defenses can be evaluated in a similar way as conventional responses. They would be an auxiliary measure in a non-nuclear world to bolster confidence that security will not be diminished dramatically if a nuclear weapons program were discovered late. It can be surmised that the willingness to accept both defenses and reasonable limits on them will grow as the process of nuclear disarmament is successfully pushed forward through a series of steps. Again, how the major powers would interpret missile defenses built by their peers would very much depend on the overall quality of their relations and the institutional (limitation and cooperation) framework in which missile defenses would exist. The vision of a complex, globally operated, modularized missile defense system is institutionally very demanding and presently beyond realistic reach, but worth exploring, as calls for a global system have already been made (by President Reagan, and by the present Russian government, for example). The technical effectiveness of current and planned systems is almost a matter of belief, but this could change with technological advances. The destabilizing potential lies in unilateral, asymmetrical pursuit that is bound to provoke offensive responses and thereby to undo the hopes for nuclear disarmament. Without agreed limits, this destabilizing effect in the process of disarmament is inevitable.

Consequences and Conclusions

Sifting through the deliberations in this paper, one thing becomes clear: To realize the vision of a nuclear weapon–free world, the relationship among the great powers must be one of cooperation and mutual trust, not one of sharp geopolitical rivalry in which the security dilemma reigns.[33] This is essential for them to give up their last nuclear weapons in the first place, it is necessary for them to stay in a non-nuclear posture and thereby to spare the rest of the world the hazardous necessity either to return to multipolar nuclear deterrence in a frenzy, or to deny a big power the return to nuclear weapons status by military force. There need not be complete harmony, which is very improbable, but rather agreed ways for managing whatever differences of interest might exist. A cooperative relationship among the great powers is a prerequisite for installing a reliable and credible enforcement system.

While it would be helpful if all great powers were democracies at the time of the transition to zero,[34] this is not a necessary condition. Most nondemocratic states abide by international law. The Soviet Union under Gorbachev was still an autocratic one-party state, but it was willing to accept intrusive verification such as that required by the INF and START I treaties. And "societal verification" can work in an autocratic state as well: it was an Iranian opposition group that revealed the existence of the Natanz enrichment construction project. In other words, it is possible for enough trust to be created to persuade the democratic governments of nuclear weapon states that they do not need nuclear weapons as insurance against the uncertainties connected with the autocratic character of their international partners.

But it is true that a great and sustained effort must be made to develop relations among the great powers that are the contemporary equivalent of the "Concert of Europe."[35] The Concert rested on relatively simple principles:

- All participating powers recognize each other as equal.
- All respect the vital interests[36] of all others and avoid intruding on them. This includes the interest in a secure regional environment for each of them.
- All conduct regular consultations on issues of common and global concern.
- All renounce the unilateral use of force.
- All agree that the network of consultation should be immediately intensified when a crisis looms.
- None seeks unilateral advantage in such a crisis.

The Concert managed to keep the peace in Europe for more than a generation among more liberal (United Kingdom, France) and more autocratic (Russia, Prussia, Austria) states. It appears that this model captures quite well the political preconditions for a nuclear weapon–free world. To realize them is a major challenge, but far from impossible. It is not a prerequisite to start the steps toward nuclear disarmament; it would most likely be necessary to take the last step(s) toward true abolition. It remains to be seen whether the institutions that will be built in this process are strong enough to bring together the "concert" as described here. It appears necessary to phase the compliance procedures discussed in this chapter and the verification system on which it is based in parallel with the nuclear arms reduction process and to have it in place for a while, testing it, as it were, during the phase when the nuclear weapon possessors rely on very small arsenals. Such a testing phase would probably be necessary to get accustomed to the system and to create the necessary confidence in its functioning to convince them that the last steps toward zero could be taken without undue risk.

A second, not so surprising, conclusion is that any enforcement system needs an excellent verification system as its basis. Verification was not the subject of this study, but effective verification is the prerequisite on which its deliberations on enforcement rest. It has to be emphasized, however, that this is really the case. In terms of technology, forensic capabilities, the quality of staff and leadership, transparency, and communication policy, as well as uncompromising support by the international community, the verification system and its organization must work without flaws. Fortunately, the IAEA as of today is a good starting point from which the verification system can evolve. Whether, in the end, the IAEA will remain the IAEA or whether it will evolve into a different organization because of the enhanced scope of mission is a matter to be resolved in the distant future.

The interface between the assessment of threat and the decision on response, then, is the crucial link. The combination of a "green light" procedure for national action, triggered by a technical finding of a neutral body, and collective decision making on top of that tries to resolve the present tension between dangerous unilateralism and a veto-blocked UNSC incapable of taking needed action.

The balance of interests in preventing nuclear proliferation looks different in a world of zero nuclear weapons where the return to nuclear deterrence might not be a viable short-term option; to realize this fact is of great importance in the assessment of whether an enforcement system that works better than today's is thinkable. Major powers would have a distinct interest in preventing the perpetrator from achieving his objective. The readiness to join forces for preventive military action, even against a major power, would most likely be considerably higher than today; not the least because a major power taking the gamble of nuclear (re-)armament would give a very ominous signal as to its future intentions. That a major power would decide so in an environment framed by the joint "concerting" among its peers, which includes respect for the power's vital interests, appears very unlikely, however. Against minor powers, the prospect of overwhelming hostile force assembled in response to a breakout attempt would, under all foreseeable circumstances, work as an effective non–nuclear deterrent. Altogether, the system of verification—thorough, well-installed procedures to respond to noncompliance; sanctions; isolation of the perpetrator; and, in extremis, conventional military action bolstered, possibly, by missile defenses—looks like a strong complex of non-nuclear deterrence in a world without nuclear weapons.

The role of ballistic missiles and missile defenses in a world without nuclear weapons is ambivalent. They could serve as a hedge against the breakout attempt of a malevolent government. They could also serve as the preparation and platform for such a breakout. It might be possible to configure them in a way as to enhance the first and diminish the second possibility. At present, strict limits on missile defenses would be advisable to start the disarmament process.

Notes

1. *Virtual arsenal* means the following: the essential parts of nuclear weapons and their delivery systems would still be around, but weapons would be disassembled and separated from delivery systems. See Michael Mazarr, "Virtual Nuclear Arsenals," *Survival* 37, no. 3 (1996): 7–26. I stick to this definition of virtual arsenals as requiring some hardware background. Blueprints

and computer data relating to weapons will probably be around for a long while, though the problems to transform them into physical reality might mount as practical experience fades out. Virtual arsenals exert their destabilizing potential through the combination of existing soft- and hardware.

2. James Leonard, Martin Kaplan, and Benjamin Sanders, "Verification and Enforcement in a NWFW," in *A Nuclear-Weapon-Free World. Desirable? Feasible?* ed. Joseph Rotblat, Jack Steinberger, and Bhalchandra Udgaonkar (Boulder, CO: Westview, 1993), 132–144, argue that the perpetrator will draw little benefit from his act (see 139).

3. David Malone, "Goodbye UNSCOM: A Sorry Tale in US-UN Relations," *Security Dialogue* 30, no. 4 (1999): 393–412.

4. Hans Blix, *Disarming Iraq* (New York: Pantheon, 2004).

5. Bruce Jentleson and Christopher A. Whytock, "Who 'Won' Libya? The Force-Diplomacy Debate and Its Implications for Theory and Policy," *International Security* 30, no. 3 (Winter 2005/2006), S. 47–86; Wyn Q. Bowen, "Libya and Nuclear Proliferation, International Institute for Strategic Studies," Adelphi Paper 380 (London: 2006); Harald Müller, "The Exceptional End to the Extraordinary Libyan Nuclear Quest," in *Nuclear Proliferation and International Security*, ed. Morten Bremer Maerli and Sverre Lodgaard (London: Routledge, 2006), 73–95.

6. Mike Chinoy, *Meltdown: The Inside Story of the North Korean Nuclear Crisis* (New York: St. Martin's, 2008).

7. Christoph Bertram, *Rethinking Iran: From Confrontation to Cooperation*, Chaillot Paper 110 (Paris: Institute for Security Studies, 2008).

8. Blix, *Disarming Iraq*; Richard Butler, "Improving Nonproliferation Enforcement," *Washington Quarterly* 26, no. 4 (2003): 133–145.

9. Andrew Mack, "Nuclear 'Breakout': Risks and Possible Responses," Australian National University, Department of International Relations Working Paper No. 1997/1 (Canberra: Australian National University, 1997).

10. Rebecca Johnson, "Incentives, Obligations and Enforcement: Does the NPT Meet Its States Parties' Needs?" *Disarmament Diplomacy* 70 (April–May 2003); Butler, "Improving Nonproliferation Enforcement"; John Burroughs, "The Role of the Security Council," in John Burroughs et al., *Nuclear Disorder or Cooperative Security? An Assessment of the Final Report of the WMD Commission and Its Implications for U.S. Policy* (New York: Lawyers Committee on Nuclear Policy, 2007), 35–44.

11. George Perkovich and James M. Acton, "Abolishing Nuclear Weapons," Adelphi Paper 396 (London: IISS, 2008), 85.

12. George Perkovich, Jessica T. Matthews, Joseph Cirincione, Rose Gottemoeller, and Jon B. Wolfsthal, *Universal Compliance: A Strategy for Nuclear Security* (Washington, DC: Carnegie Endowment for International Peace, 2005), 68.

13. See "Multilateral Disarmament and Nonproliferation Regimes and the Role of the United Nations: An Evaluation," Contribution of the Advisory Board on Disarmament Matters to the High-Level Panel on Threats, Challenges and Change, New York, United Nations Department of Disarmament Affairs Occasional Paper 8, 2004.

14. This procedure appears to me more reliable and less prone to errors of national assessment or misuse than guidelines for assessing the "imminence" of a threat, which still leaves much to the subjective interpretations of national governments, cf. Perkovich et al., *Universal Compliance*, 76–77.

15. Perkovich and Acton, "Abolishing Nuclear Weapons," 92–93.

16. Model Nuclear Weapons Convention, Section 3, 109, www.reaching criticalwill.org/legal/nwc/nwc.pdf.

17. Model Nuclear Weapons Convention, Section 3, 110, www.reaching criticalwill.org/legal/nwc/nwc.pdf, November 6, 2008.

18. Ibid.

19. Maxwell Bruce, Horst Fischer, and Thomas Mensah 1993: "A NWFW Regime: Treaty for the Abolition of Nuclear Weapons," in Rotblat et al., *A Nuclear-Weapon-Free World*, 119–131, 122.

20. Tom Milne and Joseph Rotblat, "Breakout from a Nuclear Weapons Convention," in *Nuclear Weapons: The Road to Zero*, ed. Joseph Rotblat (Boulder, CO: Westview, 1998), 145–154, 146.

21. Maxwell Bruce, Horst Fischer, and Thomas Mensah, "A NWFW Regime: Treaty for the Abolition of Nuclear Weapons," in Rotblat et al., eds., *A Nuclear-Weapon-Free World*, 119–131, 121–122.

22. Kenneth Waltz, "Thoughts about Virtual Arsenals," *Washington Quarterly* 20, no. 3 (1997): 153–161; National Academy of Sciences, *The Future of U.S. Nuclear Policy* (Washington, DC: National Academy Press, 1997), 92.

23. Paul Nitze, "Is It Time to Junk Our Nukes?" *Washington Quarterly* 20, no. 3 (1997): 97–101.

24. Paul C. White, Robert E. Pendley, and Patrick J. Garrity, "Thinking about No Nuclear Forces: Technical and Strategic Constraints on Transitions and End Points, in *Security without Nuclear Weapons? Different Perspectives on Non-Nuclear Security*, ed. Regina Cowen Karp (Oxford, Oxford University Press, 1992), 103–127.

25. Harold Feiveson, Bruce G. Blair, Jonathan Dean, Steve Fetter, James Goodby, George Lewis, Janne E. Nolan, Theodore Postol, and Frank von Hippel, *The Nuclear Turning Point: A Blueprint for Deep Cuts and De-alerting of Nuclear Weapons* (Washington, DC: Brookings Institution Press, 1999), 299.

26. Ibid., 297–298.

27. See Generals Charles Horner and Lee Butler in conversation with Jonathan Schell, in Jonathan Schell, "The Gift of Time: The Case for Abolishing Nuclear Weapons," *The Nation*, February 2–9, 1998, 23, 56.

28. Michael Krepon, *Cooperative Threat Reduction, Missile Defense, and the Nuclear Future* (Houndmills, Basingstoke, U.K.: Palgrave Macmillan, 2003), 9/10.

29. Schell, "The Gift of Time," 24.

30. Jürgen Scheffran, "Elimination of Ballistic Missiles: An Important Step towards a Nuclear-Weapon-Free-World," in *Towards a Nuclear-Weapon-Free World. Proceedings of the 45th Pugwash Conference on Science and World Affairs*, ed. Joseph Rotblat and Michiji Konuma (Singapore: World Scientific, 1997), 310–326.

31. Perkovich and Acton, "Abolishing Nuclear Weapons," 87.

32. See the considerations of Krepon, *Cooperative Threat Reduction*, chap. 8.

33. Ken Booth and Nicholas J. Wheeler, "Beyond Nuclearism," in *Security without Nuclear Weapons? Different Perspectives on Non-Nuclear Security*, ed. Regima Cowen Karp (Oxford, Oxford University Press, 1992), 21–55; National Academy of Sciences, *The Future of U.S. Nuclear Policy* (Washington, DC: National Academy Press, 1997).

34. Feiveson et al., *The Nuclear Turning Point*, 293–295.

35. Henry Kissinger, *A World Restored* (New York: Grosset & Dunlap, 1964); Carsten Holbrad, *The Concert of Europe* (London: Longman, 1970).

36. On this term, see Lawrence Freedman, "Great Powers, Vital Interests and Nuclear Weapons," *Survival* 36, no. 4: 35–52.

3. Verifying the Nonproduction and Elimination of Fissile Material for Weapons

ANNETTE SCHAPER

Fissile materials can be categorized according to their technical suitability for nuclear warheads, since all isotopes have certain technical advantages and disadvantages in this respect. Different categories are plutonium, various enrichments of uranium, and other isotopes or mixtures. Fissile materials can also be categorized politically according to their past and present use and their legal status. These categories are fissile materials under safeguards; civilian fissile materials and fissile materials declared excess to defense needs, but not yet under safeguards; fissile materials considered excess to defense needs but not declared as such; naval fuel; and fissile materials intended for use in nuclear explosives. In a nuclear weapon–free world, the civilian industry will still use some weapons–usable materials. Comprehensive disarmament therefore requires putting all fissile materials under international safeguards. In a nuclear weapon–free world, the verification task is to assure that any diversion and any clandestine production would be detected.

Once a nuclear weapon-free world has been achieved, safeguards and verification will largely resemble the safeguards in place today for non-nuclear weapon states (NNWS). The main methods are material accounting, containment and surveillance, inspections and managed access, and national technical means (NTM). The methods employed would vary depending on the type of facility being monitored. Together, these methods in their synergy should make it possible to detect non-compliance with a high probability. The most difficult activity to detect is clandestine enrichment at an unknown location.

The verification of the disarmament process during the transition period poses special challenges: The problems are frequently cited by skeptics who do not believe in the feasibility of a nuclear weapon–free world. Moreover, they often play a role in discussions on important contributing endeavors such as negotiation of a verifiable Fissile Material Cutoff Treaty (FMCT).

The first challenge is the fact that there will be facilities that are not designed for safeguards; for example, access to material streams might be difficult, and material accountancy will be incomplete. Each such facility that will not be shut down but converted for future civilian use will need an individual study and negotiation of how to establish some satisfactory verification. The precision of material accountancy could be gradually increased with methods like examining records, measuring inventories, and engaging in nuclear archeology.

The second challenge is sensitive information. A major problem in establishing verification regimes is the fear of the nuclear weapons states that sensitive information will be compromised. This applies not only to enrichment and reprocessing plants but also to warhead assembly, dismantling, and storage facilities. During the transition period, rigorous verification methods must be applied to both sensitive fissile materials and warheads that are not yet dismantled.

Sensitive information can also pose a challenge at fissile material production sites. Several historic precedents demonstrate how such problems have been dealt with in the past. In the Hexapartite Project, safeguards were successfully applied to centrifuge enrichment plants in a manner that protected proprietary commercial information. The lesson of this case is that the middle ground between secrecy and transparency must be developed and negotiated individually for each technology. Similar tensions apparently played a role in a second case—that is, Brazil's hesitation to sign the Additional Protocol. There is still disagreement regarding where to draw the line between intrusiveness and protection of sensitive information regarding centrifuge enrichment. The lesson of this second case is that managed access procedures must be worked out flexibly for each individual plant, even in case of comparable technologies. The third case is South Africa's nuclear disarmament. The precedent in this case was that cleanup and removal of sensitive information preceded the application of verification procedures, and when verification measures were applied, any sensitive information that remained was adequately protected. The fourth case is that of Euratom safeguards on the entire civilian nuclear energy enterprise in the European Union (EU), to include two nuclear weapons states (NWS) with dual-use production plants for both nuclear weapons fuel and fuel for the civilian nuclear industry. The lesson from this case is that NWSs can get used to civilian safeguards even at former military production plants. The fourth case is the Trilateral Initiative, which resulted in proposals for subjecting to International Atomic Energy Agency (IAEA) verification and monitoring excess nuclear material still in classified form.

As a separate matter, it is fair to ask whether much of the secrecy related to nuclear weapons has become counterproductive to the requirements of national security and nonproliferation. In this context, nuclear weapons states should be encouraged to rethink and update their classification regulations.

The third challenge is a scenario frequently cited in discussions of a nuclear weapon–free world—namely, that of a country hiding undeclared weapons or materials while pretending to disarm comprehensively. Therefore, verification must create confidence that there is a high probability of detection of any clandestine stocks, in order to deter cheating. A prerequisite is the accounting of all nuclear materials possessed by a country. The most effective cheating scenarios could occur if the decision to hide material were made at the beginning stages of the disarmament process—for example, at a stage before the initial declarations of all quantities and locations of materials. The most promising detection scenario against such cheating is "societal verification," because it is unlikely that a cheating state could keep everyone involved in the process from learning about and divulging the cheating behavior.

The fourth challenge is the detection of clandestine production, especially centrifuge enrichment that has only low effluents. In this case, societal verification and intelligence are crucial to establishing initial suspicions of a location where inspections can be conducted.

The fifth challenge is accounting of all naval fuel, which includes direct-use highly enriched uranium (HEU) but also entails other elements that remain secret. It is recommended that further research be conducted to address the problem of how to account for naval fuel, and to determine to what extent some of the secrecy surrounding the production of naval fuel could be reduced to ensure adequate verification. An approach to this problem could be developed in a manner similar to that used by the Trilateral Initiative just described.

Background

Key to the goal of a nuclear weapon–free world is credible verification of the elimination of all warheads and confidence that no warheads exist clandestinely. The key ingredient of nuclear weapons is fissile material.[1] The acquisition of ignition technology is easier than the acquisition of fissile material production technology, but it is more difficult to verify. Therefore, key to the verification of a world free of nuclear weapons is the verification of the nonproduction and the elimination of fissile materials for nuclear weapons. This task is twofold. First, huge existing stockpiles of fissile materials must be eliminated, and it must be credibly assured that there are no clandestine stockpiles. The quantities of material existing today would be sufficient to produce warheads in numbers exceeding the peak stockpiles of the Cold War. The second task is the verification of nonproduction, which must start in parallel with the elimination process and continue after the last warhead has been dismantled to address proliferation concerns that will remain even in a nuclear weapon–free world.

Although these tasks are daunting challenges, we do not start from scratch in addressing them. For decades, the international community has gained experience in verifying that NNWS under the Non-Proliferation Treaty (NPT) do not produce fissile materials for weapons. Despite large nuclear industries in many of those NNWS, verification has created high confidence that these states comply with the treaty and that their production activities and nuclear industries serve only civilian purposes. During the many decades of nuclear safeguards in these countries, many lessons have been learned and invaluable technical and political experience has been gained that could be useful for future verification.

Nevertheless, the application of past experience to verification of the transition to zero nuclear weapons is ambitious. Only after a nuclear weapon–free world has been achieved and high confidence has been created that no warhead and fissile material storage or production site has escaped verification, will the continuing verification task become comparable to that in NNWS today. At that point, the task will be to verify that no material is being produced for undeclared purposes. Until that time, there will be a transition period posing many additional challenges: Materials from dismantled nuclear warheads or those designated for dismantlement must be either eliminated or redirected to other uses. Verification must create high confidence that this is happening, while at the same time ensuring that no proliferation-sensitive information is leaked. Similarly, production facilities must be dismantled or put under safeguards. Several of those facilities entail proliferation-sensitive secrets. Furthermore, they were not designed for safeguards, in contrast to most modern production facilities in NNWS. Verification must also ensure that no secret storage site or production facilities remain or are initiated. Some important safeguards methods that are being applied in NNWS, such as material accounting, could not be applied in the same way to NWS. These are just some examples of the challenges ahead.

This chapter will explore the challenges of the transition period since the verification methods to be applied after comprehensive nuclear disarmament are well understood. I will identify the tasks of verification and illustrate technical and political paths that might at the end lead to the goal of mastering these tasks. I will also identify problems that will need additional research and analysis. The first section provides an overview of existing weapons-usable materials, categorized according to technical criteria, and then according to political criteria. The next section describes existing verification methods and explores how to extend them to the phase of transition to a nuclear weapon–free world. The last section explores special problems that pose particular challenges and illustrates some paths for coping with them.

Categorizing Weapons-Usable Materials

Nuclear materials that have been used for warheads are plutonium (Pu) and HEU. The existing quantities of Pu and HEU, for both nuclear weapons and other uses, are by far the largest. Other isotopes might potentially also be suitable for warheads—namely, U-233, or neptunium-237 (Np-237) and americium-241 (Am-241). However, the existing quantities of those isotopes are comparatively smaller. In principle, the production and use of all such isotopes must be included in the verification scheme. The disarmament process, however, will focus mainly on Pu and HEU.

Nuclear materials can be categorized according to various criteria; two will be presented here. The first is the technical suitability for nuclear warheads, since each isotope has certain technical advantages and disadvantages in this respect. The second is a political categorization based on past and present use of the material and its status under various international regimes and treaties. Technical and political problems associated with verification and safeguarding will be discussed in subsequent sections.

Technical Categorization

Plutonium

Plutonium does not occur naturally but is the product of nuclear reactions, mostly when uranium-238 (U-238) is hit by neutrons. This can happen in a nuclear reactor or in any other neutron source. The plutonium isotopes are separated from the spent fuel by a process called *reprocessing*. It is a combination of mechanical and chemical methods and radiation shielding technologies. On a laboratory scale, reprocessing is possible in so-called *hot cells* but will yield only small quantities. On an industrial scale, *reprocessing facilities* are much larger. The production of plutonium sufficient for a nuclear arsenal larger than a few warheads requires a reprocessing facility. The quantity of material needed for one warhead can be estimated as one to a few kilograms.[2]

Normally, plutonium consists of a mix of various isotopes whose composition depends on the type of production facility (more precisely, the energy distribution of the neutrons and the composition of the fuel), and the time the fuel has been exposed to the neutrons. The IAEA definition of *direct-use material* includes all Pu isotopes and compositions except of Pu containing more than 80 percent Pu-238, which is highly radioactive.[3] It also includes chemical mixtures containing Pu. In the past, the weapons usability of different isotope compositions has been subject to debates because different categorizations imply different safeguards and nonproliferation measures.[4] Plutonium that has remained in a power reactor for a rather long period consists of a substantial fraction of "higher" isotopes that are more radioactive than the comparatively stable Pu-239. *Reactor-grade plutonium* therefore emits more unwanted radiation, including neutrons, and develops unwanted heat. These effects must be taken into account and pose technical challenges in all uses, be they nuclear weapons or civilian fuel.

In contrast, *weapons-grade plutonium* consists of a large fraction of Pu-239 and only small parts of higher isotopes. Therefore, the unwanted side effects (e.g., radiation and heat) are smaller. It can be gained by exposing fuel in a reactor only for a short time, with the side effect that the quantity produced is small. This is not economic for civilian nuclear industry whose main goal is the profitable production of energy. But for warhead fuel production in the established NWS, this was the major production method. Weapons-grade plutonium is also a by-product in a fast breeder reactor, due to the different nuclear processes. Theoretically, weapons-grade plutonium could also be produced with the aid of other advanced fast neutron generators.

Since the established NWS prefer weapons-grade to reactor-grade plutonium, it had been reasoned that the latter could not be used at all for nuclear explosives. These debates have largely ceased, due to publication of plausible technical arguments that illustrate the feasibility of nuclear explosives made from reactor Pu.[5] Today, it is widely recognized that all kinds of plutonium, except Pu-238, can be used for nuclear explosives and must be safeguarded accordingly. Nevertheless, most existing nuclear warheads are made from weapons-grade plutonium. Explosives made from reactor-grade plutonium would require a different design. The plutonium created and used in civilian nuclear industry is mainly reactor-grade plutonium.

Uranium

The other isotope that has been used on a large scale for nuclear weapons is uranium-235 (U-235). Natural uranium contains 0.7 percent U-235 and 99.3 percent U-238, which is not fissile. For nuclear explosives, the U-235 content must be much higher. The lower the U-235 content, the larger is the mass needed for one explosive. NWS prefer a U-235 content well above 90 percent. But a crude nuclear explosive can also be constructed with a U-235 content well below this value, however, with more mass. The IAEA names uranium enriched to 20 percent or more as *highly enriched uranium* (HEU) and enriched uranium below this level as *low-enriched uranium* (LEU). HEU is classified as direct-use material. LEU and natural uranium cannot be used for nuclear weapons.

In contrast to plutonium, uranium is less radioactive and emits fewer spontaneous fission neutrons. This allows for less sophisticated ignition technologies and easier handling, provided enough HEU is available. For these reasons, HEU poses special proliferation dangers and needs careful safeguarding.

Ordinary power reactors use only LEU or natural uranium. The only civilian application of HEU is in research reactors. To reduce proliferation dangers, the international community has worked with great success to convert research reactors from HEU fuel to LEU fuel.[6] Yet another application of HEU other than for warheads is for fuel for naval propulsion, which is currently used only by the United States and the United Kingdom.

Enrichment technology is used to produce HEU and LEU. The two main processes that are used on an industrial scale are gaseous diffusion, which is being phased out, and centrifuge enrichment, which is the more advanced technology. However, centrifuge enrichment can be used for clandestine HEU production more easily than gaseous diffusion.

Another fissile uranium isotope is U-233. It does not occur naturally but, analogous to plutonium, is produced as a result of nuclear reactions when thorium is hit by neutrons. There are concepts for civilian nuclear fuel cycles using thorium and U-233, which principally could also be used for nuclear explosives. But up to now, U-233 has not been produced on an industrial scale.

Other Isotopes and Other Mixtures

Other isotopes potentially could be used for nuclear warheads—namely, neptunium (Np-237). The viability of americium (Am-241) for nuclear explosives is disputed because it is very radioactive.[7] Both neptunium and americium arise in spent light-water reactor (LWR) fuel, but none has been separated in larger quantities, unlike plutonium. Reprocessing would yield considerable quantities of these isotopes, but so far they have not been produced on an industrial scale. Nevertheless, they are included in IAEA safeguards regulations because they have the potential to become a proliferation danger.

Not only fission but also fusion processes produce energy during a nuclear explosion, in boosted and thermonuclear warheads. The most important materials for fusion are tritium, deuterium, and lithium. They are also used in civilian fusion research. But without fissile materials, they are not sufficient for nuclear explosives.

The isotopes discussed so far can occur in various mixtures, some of which can be used directly for nuclear weapons or with only moderate technical efforts. The IAEA classifies them as direct-use material. This includes not only HEU and separated plutonium, but also plutonium contained in mixed oxide fuel (MOX) for nuclear reactors. As long as MOX is not irradiated, the plutonium can be extracted rather easily. Similarly, chemical compounds of isotopes do not change their IAEA classification. Spent fuel or LEU fall into a broader category of "special fissionable materials," which is defined as all those materials that contain any fissile isotopes. Such material is safeguarded, though with different intensity, because with significant technical effort, the fissile isotopes could be extracted. An even broader category is simply called "nuclear materials."[8]

Figure 3.1 gives an overview of these isotopes and some mixtures, their different categories according to the IAEA (which imply different

Figure 3.1 Materials, Their IAEA Categories, and Their Role for Nuclear Explosives.

Material	IAEA Categories	Role for Nuclear Explosives
"Weapon-grade Pu": high content of isotope Pu-239	Nuclear material / "Plutonium" with no legal distinction / Direct-use material / Special fissionable material	Explosive can be made from it
"Reactor-grade Pu": Pu-239 + substantial fractions of other isotopes (Pu-240, Pu-241, etc.)	Nuclear material / "Plutonium" with no legal distinction / Direct-use material / Special fissionable material	Explosive can be made from it, but with some technical disadvantages
Pu-238 mixtures (>80%)	None	None
"Weapon-grade" HEU: content of U-235 very high (>90%)	Nuclear material / HEU with no legal distinction / Direct-use material / Special fissionable material	Explosive can be made from it
Lower grades of HEU	HEU with no legal distinction / Direct-use material / Special fissionable material	Explosive can be made from it, but this is more difficult than with 90% HEU
LEU: U-235 enriched to <20%	Special fissionable material	Enrichment necessary to make HEU, or neutron irradiation for transmutation into Pu
Natural U: U-238 with U-235 content = 0.7%	Source material	
D = Depleted U: U-235 content < 0.7%	Source material	
U-233	Nuclear material / Direct-use material / Special fissionable material	Explosive can be made from it
Mixtures containing U-233	Direct-use material / Special fissionable material	First separation from other mixture components to get U-233
Thorium (Th-232)	Source material	Neutron irradiation to produce U-233
Neptunium (Np-237)	Without classification but accountancy	Explosive can be made from it
Americium (Am-241)	Without classification	Explosive can be made from it with extreme technical sophistication
MOX: mixture of U and Pu	Direct-use material / Unirradiated / Special fissionable material	Pu must first be chemically separated
Fresh spent fuel: U-238 + U235 + Pu + highly radioactive isotopes . . .	Direct-use material / Irradiated / Special fissionable material	First reprocessing to gain Pu
Older spent fuel (>10–20 years): U-238 + U235 + Pu + less radioactive isotopes . . .	Direct-use material / Irradiated / Special fissionable material	Reprocessing and handling is easier
Ore, ore residue (e.g., yellow cake)	None	Natural U is made from it
Tritium	None	For fusion processes during a nuclear explosion

regulations for safeguarding), their technical roles for nuclear explosives, their production methods, and their civilian use or appearance. The diagram in figure 3.2 shows an example of a typical fuel cycle. It includes material streams containing uranium and plutonium, the current IAEA definition of material classes, and the related technical processes. Verification requires a high probability of detection of any diversion or clandestine production.

Disarmament in Terms of Technical Categorization

Direct-use material, as the IAEA appropriately names it, is material that is technically easy to use in nuclear weapons. Other sources of direct-use material (e.g., natural uranium, LEU, or spent fuel) pose greater technical challenges, such as reprocessing or enrichment, before the material could be used in nuclear explosives. The concept of disarmament when applied to plutonium or HEU means, in technical terms, the creation of technical obstacles to its being used for nuclear weapons, and the reduction of the overall quantity of direct-use nuclear material. In the case of HEU, efforts are under way to dilute it with natural or depleted uranium in order to obtain LEU for civilian power reactors.[9] In the case of plutonium, similar thinking underlies various scenarios for disarmament. The preferred scenario is to mix it with uranium for MOX fuel that after irradiation in power reactors is turned into spent fuel. However, it will probably take decades and large sums of funding until these projects are completed. Examples in terms of nonproliferation policy are the U.S. efforts to discourage states from using plutonium in their civilian fuel cycles, and the international efforts under way to phase out the use of HEU in research reactors and replace it with LEU.

Political Categorization

In this section, fissile materials are characterized according to their use and status, such as under international safeguards; for civilian use; declared excess; excess to explosive needs; or designated for other military needs such as naval fuel, in the warhead fabrication line, or in warheads.[10]

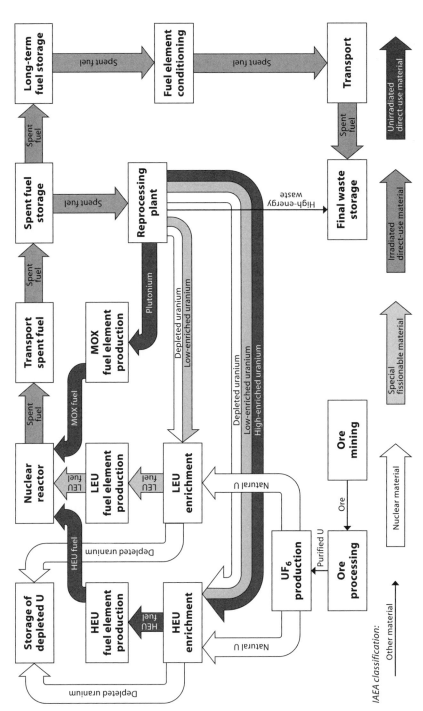

Figure 3.2. Facilities and Material Flows in Nuclear Fuel Cycles.

Fissile Materials under Safeguards

What does "disarmament" or "elimination" of fissile materials mean? Materials with nuclear explosive capabilities principally can also be used in the civilian nuclear fuel cycle or for military purposes other than explosives (e.g., naval fuel). Some of it will be transferred to final disposition by various technical means, but some of it will be used or designated for use in other applications. In non-nuclear weapon states and in a future nuclear weapon–free world, it must be assured that any attempt to use nuclear materials for other than civilian and declared purposes would have a high probability of being detected at an early time. The means to this end is to impose international safeguards, as has been done in all NNWS. Therefore, "disarmament" or "elimination of fissile material for weapons" is synonymous with "submitting fissile materials to appropriate international safeguards." Effective verification requires that, once material is under safeguards, it may never again be withdrawn from safeguards, so that the disarmament process is *irreversible*. In a nuclear weapon–free world, all fissile materials must be so safeguarded.

Plutonium is used in large quantities for civilian energy production in a number of countries. Most of it is reactor-grade plutonium, but weapons-grade plutonium can be produced by fast breeder reactors. Some countries reject plutonium use and pursue direct disposal of spent fuel, but others seek fuel cycles involving fast breeders. Since there is a wide variation of policies concerning civilian nuclear energy in various countries, this chapter assumes that nuclear disarmament should be pursued independently from civilian energy policies and that in a nuclear weapon–free world, the use of civilian separated plutonium and reprocessing might be possible.[11]

HEU is a different matter. The only civilian use for HEU is fuel for a small number of research reactors. Most research reactors are fueled with LEU, and in recent years, the international community has been working to convert all research reactors from HEU to LEU. Ideally, the use of HEU in research reactors will be phased out, once any remaining unconverted research reactors reach the end of their design life. HEU is the most proliferation prone direct-use material, as it is easier to handle than plutonium because of its lower radioactivity and fewer technical problems with metal machining. In contrast, detection methods for smuggled uranium are more difficult. Therefore, it is also easier to smuggle and hide HEU than plutonium. Verification of a nuclear weapon–free world would be easier if the production and possession of military and civilian HEU were banned. Existing stocks of HEU could be diluted with natural or depleted uranium in order to make LEU fuel for power reactors.

The direct-use material possessed by NNWS is mainly MOX and plutonium for MOX production, and small quantities of HEU for research reactors. Most of the nuclear material under safeguards is not direct-use material but special fissionable material (e.g., spent fuel and LEU). The entire nuclear fuel cycles of NNWS are under safeguards.

France and Britain are the only nuclear weapon states whose entire civilian nuclear fuel cycles are subject to safeguards by Euratom, though not by the IAEA. Euratom safeguards are at least as intrusive and detailed as those of the IAEA.[12] All NWS can submit fissile material and facilities to IAEA safeguards, but they are also free to withdraw from such safeguards, according to their voluntary offer agreement with the agency. To date, IAEA safeguarding in NWS has taken place only to a very limited extent. The United States and the United Kingdom. have submitted a few tons of formerly military HEU and plutonium to safeguards; the other NWS have submitted nothing to safeguards.[13]

Civilian Fissile Materials and Fissile Materials Declared Excess to Defense Needs but Not Yet under Safeguards

The United States, Russia, China, India, Pakistan, and Israel have large inventories of nuclear materials in their civilian nuclear industries that are not under international safeguards. Most of the material is in the form of LEU and spent fuel, as in the civilian fuel cycles of the NNWS. In addition, the United States and Russia have large quantities of HEU and separated plutonium (e.g., direct-use materials), which they have declared excess to defense needs but have not put under safeguards. Most of that material is from dismantled nuclear weapons or from the nuclear weapons fabrication pipelines. Some of the civilian direct-use material in the United States and Russia has been returned from countries that used the material in their civilian reactors.[14]

The United States and Russia, together with some other states, have collaborated on plans to dispose of some of these materials. HEU is normally diluted to LEU and subsequently either used in the civilian fuel cycle or disposed as spent fuel. The technical methods for disposition of separated plutonium are less obvious than those for HEU and have been studied and discussed for years.[15] The discussions take into account not only technical feasibility, costs, and nonproliferation but also acceptance and the arguments of the debates on the future of civilian nuclear energy. Today, the most realistic and advanced disposition option seems to be the use of plutonium in MOX fuel for civilian nuclear energy. Efforts to demonstrate this disposition method on a large scale are only just beginning.

For economic and technical reasons, such technical disposition efforts will take decades, and the timetable and means are only partly clear. In the meantime, the direct-use materials must be stored, where they remain at risk for rearmament and proliferation. An important disarmament step would be to irreversibly submit this material to international safeguards.

The demand for universal safeguards is not new. Declarations of intent to place excess nuclear material from dismantled warheads under international verification have been made on several occasions—for example, at the G8 summit in Moscow 1996,[16] in the Guidelines for the Management of Plutonium, which were agreed between the most important plutonium-using states in 1997,[17] and at the NPT Review Conference in May 2000:[18] "We are committed to placing as soon as practicable fissile materials designated by each of us as no longer required for defense purposes under the IAEA or other relevant international verification." The same has been asked by the EU Council at the NPT Review Conference in 2000.[19] The call has also been repeated in several UN General Assembly resolutions, the latest in November 2001.[20] However, key to this phrasing is the term *practicable*, which remains undefined and does not necessarily imply near-term action. There has been no visible attempt to place international safeguards on excess materials. A variety of informal U.S.-Russian transparency commitments were undertaken in the 1990s but have never been fulfilled.[21]

On the contrary, in discussions on a FMCT, diplomats of the NWS up to now categorically refuse to consider any obligations whatsoever on existing fissile materials.

A discussion of the many possible reasons why the NWS avoid strong binding commitments is beyond the scope of this chapter. But one obstacle that is frequently cited as an argument against safeguards and even against some transparency measures must be examined in detail:[22] The owners claim that their excess fissile materials are in physical forms that reveal too much sensitive information. This information must first be removed or adequately protected before these countries would consider the imposition of any international safeguards. Only with progress on this problem could we expect to make progress in promoting universal safeguards. Technical disarmament measures that could be applied to this challenge are discussed in the earlier section, "Disarmament in Terms of Technical Categorization."

Fissile Materials Considered Excess to Defense Needs but Not So Declared

In addition to the materials the NWS have declared, they possess even more fissile materials they probably consider excess but have not so declared. Considering the reductions of the nuclear arsenals after the end of the Cold War, hundreds of tons of weapons-usable materials must have become excess at least to explosive needs, sufficient for many thousands of warheads. Some of the HEU is allocated to future use in naval fuel, but there are also considerable quantities of plutonium that could be either directly disposed of or used in civilian industry.

Declaration of excess quantities and international transparency of all fissile material holdings including military use materials is a prerequisite for safeguards.

Information that would be useful for nuclear disarmament and verification includes the quantities of plutonium and HEU, broken down in the political categories of "reserve material," "remanufacturing pipelines," or "still under military control but considered excess to weapons needs." Materials in these categories should be further described according to their technical characteristics including isotopics, chemical composition, physical shape (e.g., pits, recast metal objects, oxide powder, or scraps and residues), and according to their location (e. g., at storage and manufacturing sites or in various disposition processes). Also of interest would be information on additional civilian stocks and HEU for naval propulsion, and an overview of all production capabilities, including reprocessing and enrichment, reactors, fuel fabrication facilities, and other elements of the nuclear fuel cycle. Documentation of production history would contribute to a clearer picture, but such information is still considered too sensitive to be shared.

The quantities in the category "excess but not so declared" are greater than the quantities of declared materials. They constitute an additional reserve for potential rearmament. A first step toward disarmament would be to expand the amount of declared quantities and to create a strong legal mechanism to make such declarations irreversible, so that material declared excess will never be reused for explosive purposes. The next step would be to apply irreversible international safeguards to this material.

Naval Fuel

The nuclear submarines of the United States and the United Kingdom are propelled by nuclear reactors that are fueled with HEU enriched to 97 percent, the most optimal nuclear weapons-usable material. The quantity of HEU the United States has dedicated to naval reactors is about 100 metric tons, which is 97 percent enriched. Russian naval reactors are reported to use various enrichments from 20 to over 90 percent; the U-235 content is estimated between 47 and 190 metric tons. Most of them use 21 to 45 percent with only few exceptions.[23] Britain purchases HEU for its naval reactors from the United States; the total is estimated to be 5– to 7–metric tons of weapon-grade HEU.[24] France's submarines have always used LEU fuel with an estimated average enrichment of 7 percent.[25] China is believed to use only LEU fuel for its submarines.[26]

Nuclear reactors are used in submarines because they are relatively quiet. HEU fuel is preferred for these reactors because it powers small and long-lasting reactor cores. While many educated discussions have taken place in academic and diplomatic forums on the nuclear disarmament of fissile materials for explosive as well as for civilian purposes, very few discussions on naval fuel have taken place, and they probe only vaguely at the surface of the problem. The reason is the secrecy that the owners assign to their submarines and their naval fuel. A contrasting and prominent example of discussions on the civilian use of HEU is the case of the research reactor FRM-II in Garching, Germany. This discussion featured not only political arguments but also technical considerations such as the small size of an HEU-fueled reactor core that the proponents cited as important, but the opponents considered rather marginal.[27] In principle, similar discussions could take place on fueling naval reactors with HEU or LEU; however, such discussions are not possible for outside analysts because the technical details are classified. Nevertheless, it may be assumed that some considerations on HEU-fueled research reactors and their conversion to LEU fuel would be applicable to the consideration of the use of LEU to fuel naval reactors.

In analyzing the prospects for a nuclear weapon–free world, naval fuel poses particular challenges because there exist large quantities which are not under safeguards. Should the United States (and the United Kingdom and perhaps others) decide to resume production of naval fuel, the verification of this production would pose special problems as long as the secrecy related to HEU fuel is maintained.

Fissile Materials in Use for Nuclear Explosives

As long as there are still nuclear weapons, there is fissile material for explosive use. Such material can be in weapons, warhead components, reservoirs, or production pipelines. If there is a commitment to nuclear disarmament, the warheads will be dismantled and more of this material will become excess, entering one of the other categories of fissile materials already described.

Disarmament in Terms of Political Categorization

According to the terminology used in this chapter, *disarmament* means moving fissile materials into other categories—for example, considering and declaring them excess, with the final goal of subjecting them to international safeguards.

Depending on the two different categorizations, there can be nuclear material that is considered "disarmed" in political but not in technical terms, or vice versa. Depending on the political background, states might assign different emphasis to these categories. For example, the United States and Russia, the largest nuclear weapon states whose nuclear industries are barely under safeguards,[28] pursue nuclear disarmament efforts in technical terms (e.g., plutonium disposition and HEU dilution). An alternative example would be NNWS with civilian nuclear industry using direct-use material under full scope safeguards. These states would not accept the idea that their industry would still need "disarmament measures," although they are likely to cooperate with technical nonproliferation measures such as minimizing the use and trade of HEU.

There are two prerequisites for the usefulness of a definition, such as "Disarmament of fissile materials means placing it irreversibly under international safeguards." First, the safeguards must be credible. There must be a very high probability that the material accounting is accurate, and any diversion would be detected. Second, all states must be strongly deterred from challenging the authority of the IAEA and the international community that backs it, so that any withdrawal from safeguards would entail severe consequences and therefore becomes extremely unlikely. This is already the case for the large majority of NNWS. Not surprisingly, these states are unlikely to have problems with a political categorization of fissile materials. There will always be a few exceptions such as North Korea and Iran that fail to cooperate properly with the IAEA. The discussion of how to deal with such cases is beyond the scope of this chapter. But the NWS pose a bigger problem. The authority of the IAEA, which is hardly unquestioned elsewhere, is not yet implemented in the NWS and the states outside the NPT. Not surprisingly, these states and their educated communities place all emphasis on technical disarmament measures and fail to appreciate the disarmament merits of safeguards.

Extending Established Verification Methods

Once the disarmament process is complete, the verification of nonproduction and nondiversion of fissile material for explosive purposes must continue, but it will be easier. The methods will resemble those used currently in NNWS. International safeguards and verification have been in existence almost as long as the civilian use of nuclear energy. The IAEA and Euratom, both founded in 1957, were motivated by the desire to use nuclear energy without rising proliferation.[29] From the start, the founders of Euratom subjected their civilian nuclear industries to intrusive safeguards. Therefore, some member states, such as Germany, started their nuclear energy use with safeguards.[30] This history demonstrates the technical value of incorporating safeguards in the original design of any nuclear system. This has also been the case with the civilian nuclear industries of two nuclear weapons states: the United Kingdom and France. Another positive effect is a sociological one: the industry, the nuclear decision makers, and the public view safeguards as a natural feature of the system. The nuclear culture is based on the notion that civilian fissile materials are a matter of international responsibility, not a matter of only national concern. The same is the case in states with full-scope IAEA safeguards—namely, the NNWS under the NPT. Throughout the history of safeguards, methods have been further developed and refined. There is a worldwide community of safeguards experts who work in various research centers, meet regularly in conferences and commissions, and publish numerous studies and papers.

There are various methods of verification that in their synergy comprise safeguards as currently applied by the IAEA in NNWS. This section gives an overview on established verification and safeguards methods and how they could be applied in disarming NWS. I will first present the various safeguards methods, and then discuss specific production facilities. All of this has been extensively described in numerous publications and textbooks; therefore the following is a rather short summary. It is nevertheless included in this report because without this knowledge, discussions on the verification of a nuclear weapon–free world would not be possible.

Verification Methods in NNWS and Their Potential Application in Former NWS

Material Accountancy

Principally, a NNWS makes regular and detailed declarations of its fissile materials and nuclear installations, and the IAEA verifies whether these declarations are correct and complete. Declarations include the status of facilities (e.g., under construction, closed down, decommissioned, or operating). Detailed design information of a facility must also be declared, which is then verified. This is necessary in order to understand the production capacities. Also, states must establish accountancy records of inventories and production at all facilities, and then report about them to the verification agency.

In the case where states have been subjected to safeguards from the first beginnings of their nuclear industry, confidence is high that the nuclear inventory is correctly accounted for with small error margins and therefore low probability of illegal diversion. In cases where verification has come in later, the first task is to take an inventory of all fissile material and to verify that the accountancy is complete and accurate. There have been historic precedents, the most prominent being the case of South Africa.[31] Initially, there were discrepancies between the declared and the actual measured inventory of U-235. The declarations were based on past production records. It seemed as if significant quantities of U-235 were missing. However, the missing isotopes were found: they were still contained in depleted uranium stemming from enrichment. The methods of verification were a detailed examination of production records together with measurements not only of HEU and LEU but also of all other uranium inventories. This was possible because South Africa offered maximum transparency of its nuclear installations and past activities. The lessons that can be drawn from this case are first, to create assurance that the accountancy of an inventory is complete, verification needs to cover not only all HEU and LEU but all nuclear materials in the possession of the state; and second, past production records must be transparent. Today, the completeness of the South African declaration is generally accepted due to South Africa's transparency and cooperation.

Can this example be transferred to the future task of taking an inventory of the five nuclear weapons states? Skeptics may raise the following objections. First, the quantities produced are much larger, especially in the United States and Russia; second, the production was much more complex, taking place over decades at various locations with different production technologies and many material streams; and third, the production records are probably incomplete, and a reconstruction from files is unlikely to be satisfactory.

The first objection is the easiest to be countered. The technical means for measuring inventories of smaller quantities of nuclear materials are principally the same for measuring larger ones, and the technical means are available for all sorts of isotopic and chemical compositions of material. In fact, they have been refined for years in safeguarding the civilian production of plutonium and uranium fuels, which are generally more complex than those for explosive use. A promising approach of verifying past production is nuclear archaeology:[32] special isotopes in permanent components of reactors, reprocessing plants, or tails of enrichment can be used to reconstruct past production records. Nevertheless, even if the error margins were small, they would exceed many significant quantities.

The second objection—the complexity of the task—is not a principal one. A prerequisite for success, however, is the knowledge of all locations of past production and storage, and the possibility for access to these locations. It then could be possible to measure the inventories present at each location. Initially, some of the locations and the material may contain very sensitive information from a proliferation point of view. Examples are reservoirs and pipelines with fissile materials and components for nuclear warhead uses, in addition to warheads in deployment and reserve. Until this information is removed, such as by transforming warhead components into another form, managed access provisions must be used. Or, for an intermediate period, it must be assured that no unrecorded material leaves or enters a specified area. The task of taking an inventory could then be completed later, when the too sensitive information has been removed or protected. South Africa, for example, invited the IAEA after the physical disarmament of its nuclear weapons had been accomplished.

The third objection—the incompleteness of production records—is a fact that must be accepted. Production records in the past might have been sloppy or missing, or they might have been created without actually verifying them by measurements. Their credibility therefore is limited. Nevertheless, this is not a true objection: although production records are of great help in order to confirm the accounting of inventories, the primary methods for such accounting are physical measurements. Inventory taking can produce results that contradict production records; that is not unexpected, so long as there are plausible explanations for any such contradictions. It must be anticipated and accepted that there will be contradictions between historical records and measured quantities that probably well exceed many significant quantities. And owners should not fear critics of such discrepancies to the point where they resist transparency measures. Instead, confidence must be created that the discrepancies can be plausibly explained. It is therefore extremely important that the verification process occur in a friendly, patient, and cooperative atmosphere.

A promising confirmation of the feasibility of taking inventories is the U.S. publication in February 1996 of the history of its plutonium production and use from 1944 through 1994.[33] In 2006, the United States also published a history of its HEU production and use from 1945 to 1996.[34] Taking an inventory by national means is the first step to prepare for international verification.

Parallel to inventory taking, administrative processes must be prepared. NNWS have set up offices, so-called State's Systems of Accounting for and Control of Nuclear Material (SSAC), whose task is the national material accountancy and the reporting to the IAEA.[35] They comply with specified standards. Similar bodies must also be set up in former NWS, especially in the states outside the NPT. While they certainly have national authorities in charge of supervision of nuclear installations and inventories, those authorities might still need to adopt international standards, a task that can best be accomplished through international cooperation.

Containment and Surveillance Techniques

A major technique in safeguards in NNWS is "containment and surveillance," which refers to technical equipment that the verification authority installs in the facilities. It includes seals, detectors, monitors, and cameras recording any action occurring in a particular area of a nuclear installation. Such devices provide for the detection of undeclared movements of nuclear material and potential tampering with containment or surveillance devices. In light-water reactors, for example, cores are usually not opened more than once annually. Therefore, it is often possible to seal the reactor pressure vessel head. In so-called bulk facilities (e.g., those that process various material streams), quantities and isotopic compositions are measured at various locations. The more sophisticated such an installment, and the more automatization it incorporates, the less on-site inspections are necessary for the same level of assurance that no material has disappeared. Automated data transfers to the verification agency further reduce the need for on-site inspections.

Inspections and Managed Access

The verification process is completed by inspections to confirm the integrity and functioning of the containment and surveillance techniques, control the operational status and design of facilities, and take samples for analysis of isotopic compositions. In particularly, they assist in verification of material accountancy. The methods used to achieve the inspection goals depend on the type of the facility. The details of activities during an inspection depend on the plant and will include combinations of the following:

- Observations, measurements, and tests to confirm that the design information is correct
- Installation of containment and surveillance technologies
- Installation of detection technologies for proscribed activities
- Audits of accounting records and comparison with reports to the agency
- Measurements for the control of accountancy, which include volume and concentration and enrichment measurements of nuclear materials in streams, tracking the movement of solutions, and taking samples in case of bulk facilities, or in case the material is in the form of countable items as in a reactor, counting, identifying, and examining them by nondestructive means to verify their continued integrity
- Possibly also environmental samples, as a means to detect additional undeclared operations.

Samples taken must be shipped to a laboratory such as the IAEA Safe-guards Analytical Laboratory, located in Seibersdorf, Austria, for anal-ysis. Measurement data taken from inspections and from laboratory analyses are used to establish a material accountancy that is compared to the operator's declaration.

There are several variations of the operational status of a facility. In case a facility is *decommissioned*, the status can be confirmed by complimentary access. Often, inspections can be replaced by satellite imagery. In a *decommissioning* facility, the verification task is sim-pler the more that has already been dismantled and the longer the time for the resumption of operations. A *stand-by* facility theoretically can resume the operation very quickly. However, as long as it is not run-ning, inspections are much easier than in an *operating* facility, which must provide assurance that it is working as declared (e.g., that LEU enrichment facilities do not produce HEU, or that operating installa-tions at reprocessing plants are as declared).

In INFCIRC/153, which is the legal basis for safeguards in NNWS, ad hoc inspections, routine inspections, and special inspections are pro-vided for. Most IAEA inspections are routine inspections in nuclear facilities with a facility attachment agreement between the state and the IAEA, which lays down the rights and obligations of each side in detail for each facility under safeguards. In nuclear facilities without such an attachment, these inspections are called *ad hoc inspections*. Special inspections take place only when the IAEA considers information as not adequate.[36] INFCIRC/540, also called "the Additional Protocol," was negotiated later and has not yet been ratified by all NPT members. Among other features, it allows access beyond nuclear sites, using the existing right to access on "short notice" or "no notice" during routine inspections.

Together with the Additional Protocol, the concept of "managed access" has been introduced into safeguards because it gives the inspec-tors the right to go to more locations than the declared ones.[37] But this could conflict with commercial interests. Managed access means that access is not unlimited but must follow procedures in which the owner can protect certain sensitive information. It must find a compromise between credible assurance of the absence of undeclared activities and the protection of commercial interests. The details within the framework of IAEA safeguards depend on the specifics of the technology and also on the political circumstances.

Societal Verification and National Technical Means (NTM)

In contrast to traditional verification concepts, societal verification relies on the participation of the entire population of a state and is not confined to highly specialized, technically well-equipped teams of experts. In contrast to the methods already described, it is not yet regulated in legal documents. Nevertheless, it contributes to a synergy of the various methods and might be important in case of loopholes.

Societal verification means that citizens are encouraged to pass on all information on treaty violation or attempted treaty violation which might come to their attention to a competent international authority. This would be not only the right but also the duty of every citizen and would therefore have to be incorporated into the legislation of states. The passing on of information must, therefore, not be treated as a punishable offense, either as treason or any other crime, in the states concerned. This concept of involving the whole population is also know as "Citizens Reporting."[38] In practice, such whistle-blowers will often be individuals who come to know of secret projects in one way or another because of their training (specialists, engineers, scientists). It must be made possible for such informants to disclose their knowledge without incurring any risks.

Confidence in societal verification will be easier in democratic states. Therefore, mechanisms could be set up for offering protection to whistle-blowers. This protection could range from providing legal support in conflicts concerning industrial law to the creation of an international relief fund, including secret service methods of hiding fleeing informants. The former approach is more relevant in democratic states, the latter in states where basic rights are not guaranteed and where a threat to life and limb exists.

In democratic states, there is a good chance that deception will be detected. If a party to a convention would intend to cheat by withholding undeclared nuclear materials, extreme secrecy would have to be maintained. The maintenance staff would have to be carefully selected and controlled. Furthermore, social and psychological methods such as indoctrination and intimidation, as well as the offering of rewards and honors, would be needed in order to guarantee the reliability of employees and of those knowing about the deception and to prevent whistleblowing. A mythology would have to be created to conceal the real nature of the activities. This set of lies would largely be of a technical nature. The North Korean violation of the NPT was uncovered not least by inconsistencies between analysis results and North Korean explanations. Deception would have to be coordinated between all participants; and the employees must be trained in such a way that they, too, believe as much of it as possible. However, it would be unavoidable that certain key employees would become aware that they are violating national legislation. Such legislation would exist in the case of an international treaty because of national implementation commitments. In a democracy, violations would require people with a high motivation to pursue criminal acts. In nondemocratic states, the initial motivation would not need to be so high. Social and psychological methods could be more easily applied to persuade people to commit violations, people who would lack the motivation to carry out criminal activities had they lived in a society with democratic traditions.

The motivation for a defector can be the absence of criminal energy, which would evolve most likely in a modern democratic society, opposition against an undemocratic regime, or the prospect of rewards and protection.

If suspicion came to be voiced by the international community, a cheating state would react in certain ways: it might deny access during inspections, as happened in both North Korea and Iraq, or use delaying tactics by means of adjourned diplomatic negotiations, in order to allow time for the removal of telltale clues, as did Iraq. The more often observations of this kind are made, the stronger the suspicion becomes. This could then trigger additional, more intrusive verification methods such as, for example, interviews with staff at suspected plants and establishments. It might be the case that such staff feels intimidated. In this case there should be a mechanism for their protection. Variations of such mechanisms could be legal aid, financial assistance, or typical secret service methods of protection of informants.[39]

National technical means is a well-accepted additional tool of verification that is carried out by states, initially without visible international cooperation. The term is officially included in many arms control treaties and denotes various monitoring technologies, especially satellite observation, or other additional verification measures. Examples are the collection and analysis of environmental samples, or the monitoring of the international trade of a country. More broadly, it is understood as collecting any information that could help draw conclusions regarding a treaty partner's compliance, including potential societal verification. Although not officially acknowledged in diplomatic communities, NTM in fact means typical intelligence measures.

Societal verification and, more broadly, NTM increase the probability of the detection of noncompliance and therefore constitute an important deterrent.

Verification Methods at Different Facilities

The verification methods vary substantially depending on the type of facility. Some major differences are illustrated in the following sections.

Verification of Facilities Containing Bulk Plutonium

Civilian facilities containing bulk plutonium are reprocessing and fuel fabrication plants.[40] They contain separated plutonium in bulk form that can be used directly for nuclear weapons. Reprocessing extracts various chemical elements from radioactive mixtures, but it does not separate different isotopes of the same element. The means are mechanical and chemical processes together with various radiation protection technologies; the output are compounds destined for further uses and highly radioactive waste to be disposed of. The major reason for reprocessing is the intended use of some elements contained in the spent fuel. Today these elements are mainly plutonium and uranium for energy or nuclear explosive uses, but theoretically also neptunium, americium, and others can be separated.[41] Principally, spent fuel from nuclear reactors could be disposed of without reprocessing. There may still be cases of reactors that produce spent fuel that needs to be reprocessed because otherwise there would be corrosion problems during storage.

Safeguards at reprocessing plants are more complex and more expensive than at any other facility.[42] The reasons are first, that reprocessing requires dealing with very high radioactivity, and a plant consequently contains a lot of special equipment for its containment; and second, this process involves many material streams of different compositions in shielded pipes, tanks, and reservoirs. All these various flows contain plutonium isotopes whose quantities and compositions must be measured in order to keep track of the whole inventory. Any illegal diversion from these flows must be detected.

In all plants to be subject to safeguards, there are *key measurement points* at which nuclear material is present in a form enabling its measurement to determine the material flow or the inventory. There are also *material balance areas* where the quantity of every transfer can be determined with fixed procedures. This way, material balances for each area and consequently for the whole plant can be established. Safeguard-friendly facilities provide for better-defined and -instrumented key measurement points.

Nevertheless, some uncertainties persist in results. Errors in calculated plutonium contents can at times exceed a significant quantity. They stem from biases in solution measurements, difficulties to determine the exact Pu content in spent fuel going into the plant, time delays of sample analyses, and measurement limitations because of radioactivity. An important means to achieve better precision is the incorporation of information on the production history of the spent fuel that goes into the plant. This means material accountancy and safeguards also in nuclear reactors. In plants that are subjected to safeguards only later, the key measurement points and material balance areas must be added. It is not clear whether this is possible for every plant. A historic precedent is a British large reprocessing plant (B205 at Sellafield) that came under Euratom safeguards some 20 years after it was designed. Euratom is satisfied that it can verify nondiversion. For every operating plant that is subjected to safeguards, it must be studied whether and how safeguards may be implemented. An obstacle could be the presence of sensitive information that is not yet removed. This is the case especially at plants that formerly have been used for the production of nuclear explosives and are now being converted to civilian use.

The other verification task is the detection of undeclared production facilities. Reprocessing releases several characteristic effluents that can be detected and monitored from outside. They include particulates and gaseous fission products, especially noble gases that are not bound chemically. Reprocessing produces far more emissions than the operation of a reactor or enrichment, so it is possible to create a high probability of detection of clandestine reprocessing.[43] Even with shielding, there is a significant risk of being detected.

Verification of Enrichment Facilities and Other Facilities Containing Bulk Uranium

Apart from fuel fabrication facilities, the most important civilian facilities containing bulk uranium are enrichment plants. A uranium enrichment facility changes the isotopic composition of uranium. The enrichment technology that is increasingly used on an industrial scale is gas centrifuge enrichment.[44] Today, there is no other technology that would be economically competitive. It will soon replace older diffusion plants in the United States and France. Its sophisticated technology has spread into many countries, and more are pursuing ambitious development projects, including Iran and Brazil.[45]

Centrifuge enrichment has disadvantages with regard to nonproliferation and poses special challenges to safeguards.[46] First, it allows rapid breakout scenarios, which means that a plant can be used to produce higher enrichment levels. This can be done by reconfiguration of the cascades, which is verifiable, but can be accomplished quickly. If a country has pre-enriched uranium (e.g., LEU), a fast breakout is also possible by further enrichment even without reconfiguration.[47] These breakout scenarios involve short timelines that must be undercut by verification. The means for verification are design verification, environmental sampling, and material accountancy in time intervals shorter than the breakout scenarios would permit, as well as permanently installed features. In cases where HEU traces are found, their origin must be clarified. In the case of a nuclear weapon–free world, the verification method of looking for HEU traces would hold only in

LEU facilities where no previous HEU production had ever taken place. It would cause false alarms in former military facilities that have been converted to LEU production. Nevertheless, some methods offer promising prospects for conducting forensics on uranium samples to facilitate identification of the origin of a sample.[48]

Material accountancy is an indispensable verification technique. Otherwise, clandestinely diverted LEU could quickly be further enriched with only a low detection probability. In NNWS, the IAEA not only verifies the design of enrichment plants but also takes an inventory of the overall U-235 content that goes in, that is contained, and that comes out, including the isotopes in LEU or depleted uranium. An especially high precision of accounting is required at plants that produce the uranium hexafluoride (UF_6), which is the key ingredient to centrifuge plants. It must be ensured that there is no unaccounted uranium available, which means full-scope safeguards on the entire fuel cycle of a country.

The second problem is that it is difficult to detect clandestine enrichment. A satellite image could not distinguish between a centrifuge and a normal industrial plant. Energy consumption of a centrifuge plant is rather low, so that there would be no significant infrared signal, and its effluents are so low that they allow detection in a radius of only a few kilometers.[49] In contrast to reprocessing, wide-area environmental monitoring therefore is not an option. In other words, only in case of suspicion and a known location is detection likely and could evidence be established. The problem of detecting undeclared activities is dealt with in the Additional Protocol (INFCIRC/540), which gives the IAEA the right to inspect at undeclared locations on the basis of any information that arises. This would include NTM or societal verification. Any noncompliance therefore entails a certain detection probability. In the case of a nuclear weapon–free world, these methods must be applied universally.

A further complication is that centrifuge enrichment involves proliferation-sensitive information and commercial secrets, which is why the owners have problems with unlimited access to the enrichment cascade halls. To solve this problem, the so-called Hexapartite Safeguards Project was started in 1980 by Germany, The Netherlands, and Britain, as well as Japan, Australia, the United States, the IAEA, and Euratom.[50] The group devised and agreed on a concept of "Limited Frequency Unannounced

Access," with three conditions: All measures would be applied similarly in the NWS and NNWS, individual verification activities would be clearly defined in advance, and the secrecy problems resulting from inspector access would be resolved satisfactorily. On the one hand, unannounced inspector visits could detect any undeclared illegal activity; on the other hand, overly detailed intrusion would be avoided. The possibility of unannounced inspections at any time is a strong deterrent against reconfiguration and HEU production between two regular inspections. The application of similar measures in the United States is an important prerequisite for future verification scenarios. An interesting option would be to broaden this agreement to include Russia and China.

A new enrichment technology is laser isotope separation whose operation, in contrast to other enrichment methods, has a much lower detection probability. However, there is no commercial use of this technology because it is uneconomic, and proliferation is unlikely because the level of technical sophistication is very high, and substantial investment of research and development would be necessary. The probability of detecting construction and operation of such a facility, however, is low, and safeguards for such a facility have not been studied. In principle, it is always possible that a new enrichment method will be invented. No matter the method of enrichment, the indispensable verification tools are material accountancy and societal verification.

Verification of Reactors

Verification at reactors is much easier than at reprocessing or enrichment plants, because all nuclear material consists of large countable items. Accordingly, undetected diversion is much more difficult and unlikely. Nevertheless, to establish the total inventory of nuclear material in a country, and to facilitate material accountancy at reprocessing plants, material accountancy of reactors must be included.

Depending on the type of the reactor, the fresh fuel can consist of LEU, MOX, HEU, or natural uranium. Verification must confirm that the quantities entering and exiting a facility are as declared.[51] This is done by item counting and identification, nondestructive measurements, and examination to verify the continued integrity of the item, assuming that the fuel is received from an IAEA safeguarded facility. Much of this can be automatized.

Today, the frequency of routine inspections of reactors depends on the size of the fuel cycle. As a result, most inspections take place in countries where confidence is high anyway, e.g., Canada, Japan, or Germany. Since all NWS have large civilian nuclear industries, an extension of safeguards would raise the costs. But costs could be substantially reduced if routine inspections were replaced by a random system of inspections for nuclear reactors in which material accountancy and verification is easy anyway. The goal of verification is the deterrence of noncompliance by creating a certain risk of detection. Unannounced random inspections that would take place with a certain probability would serve the same goal. The facility operator would need to be prepared for an unannounced inspection at any time. The benefit is that the absence of undeclared activities at the facility at the time of the inspection implies that this has been the case with certain probability over the whole time interval since the last on-site inspection. Since the most expensive component of verification is the cost of inspectors, a random inspection regime for civilian power reactors could substantially reduce the overall costs without raising the risk of undetected diversion.

Verification of Other Neutron Sources and Innovative Fuel Cycle Technologies

Plutonium and other fissile isotopes are created by nuclear reactions involving a neutron. Therefore, any installation that produces neutrons may potentially be used for the production of direct-use material and needs to be verified. Today, such installations are mostly reactors, but, in the future, other machines and technologies may be available. The most prominent examples for future large neutron-producing machines are powerful spallation neutron sources and fusion experiments, which could be used for research, for isotope or energy production, or for transmutation. There is the possibility of measuring neutron flows directly, but since the precision of this may vary, additional other quantities must be measured to draw conclusions—namely, heat production, and isotopic compositions and mass of materials that go in and out. Taking these quantities together would provide for material accountancy.

There are many more suggestions for new nuclear energy systems, most of them still in very early research and design phases. Scientists have proposed various innovative ideas, some of which are praised for posing far less proliferation risks than the traditional systems. Examples include thorium fuels for light-water reactors, nonfertile plutonium burners that only burn but do not breed plutonium, accelerator-driven plutonium burners, pyro-metallurgical reprocessing, recycling of spent fuel without reprocessing that maintains the radiological barrier throughout the cycle, and small or long-lived reactors without recycling. But other proposals might entail similar proliferation risks as the current systems. A framework for international cooperation in research for a future generation of nuclear energy systems is the U.S.-led Generation IV International Forum (GIF).[52] The GIF undertaking investigates a selected set of new nuclear energy system proposals according to various criteria, one of which is proliferation resistance.[53] Detailed and to a large extent similar criteria have earlier been developed by the IAEA.[54] One of the elements in both catalogs is the insistence on safeguards. There will be no technology that could be proliferation resistant without them. But it is important— whether it is difficult or easy— to put a system under international safeguards. In the decision making for new nuclear energy systems, this should be an important aspect, according to criteria of proliferation resistance.

As long as the planning incorporates the technical features for safeguards in an early stage, this is as possible for future nuclear energy systems as for existing ones. The principal technical elements are the same as described in the preceding sections: material accountancy, containment and surveillance, and inspections with or without managed access. Safeguards are easier in the case of countable items than in case of bulk material, and a potential diversion entails more acute proliferation risks in the case of direct-use material than in the case of other material.

Verification Problems during the Disarmament Process

The preceding section describes the verification methods in the absence of a nuclear weapon program and the less problematic parts of verification before and after the transition toward a nuclear weapon–free world.

But the transition period entails several specific problems—problems that are frequently cited by skeptics who do not believe in the feasibility of a nuclear weapon–free world. Moreover, these problems sometimes also play a role in discussions on less ambitious endeavors such as verification of a Fissile Material Cutoff Treaty (FMCT). Plausible answers regarding how to address these problems is key to whether confidence into the feasibility of a nuclear weapon–free world can be established.

I describe and discuss these major challenges in the following sections, with the aim of identifying them and noting where to invest further research, technical analysis, or political change.

Facilities Not Designed for Safeguards

In NNWS, implementation of safeguards is taken into account early in the design stage of a plant, and elements designed for verification are included during construction. This makes it much more difficult for a country to pursue unmonitored diversion paths. Plants in NNWS are well understood, and all their potential diversion paths are known and monitored.

In contrast, facilities in states without full-scope safeguards pose potential challenges. For instance, they might be constructed in a way that the installation of material balance areas and key measurement points would be physically difficult or difficult due to material flows and contamination issues. This is especially the case for bulk facilities. Such problems, however, seem to be more of a technical nature. Remedies might be costly, but not technically impossible. Each such facility that will not be shut down but converted for future civilian use will require an individual study and negotiation of how to establish some satisfactory verification. Most likely, initial safeguards would treat the whole plant as a "black box."

Furthermore, it will be difficult to measure the initial inventory in a plant that had been in operation before being subjected to safeguards. Inside such a plant, there will be various material reservoirs in many different pipes and containers, posing difficulties for measurement of quantity and isotopic composition. Measurements could be incomplete with high error margins. The documentation of past production might be unsatisfactory and contradictory. Even in NNWS, the IAEA sometimes declares material unaccounted for (MUF) but seeks to clarify it later, with the help of material accountancy. The MUF is not diverted, but it is hidden somewhere inside the plant. Clarification requires that inspectors get access to the plant. Even so, there is a limit to the accuracy of this accounting.

For some intermediate period, it must be accepted that the accountancy of the inventory will not be up to the standards of that in NNWS due to such uncertainties in the inventory. Nevertheless, it must be ensured that no additional undeclared operations are taking place in operating declared facilities. The error margins are reduced when the material going into a plant, such as spent fuel, was accounted for at the plant where it originated, such as a nuclear reactor.

The concern that there are facilities not designed for safeguards holds similarly for verification of an FMCT. Since 1994, discussions on FMCT verification have taken place in various diplomatic and academic forums. While there is no consensus on the extent and details of verification, it is clear that reprocessing and enrichment facilities must be included, unless verification is renounced altogether.[55] In the context of discussions regarding FMCT verification, this problem will play a prominent role and will need to be studied in detail.

Cooperative studies to identify such facilities and investigate specific verification methods for them are highly recommended. This would include taking inventories, developing managed access procedures, and permanently installing measurement systems.

Sensitive Information

In NWS, the problem with such plants is less the technical challenge of adding measurement systems for material accountancy, but more the fear that sensitive information cannot be protected. This applies not only to enrichment and reprocessing plants but also to former warhead construction, dismantling, and storage facilities.

Sensitive Information at Warhead Construction, Dismantling, and Storage Sites

As long as warhead construction, dismantling, and storage sites are still operating, they pose a problem for verification because it is difficult to ensure that no clandestine material production is taking place inside. It is evident that on-site inspection or other intrusive verification activity would reveal too much sensitive information. This problem arises especially in FMCT verification scenarios, since remanufacturing of warheads would continue in case of an FMCT.

To a lesser extent, this problem also arises during the transition period toward a nuclear weapon–free world, because of dismantlement activities for warheads. During this period, in addition to the verification of undeclared production of fissile materials, it must be verified that warheads are being dismantled but not produced.[56] This requires accounting of fissile material going in and out, among various other technologies and processes that compromise between secrecy and assurance of compliance. In principle, it is possible to identify and account for all warheads passing a gate without revealing information of their design.[57] With these methods, described in other contributions to this volume, it is also possible to distinguish between warheads and other fissile materials without revealing sensitive information. Therefore, unmonitored processes could take place inside such facilities as long as it is ensured that no additional fissile material is entering and that all fissile material that leaves is accounted for. When the plants are later shut down, verification must ensure that operations have ceased and that cleanup is completed.

Sensitive Information at Fissile Material Production Plants

In facilities formerly used for fissile material production for nuclear explosives and later being converted to civilian production, sensitive information could also pose problems. Some NWS will not reveal the isotopic composition of their warhead materials. Although the isotopic composition would be different for civilian applications, traces of the former material could perhaps be detected and analyzed. In some cases, civilian and military uses are integrated and collocated at one site. An example is the Russian Ural Electrochemistry Plant at which both uranium enrichment and warhead fabrication have taken place.[58] Tools, machines, or nuclear materials in various forms could be around that might reveal sensitive information, in addition to the proprietary information surrounding the civilian processes themselves. Secret information could include not only the isotopic composition of fissile materials but also other physical properties, such as the crystalline phase and other constituent elements.[59] Apparently, conversion of such a dual use facility to an exclusively civilian facility is difficult. Some owners claim that it is virtually impossible to remove the sensitive information.[60]

Examples for secrets in centrifuge enrichment are details of the rotors, their bearings and acceleration, and so forth. Revealing this information could contribute to proliferation and could compromise commercial secrets. But the information needed for safeguards is different (e.g., quantities and isotopic composition of the material streams). To ensure that additional material cannot be hidden and accumulated, inspections need to come close to the centrifuges and need to take measurements in pipes, but they do not need to look inside at a rotor.

Historic Precedents

Lessons can be learned from historic precedents involving the tensions between intrusiveness of safeguards and the desire of the technology owner to protect secrets. One example is the history of enrichment safeguards, when such problems were successfully solved by the Hexapartite Project discussed previously in this chapter. The lesson of this precedent is that a middle ground between secrecy and transparency must be developed and negotiated individually for each technology.[61]

Similar tensions apparently play a role in Brazil's hesitation to sign the Additional Protocol.[62] There is still disagreement regarding where to draw the line between intrusiveness and protection of safeguards on centrifuge enrichment. Brazilian experts claim that the methods of the Hexapartite Project could not be applied in some special exceptions and asked for alternatives.[63] Comparable initial disagreements existed in many other states with nuclear industries, including Germany.[64] The lesson of this second case is that managed access procedures must be uniquely worked out for each individual plant, even in case of comparable technologies. As long as the owners are cooperative, the optimistic assumption is that a solution will be found.[65]

The third case is South Africa's nuclear disarmament. South Africa granted access to all its former production sites and fissile materials, but only after dismantlement was completed and a lot of sensitive information was removed. It also stopped its uranium enrichment. However, there was no verification during the transition period. Therefore, tensions were avoided and a credible cooperation was possible. This case is comparatively easy because South Africa has given up its military intentions and also had no commercial secrets that would have been compromised. The lesson in this case is, cleanup and removal of sensitive information came first without verification; and when verification was introduced, what little sensitive information remained could be adequately protected.

The fourth case involves Euratom safeguards on the entire civilian nuclear energy industry in the EU, including two NWS members with dual-use production plants for both nuclear weapons fuel and the civilian industry.[66] This case relates to reprocessing and to military secrets instead of commercial ones: Britain brought a large reprocessing plant (B205) under Euratom safeguards some 20 years after it was designed, which was formerly used for military production. Euratom is satisfied that it can verify nondiversion from the plant. Indeed, Euratom safeguards are applied to all civilian production in Britain and France, and it runs the full accountancy of the entire civilian fuel cycle in the IAEA. In dual-use facilities, Euratom went out for military batches but came in again for civilian production. It would be useful to study how the United Kingdom brought B205 under safeguards, and to consider the lessons for other problematic facilities. One lesson from this case is that NWS can get used to civilian safeguards even at former military production plants.

The last case presented here is the Trilateral Initiative.[67] It was a six-year (1996–2002) effort to develop a verification system under which Russia and the United States could submit classified forms of weapon-origin fissile material to IAEA verification and monitoring without exposing secrets. Sealed containers would be transported into a facility in which the sensitive information would be removed. This information removal (e.g., transforming warhead pits into other forms with changed chemical and isotopic composition) is costly and takes a long time. The Trilateral Initiative resulted in proposals for how to subject excess material to verification at a much earlier stage than would have been possible if all the classified information were first removed.

Verification measures would be applied on tagged and sealed containers that would be transported to facilities where the classified information would be removed. These methods use measurements operating behind so-called *information barriers*, which are closed devices involving computers without permanent memories that give out only the minimum information that the verification process requires while protecting additional classified information.[68] Such information barriers need authentication and certification procedures to assure both the host country and the inspecting party that the devices have not been manipulated for purposes of spying or cheating. This is not trivial, but various promising approaches have been investigated and discussed to quite a detailed extent by the IAEA and U.S. and Russian researchers.[69]

The methods investigated by the Trilateral Initiative would not be able to establish that the materials submitted actually came from dismantled nuclear warheads. But they would make it possible to verify that the amount of plutonium present in a container exceeded a specified minimum mass value. Consequently, it would be possible to create assurance that no material has been clandestinely diverted, although the verification methods are different from those used for unclassified materials.

The lesson that can be learned from this initiative is that it is possible to devise new methods to deal with sensitive information while permitting fissile materials to be accounted for. Another lesson is that the technical ideas are at a much more advanced stage than are the associated politics. A final lesson is that the more information remains secret, the more difficult verification becomes. Owners of secret information should therefore reconsider their classification guidelines.

Which Information Is "Sensitive"?

The topic of reconsidering classification criteria is a very sensitive one. The only prominent example with far-reaching results is the Openness Initiative of the Clinton administration, which was discontinued by the subsequent Bush administration.[70] Today, information denial practices seem to exceed what is required for preventing proliferation. An example is the isotopic composition of weapon plutonium that remains secret in Russia. This poses additional obstacles to disarmament and verification, as can be seen in the Plutonium Disposition Agreement between the United States and Russia of 2000.[71] To circumvent the declassification of the plutonium isotopics, the agreement regulates how the weapon plutonium may be diluted by up to 12 percent with so-called blend stock plutonium, which is of different isotopic composition and from a non-weapon origin. Although the agreement is better than no efforts at all, the extensive secrecy seems to be an unnecessary complication.

There are several motives for secrecy: One, obviously, is nonproliferation. A second motive is commercial secrets, which also exist in civilian industry. A third is national security, which is deemed necessary to ensure the survivability of the arsenal for deterrence, maintaining uncertainty about intentions and capabilities, hiding technological weaknesses, or protecting technological superiority. NWS should reconsider what information still needs to be protected. Even before the transition toward a nuclear weapon–free world occurs, much of this secrecy may be considered obsolete. A fourth motive might be status: The disclosure of technical information is sometimes seen as a surrender of status and defeat. Again, it may be assumed that in the case of consensus on the goal of a nuclear weapon–free world, the culture and the role of status will manifest itself differently. Fifth, excessive secrecy can result from democratic deficiencies. It could serve as a cover for mismanagement, crime, or corruption. It may also be abused by certain constituencies to set agendas that serve their special interests, to preserve autonomy in decision making, to maximize their power through knowledge, and to avoid scrutiny by competitors or publics. Sixth, a reason for secrecy could also be historic traditions and inertia, including a lack of bureaucratic procedures and incentives to declassify information.

Paradoxically, the tension between secrecy and verification seems to pose fewer problems the more advanced nuclear disarmament becomes. A nuclear weapon–free world, once achieved, is easier to verify than the transition, although some transition steps (e.g., an FMCT) seem more realistic to many observers. This is not only because some problems have already been solved but also because the culture will change during the transition period as a result of past disarmament experience and achievements.

The efforts of the Openness Initiative should be resumed, and other states should be encouraged to undertake similar endeavors.

Detecting Undeclared Stocks

A scenario frequently cited in discussions of a nuclear weapon–free world is that of a country hiding undeclared stocks while pretending to disarm comprehensively. Therefore, verification must create assurance that there is a high probability of detection of any stocks, to deter such behavior.

As noted previously, all nuclear materials in possession of a country must be accounted for. It must be expected and accepted that, initially, inaccuracies and contradictions in the accounting will exist. There must be a cooperative process of clarification that will gradually reduce the error margin until it reaches the standards achieved in NNWS. It is important that these procedures are face saving for the possessors and that they take place in a culture of trust and patience. It should be possible for a state to admit that it has discovered undeclared stocks on its territory. As long as this can be explained by deficiencies in past accounting, such discoveries must be accepted and remedied. Otherwise, the state might continue to hide this material simply to avoid a scandal.

However, in the absence of a plausible explanation, it must be assumed that the case was intentional. Once suspicion of a location with hidden material is established, verification becomes easy with the methods described here. But how can a high probability be created that such suspicions will arise? The decision to hide material would most likely be made at the first stages of the disarmament process—for example, at a stage before the initial declarations of all quantities and locations. This suggests that a participant in the process was intending to cheat from the very first moment and to designate a storage site with maintenance features for this purpose. In this case, the most promising detection scenario would be societal verification, because it is likely that the cheating state would have a special and sizable staff to carry out the various technical and logistics tasks, and also to comply with the deception. This is a big difference from current situations in which the staff complies with secrecy regulations in a nuclear weapons program that is consistent with international law and with the related domestic legislation. The respective mentalities of the people involved would differ substantially from those in today's nuclear staff. Such a cheating state would always run a high risk of being detected because of a defector. The state would therefore insert various means of pressure on such staff; however, history has shown that such a situation will not last forever and that the pressure would become known sooner or later. Scenarios in which large-scale deceptions can be maintained indefinitely seem to be highly unlikely.

Another mechanism that could provoke suspicions is inconsistent material accountancy. Inconsistencies could pop up during reconstruction of past production, thanks to new methods such as nuclear archaeology.

Nevertheless, the concern about cheating cannot be dismissed easily and should be taken seriously, once more realistic steps toward comprehensive nuclear disarmament are taken. An obstacle would be still-lingering mistrust. Confidence will grow in the case of maximum transparency. A future cooperative effort to verify nuclear disarmament must incorporate procedures to facilitate societal verification.

Detecting Production at Clandestine Facilities

The methods for the detection of clandestine production are NTM, including the use of intelligence information, societal verification, environmental sampling, wide-area monitoring, and on-site inspections.[72] Since all production requires feed material, full-scope material accountancy and reconstruction of past production will also contribute. For less developed states, another verification method is observing international trade, which can be considered a method of NTM. These various methods form a synergy that creates high confidence that an illegal activity would be detected.

As discussed previously, the activity that is the most difficult to detect is clandestine centrifuge enrichment, because of its low effluents. In this case, societal verification and intelligence are crucial to establishing initial suspicions of a location where inspections could be conducted. Another method could be the detection of the feed material for centrifuge plants, such as uranium fluoride (UF_6).[73] When UF_6 is released to the atmosphere, it reacts with water vapor to form uranyl fluoride, a stable substance with an identifiable signature.

The problem of how to detect clandestine activities is not restricted to a nuclear weapon–free world but exists already today. It is inherent to the civilian use of nuclear energy. An important step to cope with it is the Additional Protocol that implements the methods mentioned in this chapter. Past cases have demonstrated that, sooner or later, illicit activities will be detected.

In the large majority of states, it is believed that no illegal production is taking place. In a nuclear weapon–free world, the former nuclear weapons states must be similarly trusted and will need to gain the confidence of other states through active compliance and transparency.

Naval Fuel

The problem of naval fuel is frequently cited in the context of an FMCT, but it might also play a role during the transition toward a nuclear weapon–free world. Naval fuel already poses a problem. It does not consist only of direct-use HEU, but all the related information is kept secret. Very little is officially known about submarine nuclear fuel designs, production technology, operational data, and naval fuel stocks.[74] The United States uses HEU in its submarines because reactor cores can be made especially small and long lasting. For those reasons, the United States is determined to continue HEU use in the future.[75] But if all reactors were converted to lower-enriched fuel, as is envisaged for civilian research reactors, the use of HEU could be phased out altogether during the transition to a nuclear weapon–free world. In recent years, new reactor fuels have been developed that allow the conversion of civilian reactors from HEU to LEU fuel. Similarly, it could be envisaged to convert all naval reactors to LEU fuel. This would also facilitate the verification of an FMCT.

In a nuclear weapon–free world, all naval fuel stocks and production, be it HEU or LEU, must be accounted for. But this seems to be a problem for the NWS, as has been shown during discussions between diplomats and academics on various occasions on verification of an FMCT. The reason is the secrecy that is still attached to the technical details of naval reactors and fuels.

Another issue is that NNWS are allowed to possess military HEU for nonexplosive purposes without safeguards as long as it is not used for nuclear explosives, although this has not happened so far. In INFCIRC/153 (§14b), it is foreseen that verification of fuel in a "non-proscribed military activity" is renounced as long as the nuclear material is in such an activity. The agency and the state shall make an arrangement that identifies "to the extent possible, the period or circumstances during which safeguards will not be applied." Thus, it is not clearly defined under what conditions safeguards of fuel would be interrupted. The interruption could be limited only to fuel in the reactor, or it could also be applied to specific naval fuel storage sites. "In any event, the safeguards provided for in the Agreement shall again apply as soon as the nuclear material is reintroduced into a peaceful nuclear activity." So far, there is no historic experience with this provision.

It is recommended that further research be invested in the problem of how to account for naval fuel and to what extent some secrecy should be abandoned. An approach could be along the lines of Trilateral Initiative, described earlier.

Convincing the Most Skeptical

As has been shown, it is possible to address the objections and provide some answers to those who remain skeptical about our ability to verify the elimination of nuclear weapons. Nevertheless, skeptics may argue that the answers do not prove that all loopholes can be eliminated. On the contrary, the answers indicate that we have to accept some loopholes, at least for a considerable time. Examples include material accountancy of huge quantities previously unaccounted for will yield error margins far larger than those acceptable for NNWS; clandestine centrifuge enrichment might not be detected for a rather long time in a non-nuclear weapon state; during the transition period, verification at special facilities will remain of a qualitative instead of a quantitative nature; mistrust might still linger among certain states that some disarmers would still cheat. Taking all these uncertainties together, one might argue that the reliability of verification does not seem convincing enough to be globally accepted.

Several counterarguments to these objections are possible. First, the overall prerequisite for the success of comprehensive disarmament is a strong and credible deterrence of breakouts. Violators will calculate the risks of their scenarios: When the probability of detection of a violation is high because of a convincing verification regime, a state will refrain from cheating. When the probability of detection of a certain scenario is low, a state is likely to consider the consequences of the possibility that the activity would nonetheless be detected. If the consequence is considered to be painful and intolerable, a strong deterrent effect would be created. It is therefore critical to impose strong consequences for noncompliance with the nuclear free world.[76] Then even small risks of being detected would have a strong deterrent effect.

Second, safeguards improve with time, as has been shown by history: North Korea devised a cheating scenario when it entered the NPT. The North Korean nuclear experts anticipated IAEA safeguards as they had been before the detection of Iraq's clandestine proliferation effort that had been detected in 1991. But in the meantime, the IAEA had learned to look for undeclared activities and to consider additional information. This led to the detection of inconsistencies and, subsequently, to the discovery of North Korea's illegal activities. North Korea failed to trick the IAEA.

Third, detection also depends on pure chance and on the risks that proliferators are prepared to take and that cannot be eliminated entirely. No cheater can be safe from accidental detection because of societal verification or NTM such as observation by satellite. Nongovernmental organizations can also provide evidence. Even in a dictatorship, no one can be absolutely immune from societal verification and NTM. In the case of North Korea's cheating attempt, information obtained by satellite imagery triggered the first suspicions.[77]

Recommendations

So far, the world has not yet taken the decision to go down to zero. But, the Obama administration gives hope that the substantive next steps will be taken. In the context of verification, the most prominent steps are an FMCT, and additional measures concerning the security of already existing materials, namely a Fissile Material Control Initiative (FMCI).

For many years, verification scenarios for an FMCT have been discussed in various academic and diplomatic forums. While the details of a future treaty are not clear, most states emphasize the benefits of verification, and the new U.S. administration is likely to revert to a similar position. Verification of an FMCT has a highly symbolic value for a paradigm shift: For the first time, the NWS would accept international verification on fissile materials and production sites on their territories and report to the international community. Fissile materials would cease to be a matter of only national concern, even if verification would be modest in an early phase. Verification of an FMCT poses special problems that to a great extent resemble the problems of verification of the transition to zero. Examples are the detection of clandestine centrifuge enrichment and the difficulty of verifying facilities that were not designed with verification in mind. Once verification of an FMCT has been mastered, more far-reaching verification measures will be easier to add on. It is highly recommended to start international collaboration now on studies on FMCT verification. Since it is likely that an FMCT will focus only on production after entry into force, it is recommended to start parallel efforts on verification of previously produced materials. A proposal that has been endorsed by several states is the FMCI.[78] In this voluntary endeavor, states would collaborate to "increase security, transparency, and control over fissile material stocks worldwide, to prevent their theft or diversion to non-state actors or additional states, and to move fissile materials verifiably and irreversibly out of nuclear weapons and into forms unusable for nuclear weapons." Working on the challenges of the FMCI and FMCT will pave the way for the challenges of the verification of fissile materials.

Several particular challenges have been identified. Each is being addressed, but further research and action is necessary. Here is a list of tasks ahead:

1. **Facilities not designed for safeguards:** Engage in cooperative efforts and studies of how to subject such facilities to national material accountancy and to IAEA safeguards or other verification.
2. **Undeclared stocks:** Start with the implementation of comprehensive material accountancy in nuclear weapons states now. Place as much fissile material under international safeguards as is possible. Subject the entire civilian nuclear fuel cycle in NWS to irreversible IAEA safeguards. Implement mechanisms that facilitate societal verification.
3. **Sensitive information:** Resume the activities of the Trilateral Initiative and implement its results. Cooperate on similar endeavors with other nuclear weapon states. Refine classification criteria to enable more transparency and to facilitate verification. Motivate other states to do the same.
4. **Clandestine centrifuge enrichment:** Pursue the goal of internationalization of fuel cycles. Invest further research in environmental monitoring that might detect clandestine centrifuge enrichment. Implement mechanisms that facilitate societal verification.
5. **The challenge of naval fuel:** Investigate the following questions: Can naval reactors be converted to LEU instead of HEU fuel? To what extent is it possible to lift the extreme secrecy surrounding naval fuel? Which results of the Trilateral Initiative can be applicable to the verification of naval fuel?
6. **Confidence:** Motivate still-abstaining states to adopt the Additional Protocol. Continue refining and strengthening its measures, and demonstrating the increased transparency. NNWS should serve as a role model in the process of ongoing improvement of safeguards.
7. **Next steps:** Identify international measures that seem realistic today, such as an FMCT and a Fissile Material Control Initiative (FMCI). Give new momentum to FMCT and FMCI. Engage in cooperative diplomatic activities to promote and implement them. Provide more money and resources to the IAEA.

8. **Cooperative background:** Promote an international atmosphere that is friendly and encouraging. NNWS should show greater appreciation for efforts by NWS, and understand that the situation for NWS in transition is different from their own, and requires their optimistic patience.

Notes

1. Examples of literature on fissile materials and the verification of its disarmament are David Albright and Lauren Barbour, eds., *The Challenges of Fissile Material Control* (Washington, DC: Institute for Science and International Security, 1999); National Academy of Sciences, *Monitoring Nuclear Weapons and Nuclear-Explosive Materials* (Washington, DC: National Academies Press, 2005); David Albright, Frans Berkhout, William Walker, *Plutonium and Highly Enriched Uranium 1996—World Inventories, Capabilities and Policies*, SIPRI (Oxford: Oxford University Press, 1997). For updates, see also the Web site of the Institute of Science and International Security (ISIS), www.isis-online.org; Alexander Glaser and Zia Mian, "Fissile Material Stockpiles and Production," *Science & Global Security* 13, no. 3 (2008): 55–73; A. Schaper and K. Frank, "A Nuclear Weapon Free World—Can It Be Verified?" PRIF Reports No. 53, Frankfurt, December 1999; International Panel on Fissile Materials, "Global Fissile Material Report 2008: Scope and Verification of a Fissile Material (Cutoff) Treaty," www.fissilematerials.org. See also numerous publications of Matthew Bunn et al. of the Belfer Center at Harvard University.

2. The IAEA currently defines a "significant quantity" of Pu as 8 kilograms. This is a legal term with consequences for safeguards regulations. It is a compromise between high confidence in verification, on the one hand, and costs, on the other. The "critical mass" of a bare sphere is a technical term; it describes the mass of a sphere of normal density in which the number of neutrons during a chain reaction is just constant. For Pu-239, this is 10 kilograms. The fissile material in a warhead, however, is compressed and surrounded by a reflector. Therefore, the quantity needed for one warhead is probably less.

3. International Atomic Energy Agency, *IAEA Safeguards Glossary*, 2001 Edition, www-pub.iaea.org/MTCD/publications/PDF/nvs-3-cd/PDF/NVS3_prn.pdf.

4. For a historic overview, see E. Kankeleit, C. Küppers, U. Imkeller, "Bericht zur Waffentauglichkeit von Reaktorplutonium," Report IANUS-1/1989;

this report has been translated by the Livermore Laboratory with the title "Report on the Weapon Usability of Reactor-Grade Plutonium."

5. Kankeleit made his calculations by using historic quotations from only open sources; ibid. Later, his arguments were confirmed by former nuclear weapon designer Carson Mark: "Explosive Properties of Reactor-Grade Plutonium," *Science & Global Security* 4 (1993): 111; National Academy of Sciences (NAS) and Committee on International Security and Arms Control (CISAC), *Management and Disposition of Excess Weapons Plutonium* (Washington, DC: Authors, 1994); NAS and CISAC, *Management and Disposition of Excess Weapons Plutonium: Reactor Related Options* (Washington, DC: Authors, 1995); National Academy of Sciences, *Monitoring Nuclear Weapons and Nuclear-Explosive Materials.*

6. Ole Reistad and Styrkaar Hustveit, "HEU Fuel Cycle Inventories and Progress on Global Minimization," *The Nonproliferation Review* 15, no. 2 (July 2008).

7. David Albright and Kimberly Kramer, "Neptunium 237 and Americium: World Inventories and Proliferation Concerns," June 10, 2005, revised August 22, 2005, http://isis-online.org/global_stocks/end2003/np_237_and_americium .pdf. For a table of properties of nuclear explosive nuclides, see Nuclear Energy Research Advisory Committee, *Attributes of Proliferation Resistance for Civilian Nuclear Power Systems* (Washington, DC: U.S. Department of Energy, October 2000).

8. See *IAEA Safeguards Glossary.*

9. William C. Potter, "Nuclear Terrorism and the Global Politics of Civilian HEU Elimination," *The Nonproliferation Review* 15, no. 2 (July 2008).

10. For quantities, see Institute for Science and International Security, "Global Stocks of Nuclear Explosive Materials," http://isis-online.org/global _stocks/end2003/tableofcontents.html.

11. There are considerations of new fuel cycles that are more proliferation resistant. As an example, when a fuel cycle does not include separated direct-use material, it is more proliferation resistant than a fuel cycle involving reprocessing. While it is recommendable to reduce proliferation dangers with the aid of more proliferation-resistant technologies, the discussion of proliferation resistance is beyond the scope of this chapter.

12. In fact, Euratom has more access rights than the IAEA, and in contrast to the IAEA, it has even enforcement rights by imposing sanctions.

13. ISIS, *Global Stocks.*

14. David Albright and Kimberly Kramer, "The Disposition of Excess US and Russian Military Highly Enriched Uranium (HEU)," February 2005, ISIS-Online, Global Stocks of Fissile Materials, www.isis-online.org.

15. NAS and CISAC, *Management and Disposition of Excess Weapons Plutonium*; Joint U.S.-Russian Plutonium Disposition Steering Committee, *Joint United States/Russian Plutonium Disposition Study* (Washington, DC: U.S. Department of Energy, September 1996).

16. Moscow Nuclear Safety and Security Summit Declaration, April 20, 1996, para 25.

17. INFCIRC/549.

18. Letter dated May 1, 2000, from the representatives of France, China, Russia, the United Kingdom, and the United States addressed to the president of the 2000 Review Conference of the Parties to the Treaty on the Non-Proliferation of Nuclear Weapons, www.basicint.org/nuclear/NPT/2000revcon/MC3ChairReportMay12.htm.

19. Council Common Position of April 13, 2000, relating to the 2000 Review Conference of the Parties to the Treaty on the Non-proliferation of Nuclear Weapons Official Journal L 097, 19/04/2000 p. 0001 (Document 400X0297), Article 2 (2i).

20. Resolution 56/24N of the UN General Assembly, November 29, 2001, "A Path to the Total Elimination of Nuclear Weapons."

21. Matthew Bunn, "The Next Wave: Urgently Needed New Steps to Control Warheads and Fissile Material," Report Carnegie Endowment for International Peace and Harvard University, March 2000, available at www.ksg.harvard.edu/bcsia/atom, p. 47.

22. Annette Schaper, "Looking for a Demarcation between Nuclear Transparency and Nuclear Secrecy," PRIF Reports No. 68, 2004, www.hsfk.de/publication_detail.php?publicationid=2467&language=en.

23. O. Bukharin, "Analysis of the Size and Quality of Uranium Inventories in Russia," *Science & Global Security* 6, no. 1 (1996): 59.

24. Albright and Barbour, *The Challenges of Fissile Material Control*, 118.

25. Ibid., 125.

26. Lisbeth Gronlund, David Wright, and Yong Liu, "China and a Fissile Material Production Cutoff," *Survival* 37, no. 4 (Winter 1995).

27. Annette Schaper, "HEU in Germany," unpublished manuscript; Alexander Glaser, "Neutronics Calculations Relevant to the Conversion of Research Reactors to Low-Enriched Fuel," PhD diss., Technical University Darmstadt, February 2005, elib.tu-darmstadt.de/diss/000566/aglaser_thesisrev.pdf. This dissertation was possible because the author had access to a lot of technical information of the concept.

28. Except voluntary safeguards under INFCIRC/66 that are hardly implemented.

29. 50 years of the Euratom Treaty: reflecting on the past, safeguarding the future. ENS News, Issue No.16 Spring, April 2007, http://www.euronuclear .org/e-news/e-news-16/euratom-treaty.htm

30. Wolfgang D. Müller, „Geschichte der Kernenergie in der Bundesrepublik Deutschland—Anfänge und Weichenstellungen (History of Nuclear Energy in the Federal Republic of Germany—Beginning and Setting the Course)," Stuttgart 1990.

31. Adolf von Baeckmann, Gary Dillon, and Demetrius Perricos, "Nuclear Verification in South Africa," *IAEA Bulletin* 37, no. 1.

32. Steve Fetter, "Nuclear Archaeology: Verifying Declarations of Fissile Material Production," *Science & Global Security* 3 (1993): 237–259.

33. U.S. Department of Energy, "Plutonium: The First 50 Years: United States Plutonium Production, Acquisition, and Utilization from 1944 through 1994," DOE/DP-0137, February 1996, http://apollo.osti.gov/html/osti/opennet/document/pu50yrs/pu50y.html.

34. U.S. Department of Energy, National Nuclear Security Administration, "Highly Enriched Uranium: Striking a Balance—A Historical Report on the United States Highly Enriched Uranium Production, Acquisition, and Utilization Activities from 1945 through September 30, 1996," January 2001.

35. Most EU member states do not have national SSACs; instead, their common SSAC is Euratom.

36. Wolfgang Fischer and Gotthard Stein, "On-Site Inspections: Experiences from Nuclear Safeguarding," *Disarmament Forum* 3 (1999): 45–54.

37. Ibid.

38. J. Rotblat, "Societal Verification," in *A Nuclear-Weapon-Free World: Desirable? Feasible?* ed. J. Rotblat, J. Steinberger, and B. Udgaonkar (Boulder, CO: Westview, 1993), 103–118.

39. Frank Blackaby, "Societal Verification," in *Background Papers of the Canberra Commission on the Elimination of Nuclear Weapons* (August 1996), 264.

40. Nuclear fuel containing plutonium is called mixed oxide fuel (MOX).

41. David Albright and Kimberly Kramer, "Neptunium 237 and Americium: World Inventories and Proliferation Concerns," June 10, 2005, revised August 22, 2005, www.isis-online.org/global_stocks/end2003/np_237_and _americium.pdf.

42. T. Shea, "Reconciling IAEA Safeguards Requirements in a Treaty Banning the Production of Fissile Material for Use in Nuclear Weapons or Other Nuclear Explosive Devices," *Disarmament Forum*, UNIDIR, 2 (1999): 57.

43. Martin B. Kalinowski, "Remote Environmental Sampling for the Detection of Clandestine Nuclear Weapons Production and Testing," ESARDA Training Course "Nuclear Safeguards and Nonproliferation," Ispra, April 14–18, 2008, http://esarda2.jrc.it/internal_activities/WC-MC/Web-Courses/01-Background/09-Environmental-Kalinowski.pdf.

44. There are several different enrichment technologies with different process characteristics. They include gaseous diffusion, gaseous centrifuge plants, aerodynamic enrichment, electromagnetic separation, chemical isotope separation, atomic vapor laser isotope separation (AVLIS), and molecular isotope separation (MLIS). Because of different process characteristics, the technical details of verification vary. The levels of experience that the IAEA has collected in safeguarding these technologies vary, as does the extent to which such facilities are operated commercially or on an experimental level. See Allan S. Krass, Peter Boskma, Boelie Elzen, and Wim A. Smit, *Uranium Enrichment and Nuclear Weapon Proliferation* (London: Taylor & Francis, 1983).

45. For this reason, the internationalization of the fuel cycle is being discussed. See Harald Müller, „Multilateralisierung des Brennstoffkreislaufs: Ein Ausweg aus den Nuklearkrisen?" (Multilateralization of the Fuel Cycle: A Way Out of the Nuclear Crises?), HSFK-Report 10/2006, www.hsfk.de/downloads/report1006.pdf.

46. Houston G. Wood, Alexander Glaser, and R. Scott Kemp, "The Gas Centrifuge and Nuclear Weapons Proliferation," *Physics Today*, September 2008, pp. 40–45; Dmitry Sharikov; "Verification Challenges for Safeguarding Uranium Enrichment Plants," *ESARDA Bulletin* 37 (December 2007): 75–79.

47. Alexander Glaser, "Characteristics of the Gas Centrifuge for Uranium Enrichment and Their Relevance for Nuclear Weapon Proliferation," *Science & Global Security* 16 (2008): 1–25.

48. Houston G. Wood, "Effects of Separation Processes on Minor Uranium Isotopes in Enrichment Cascades," *Science & Global Security* 16 (2008): 26–36.

40. Ibid.

50. For details on the Hexapartite Safeguards Project, see Fischer and Stein, "On-Site Inspections." Germany, The Netherlands, and the United Kingdom are partners in the centrifuge enrichment company URENCO.

51. N. Harms and P. Rodriguez, "Safeguards at Light-Water Reactors—Current Practices, Future Directions," *IAEA-Bulletin* 38, no. 4 (1996), www.iaea.org/worldatom/inforesource/bulletin/bull384/harms.html.

52. U.S. DOE Nuclear Energy Research Advisory Committee and the Generation IV International Forum, "A Technology Roadmap for Generation IV Nuclear Energy Systems," December 2002; see also GIF homepage: www .gen-4.org.

53. The Proliferation Resistance and Physical Protection Evaluation Methodology Expert Group of the Generation IV International Forum, "Evaluation Methodology for Proliferation Resistance and Physical Protection of Generation IV Nuclear Energy Systems," Revision 5, November 30, 2006, www .gen-4.org/Technology/horizontal/PRPPEM.pdf.

54. Guidance for the evaluation of innovative nuclear reactors and fuel cycles, "Report of Phase 1A of the International Project on Innovative Nuclear Reactors and Fuel Cycles (INPRO)," IAEA-TECDOC-1362, June 2003.

55. Annette Schaper, "Principles of the Verification for a Future Fissile Material Cutoff Treaty (FMCT)," PRIF Report No. 58, Frankfurt am Main, 2001, http://hsfk.de/fileadmin/downloads/prif58.pdf.

56. See chap. 4, "Going to Zero: Verifying Nuclear Warhead Dismantlement," and chap.6, "Verifying the Nonproduction of New Nuclear Weapons," in this volume.

57. Ibid.

58. O. Bukharin, "Integration of the Military and Civilian Nuclear Fuel Cycles in Russia," *Science & Global Security* 4, no. 3 (1994): 385.

59. Much of such information has meanwhile been declassified: U.S. Department of Energy, Office of Declassification, "Restricted Data Declassification Policy 1946 to the Present (RDD-7)," January 1, 2001, http://www.fas .org/sgp/othergov/doe/rdd-7.html.

60. This argument was among those raised by the United States in July 2004, when the U.S. administration announced that it would oppose verification arrangements.

61. Fischer and Stein, "On-Site Inspections."

62. Carlos Feu Alvim, "Brazil and the Additional Protocol of the Safeguards Agreement," transcription of an Article published in *Correio Braziliense*, April 19, 2004, http://ecen.com/eee43/eee43e/adic_protc_cb.htm.

63. Orpet J. M. Peixoto and Laércio A. Vinhas, "Information Protection When Applying Safeguards to Centrifuge Enrichment Facilities," *ABACC News* 4 (January 1, 2005), www.abacc.org/abaccnews/trabalhos .asp?edicao_id=3.

64. Statement by the Utilities Employing Nuclear Energy and the Nuclear Industry in Germany on the IAEA Programme 93+2, 3 June 1996.

65. Another lesson is the role that regional safeguards play in establishing confidence: Euratom safeguards are more intrusive than those of the IAEA, and for the owners of the centrifuge facilities, Urenco, it was less a problem to grant access to Euratom than to IAEA inspectors. A comparable role is played by ABACC, the regional verification authority in South America. It has already demonstrated the potential to pave the way for the IAEA.

66. Meanwhile, the production for explosive purposes had ended.

67. Thomas E. Shea, "The Trilateral Initiative: A Model for the Future?" *Arms Control Today*, May 1, 2008, www.armscontrol.org/print/2980; Thomas E. Shea, "Report on the Trilateral Initiative: IAEA Verification of Weapon-Origin Material in the Russian Federation & the United States," *IAEA Bulletin* 43, no. 4 (2001). This subject is also addressed in chap. 4.

68. Oleg Bukharin, "Appendix 8A: Russian and US Technology Development in Support of Nuclear Warhead and Material Transparency Initiatives," in *Transparency in Nuclear Warheads and Materials*, ed. Nicholas Zarimpas (Oxford: Oxford University Press, for Stockholm International Peace Research Institute, 2003), 32, also p. 16; J. L. Fuller and J. K. Wolford, "Information Barriers," Proceedings IAEA-SM-367/17/01, R. Whiteson, D. W. MacArthur, "Information Barriers in the Trilateral Initiative: Conceptual Description," Report LAUR-98-2137, Los Alamos, NM, 1998.

69. Some of the results are presented in "Session 17: Verification Technology for Nuclear Disarmament," in *Proceedings of the Symposium on International Safeguards: Verification and Nuclear Material Security*, Vienna, October 29–November 2, 2001.

70. See Schaper, "Transparency."

71. Agreement between the Government of the United States of America and the Government of the Russian Federation Concerning the Management and Disposition of Plutonium Designated as No Longer Required for Defense Purposes and Related Co-operation, September 1, 2000.

72. National Academy of Sciences, *Monitoring Nuclear Weapons and Nuclear-Explosive Materials.*

73. R. Scott Kemp, Initial Analysis of the Detectability of UO2F2 Aerosols Produced by UF6 Released from Uranium Conversion Plants, *Science & Global Security* 13, no. 3 (2008): 115–125.

74. Morten Bremer Maerli, "Deep Seas and Deep-Seated Secrets: Naval Nuclear Fuel Stockpiles and the Need for Transparency," *Disarmament Diplomacy* 49 (August 2000).

75. U.S. Department of Energy, "Striking a Balance."

76. See Müller's chap. 2 of this volume, "Enforcement of the Rules in a Nuclear Weapon–Free World."

77. David Albright and Corey Hinderstein, "Evidence of Camouflaging of Suspect Nuclear Waste Sites," in *Solving the North Korean Nuclear Puzzle*, ed. David Albright and Kevin O'Neill (Washington, DC: ISIS Press, October 2000).

78. Proposal by Robert Einhorn, "Fissile Material Control Initiative—A CSIS Proposal, December 2007: Creating a New momentum for a Fissile Material Cut-Off Treaty (FMCT)," working paper submitted by Germany, Preparatory Committee for the 2010 Review Conference of the Parties to the Treaty on the Non-Proliferation of Nuclear Weapons, NPT/CONF.2010/PC.II/WP.21, April 30, 2008.

4. Going to Zero: Verifying Nuclear Warhead Dismantlement

JAMES FULLER

An agreement to eliminate all nuclear weapons worldwide would almost certainly take considerable time to implement. The weapon states, particularly in the beginning the United States and Russia, will demand that the nuclear balance does not change during (and forever after) the drawdown. And while the United States and/or Russia can lead the way, the endeavor will not be unilateral. Trust and goodwill will not be enough. Transparency and confidence building will not be enough. Nuclear weapons constitute an incredible threat to mankind but at the same time are believed by many to be the ultimate security assurance against massive invasion, world war, and the use of other types of mass destruction weapons.[1] The processes and tools that are put in place to cooperatively eliminate nuclear warheads could very well influence the balance of power between nations. They will have to be very good. *Verification* will become the watchword, and the standards for it will need to be as *airtight* or *perfect* as possible.[2] These standards will receive considerable debate, and while it should be possible to statistically estimate the efficacy of this or that instrument or approach, ultimately there will be a considerable degree of subjectivity to the consideration because *perfection* is indeed elusive.

Several studies have been undertaken by the United States government over the years researching the issues and investigating plausible solutions for verification regimes directly involving nuclear warheads.

The net result of these studies, practical experience gained through bilateral and multilateral arms control, nonproliferation, and nuclear safety and security agreements, as well as studies by independent non-government entities, suggest a number of underlying issues associated with warhead reduction verification processes. These include (1) defining *nuclear warhead*; (2) determining an accurate baseline inventory of warheads, by state, on a worldwide basis; (3) relying on extensive and potentially very intrusive on-site inspections and perfecting new on-site inspection (OSI) tools due to the reduced efficacy of national technical means (NTM); (4) protecting state secrets; and (5) developing concomitant regimes to assure irreversibility of the dismantlement process.

A basic construct for the verification of nuclear warhead dismantlement would include (1) verifying that an item presented for dismantlement is actually a nuclear warhead, (2) accurately counting and maintaining a continuity of knowledge about all warheads until they are dismantled, and (3) verifying the physical dismantlement of the warheads. As mentioned, cooperative on-site inspection and monitoring approaches associated with these activities have received considerable study, especially since the end of the Cold War.

These studies confirm that options do indeed exist to verify warhead dismantlement. A seemingly intractable problem is assuring that there are no clandestine stockpiles of warheads as a result of incomplete initial declarations or illicit initial diversion of warhead items or nuclear materials.

Deep reductions on the way to zero of the last of the weapons of mass destruction will require new thinking by policymakers, military planners, and technical specialists. The methods, technology, and procedures envisioned today for verification must begin receiving much more critical review and assessment. Some of these may be found wanting. New methods and procedures may need to be devised to help solve some specific issues. For example, it may not prove feasible to keep protected from disclosure all that is considered classified and sensitive if we are to truly be successful in overcoming some of the more difficult verification problems. And probably the best, though not the least expensive approach to monitored dismantlement in any of the nuclear weapon states is to build (or have built by an international organization) a special new, aboveground dismantlement facility of a design that is acceptable to the other weapon states and to all others involved in monitoring or having a stake in monitoring. Such an investment not only would simplify monitoring but also would help minimize the myriad of potential problems and impacts to other legitimate defense and homeland security activities.

Specific areas that are identified as needing further work include refinement of radiation detection inspection methods for better warhead type-class differentiation while still protecting sensitive design information. Further refinement of radiation-based template matching methods is required. Independent validation and protection of reference radiation signature template data is a pivotal problem that demands further study and assessment. The possibility that non-nuclear warhead signature approaches might exist that inherently protect important warhead design information while at the same time solve certain verification problems needs considerably more attention as well. It would prove very useful if nuclear archeology techniques are explored as a way to validate both production and disposition declarations of nuclear explosive device material and items, to the same degree of efficacy that has been demonstrated for plutonium production reactor history. New, very high-security unique identifiers, extending national laboratory work from the START era, for tagging and sealing warhead items and containers needs to be undertaken, focusing on active devices utilizing cryptographic keys for authentication. Similarly, cryptographic methods to facilitate warhead counting— that is, data exchanges on warhead types and locations—need to be devised and independently assessed.

And while there has been excellent research success in the United States, Russia, and the United Kingdom in the area of radiation-based monitoring systems integrated with information barriers, the authentication of such systems (and the associated data from them) under the rigorous demands of deeper reductions has received inadequate attention. To protect state secrets, it is presumed that there will be great resistance by any of the nuclear weapons state to allow an inspectorate to use any such equipment without inspected-country certification or to allow the removal of this equipment from the country once it has been used on a warhead item. The development of essentially invulnerable authentication methods and procedures is an area of great concern and needs focused attention, including the possibility of establishing national authentication authorities to advise heads of state as they eliminate their nuclear arsenals.

Background

Verification is associated with a process of confirmation, as opposed to *transparency*, which is a process of confidence building.[3] The overall process of verification includes cooperative monitoring and inspections, intelligence community judgments and estimates based on national technical means and open sources, and political judgments based on many additional subjective factors. The focus of this chapter is on the more deterministic approaches for rigorous on-site cooperative monitoring and inspections, both because of the basic nature of the problem, and because of the difficulty in detailing private sources and methods. Also, dismantlement verification is viewed from a perspective of minimizing the need to divulge state secrets: classified information about nuclear warheads and their stewardship. This tack provides the shortest and quickest (but perhaps not the least expensive) route to the desired endpoint, though it can present some very difficult technical problems. Hopefully this focus provides an adequate benchmark of where we are today and what needs to be accomplished in the future if we are to come close to achieving airtight verification.

Much has been written in the United Sates and elsewhere in both the open and classified literature about the feasibility of directly verifying deeper reductions in nuclear weapons. This is especially true since the end of the Cold War. In some cases the views expressed about the efficacy of today's technologies have been overly optimistic. Considerable progress has occurred within official channels in the United States, Russia, the United Kingdom, and elsewhere, but many problems remain to be solved. There have even been some first attempts at making direct measurements, as well as mechanically destroying classified objects, both in the United States for foreign (particularly Russian) visitors and vice versa in Russia. There are recent publications out of China that suggest they too are looking at technical methods to support verification of deeper reductions.[4] But, as noted several years ago and remains true today, there has never been an *end-to-end* demonstration of a verifiable nuclear warhead dismantlement process.[5] And there has been a paucity of papers considering verification regimes leading to complete elimination.

Only limited actual cooperative monitoring of nuclear warheads using technical measures has taken place in the international arena even though the numbers of deployed U.S. and Russian systems has been significantly reduced from Cold War levels. Some notable exceptions include the Joint Verification Experiment in association with the Threshold Test Ban Treaty, portal perimeter neutron measurements on Russian SS25s in support of the Intermediate Nuclear Forces (INF) treaty, and RVOSI (Reentry Vehicle On-Site Inspection) under START, and New START. Heretofore, up until New START, the focus has been on delivery systems: these items are usually less sensitive and quite large and therefore much easier to observe. Deployed stockpiles have been monitored through declaration and attribution, in conjunction with national technical means. This has proved adequate with numbers of warheads still in the thousands. But at much lower levels where long-standing deterrence strategies will need to be reconsidered and where assuring strategic stability will be more challenging, parity down to a small number of warheads will likely become very important.

An early (1963–1969) secret U.S. Arms Control and Disarmament Agency/U.S. Air Force study that was eventually declassified, *Project Cloud Gap: The Demonstrated Destruction of Nuclear Weapons*, incorporated an extensive mock dismantlement exercise (called *Field Test 34*).[6] Two conclusions of this study were not only would significant amounts of classified information be put at risk and invariably lost under a cooperative regime, but also, if a treaty party tried to spoof the process, there would be a significant risk of detection. Following this, more than 25 years later, just before the Cold War ended, President George H. W. Bush was tasked by Congress through Section 3151 of the National Defense Authorization Act of 1991 to form a Warhead Dismantlement and Fissile Material Control Advisory Committee for the purpose of reporting on warhead dismantlement monitoring and the control of weapons-usable material. This report was prepared, similar to the Cloud-Gap effort, within an envelope of special information security classifications and the full report remains classified today. An unclassified executive summary has been made available, however.[7] The full effort was peer reviewed by the Mitre JASONs. They also offered an unclassified report on the subject.[8] The *3151* or *Robinson Committee Report* validated several of the known issues, in particular concluding that the utility of national technical means in directly monitoring warhead inventories and dismantlement activities would be very limited. This conclusion points to the necessity of on-site, thus more intrusive inspections for verification of warhead dismantlement. This effort, along with activities associated with early INF and START treaty negotiations, also resulted in the construct of a new warhead dismantlement verification and fissile material control technology development program within the research and development division of what is now the National Nuclear Security Administration (NNSA) Office of Defense Nuclear Nonproliferation (NNSA/NA20).

About this same time, the Office of Technology Assessment, an institution that was part of the U.S. Congress, completed a study project and issued an extensive report: *Dismantling the Bomb and Managing Nuclear Materials.* The project staff took a hard look at the challenges of eliminating thousands of nuclear warheads, with expanded focus of environmental and safety issues. The report was quite critical of the Departments of Defense and Energy, nay, the Executive Branch for not having *a clear and comprehensive national policy of nuclear warhead dismantlement.* Also, because of a lack of openness, the Departments of Defense and Energy were accused of having a *corrosive effect* on policymaking within the U.S. government. The study group contended that the drawdown efforts that were under way in the United States at the time were more an exercise in *short-term modification of existing practice* rather than a change of mission. This was an advocacy paper very early in the post–Cold War era. Its primary value was the explanations and information in official form about the U.S. warhead infrastructure. The report did not go into depth about the hard technical problems.[9]

Immediately subsequent to the Robinson Committee and OTA reports, as Russia opened, under some visionary leadership at the U.S. Departments of Energy and Defense and from within the U.S. Congress, a period of unprecedented cooperation between nuclear and military specialists in the

United States and Russia took place. Not only did considerable effort on the protection of Russian nuclear material occur, but also under the Gore-Chernomyrdin Commission, extensive discussions were undertaken on cooperative means to monitor nuclear warhead inventories and their reductions. And under the Nunn-Lugar Cooperative Threat Reduction programs, broad assistance has been provided to the Russian Federation in the area of strategic nuclear system reductions. Taken together, these experiences have added important insights to the effort of nuclear cooperation between the world's two biggest nuclear superpowers.

Specifically regarding nuclear warhead reductions, experimental work was undertaken both unilaterally in the United States, often at a classified level, and cooperatively in an unclassified manner between Russian specialists and U.S. researchers from most of larger U.S. Department of Energy (DoE) and Russian national/federal laboratories. The DoE also assembled a Dismantlement Study Group at about the same time as the March 1997 Helsinki Summit of Presidents Clinton and Yeltsin. In Helsinki it was agreed to begin START III negotiations that would include *measures relating to the transparency of strategic nuclear warheads and any other jointly agreed technical and organizational measures, to promote the irreversibility of deep reductions including the prevention of rapid increase in the number of warheads.*

An extensive and very detailed effort was undertaken by the Dismantlement Study Group to understand how either a transparency or verification regime of warhead dismantlement might be undertaken within the existing U.S. nuclear complex. The full report from that era is still limited to official use only, but general conclusions were presented and published by the study group chairman in open session at a U.S. technical meeting in 1997. The study group concluded that there are nine salient activities that could be used to develop a warhead dismantlement monitoring regime:

1. Declarations of dismantlement schedules, warheads, and components resulting from the dismantlement process
2. Spot checks of the weapons receipt and storage areas and component storage areas to confirm declarations, including the use of radiation signatures of the weapons and components

3. Remote monitoring of the weapons receipt and storage areas and component storage areas

4. Radiation signature measurements of warheads and components following dismantlement

5. Chain of custody of warheads and components

6. Portal Perimeter Continuous Monitoring (PPCM) to inspect every item that passes in and out of a segregated portion of the dismantlement area

7. Sweeping or sanitizing a disassembly bay or dismantlement cell periodically before and after dismantlement

8. Remote monitoring or direct observation of the dismantlement process (e.g., during the disassembly of the physics package and during the removal of the high explosive from the pit)

9. Monitoring of the disposition of the non-nuclear components of the warhead, such as the high explosive and warhead electronics, after dismantlement.[10]

This list of activities was constructed without regard to the level of sensitivity of the associated information. For example, the visual observation by an inspector of the actual dismantlement procedure is something that would probably be very difficult to ever get approved, anywhere. Subsequent to this study but reported separately (and described in a later section of this chapter), a warhead radiation signature measurement campaign was completed at the U.S. Pantex facility using a large number of nuclear warheads to help understand the promise and limitations of radiation signature measurements.

Cooperation with Russian Federation weapons scientists initially came as a result of the Mutual Reciprocal Inspection (MRI) Agreement between U.S. secretary of energy Hazel O'Leary and Russian MINATOM minister Victor Mikhailov. Even though MRI was never implemented, joint research and development work continued and evolved under the DoE Lab-to-Lab program, and then ultimately as part of the joint U.S. Russian Warhead Safety and Security Exchange (WSSX) Agreement. These efforts, in part, supported actual negotiations, such as the Monitoring and Inspection Agreement for the U.S.-funded Mayak Fissile Material Storage Facility (FMSF). For this agreement,

Congress mandated that the material going into storage be of *weapons origin*. An important result of all this effort was considerable common U.S.-Russian understanding related to monitoring sensitive nuclear materials and items, the possibilities, the concerns, and potential solutions. The point was reached, just prior to the de facto dénouement of WSSX under the administrations of George Bush and Vladimir Putin, where technical demonstrations took place in both the United States and Russia using classified warhead nuclear items. These items were examined using radiation-based attribute measurement systems under the watchful eyes of both Russian and U.S. specialists, without the release of sensitive information. In one demonstration at the Oak Ridge Y-12 Plant, a classified item was ground to pieces behind a special barrier in the presence of Russian and U.S. observers.

The United States and the United Kingdom have a special relationship on matters of nuclear security. In 1998 specialists from the U.K. Atomic Weapons Establishment (AWE) began a comprehensive program of research into verification measures associated with global nuclear weapons arms control. Their initial effort culminated in the publication of an overview of the issues and of verification technology. While there was not a direct overlay in the thinking represented in their initial study with that in U.S. technical circles, many of the basic conclusions about verification were similar. This report of the initial U.K. efforts in particular provides a very valuable overview of radiation signature methodologies.[11]

More recently, in 2005 the Committee on International Security and Arms Control (CISAC) of the National Academy of Sciences revitalized thinking with the publication of an exhaustive report: *Monitoring Nuclear Weapons and Nuclear-Explosive Materials*. The committee described in detail various methods that could be applied to monitoring and verification of warheads and the associated nuclear material, including much of the work from the DoE efforts described earlier. Some of the cooperative methods that were viewed favorably have not been as well accepted within the context of official U.S. government consideration. But important new ideas were also presented. These include the use of specific types of cryptographic methods to exchange data about numbers and locations of warheads and items that can contribute to random challenge and inspection protocols. Clever new ideas such as this offer considerable promise and need to be examined more thoroughly.[12]

Issues

Practical experience gained through these studies; bilateral and multilateral arms control and nonproliferation endeavors, and nuclear safety and security agreements; as well as studies by independent nongovernment and foreign entities, suggest a number of underlying issues associated with tight warhead reduction verification processes. These include (1) defining *nuclear warhead*; (2) determining an accurate baseline inventory of warheads, by state, on a worldwide basis; (3) relying on extensive and potentially very intrusive on-site inspections and perfecting new OSI tools due to the reduced efficacy of NTM; (4) protecting state secrets; and (5) developing concomitant regimes to assure irreversibility of the dismantlement process.

Defining "Nuclear Warhead"

A nuclear weapon, in very simplistic terms, consists of a nuclear warhead plus its delivery system. However, *warhead* and *weapon* are often used interchangeably in arms control and nonproliferation discussions and writings. For items such as gravity bombs and certain tactical weapons there is no significant distinction. But to be specific, in this chapter the focus is on *warheads*. In this new multifaceted world where there is heightened concern about the acquisition of any form of nuclear capability by new, formerly non-weapon states and by subnational groups, the term *nuclear explosive device* is also commonly used. The terms *nuclear warhead* and *nuclear explosive device* are taken here to be synonymous. According to the 2005 CISAC study, these terms have not been defined with much precision in any existing treaties.[13] Nuclear warhead information is often so sensitive that it cannot be discussed in either open forums or at this time even between specialists from different weapon states. It would be helpful if a definition could be found that is both technically correct and is uncomplicated enough that cooperative verification is not overly problematic and impediments to solving technical problems are minimized. A *going-to-zero* framework may be more conducive to such a definition as opposed to limited class-type reductions.

Of course, the primary hurdle in constructing any type of nuclear explosive device is the acquisition of fissile material. This material is the single most important and defining constituent of a nuclear warhead. Parameters such as the amounts of material, configuration, chemical and isotopic composition, and the presence of high explosive can help refine the definition and potentially help differentiate one type of warhead device from another. An example of a procedure requiring such differentiation would be maintaining continuity of knowledge about items belonging to a specific type-class of warhead offered up for destruction. Their limiting values are the stuff of warhead design and thus are often too sensitive to discuss with others in any detail. While it is generally acknowledged that some form of high explosive is also needed to generate substantive nuclear yields, adding such material to a configuration of fissile material is not inherently problematic.

In a world where we are committed to going to zero, the basic definition of a *nuclear warhead* or *nuclear explosive device* is proposed to be *any compact configuration containing a significant amount of fissile material.* (It is left to specialists in the future to quantify *significant*). The presence of containerized fissile material can be directly and nondestructively detected and confirmed using nuclear radiation characterization techniques. Other military and nonmilitary items that might meet this definition could be allowed by exemption. But in a world where we have almost reached zero or have been at zero for a considerable period of time, the discovery of an unallowed compact configuration of fissile material would be quite troublesome. Defending and taking this definition further is very difficult due to the sensitive nature of the subject. However, it is offered here as being appropriate for a regime of *going to zero.* There is a huge difference between this simple fissile-material-configuration definition and the sophistication of modern warheads. It is highly unlikely that drawdowns would be precipitous enough in the beginning for such a simple definition to provide the confidence needed. In fact, the situation would be just the opposite. So even with this definition, it would certainly be required that inspection methods that provide better refinement and differentiation be considered so that type-class reductions could be monitored. Methods to effect this will be discussed later in this chapter.

Determining Baseline Inventories

Assuming that items presented as nuclear warheads can be confirmed as such, whether using a very basic definition or one that includes additional differentiating features, accurately and confidently determining the absolute number of nuclear warheads possessed at any given time by any of the nuclear weapon states or states suspected of proliferating is arguably the most significant challenge to overcome. Nuclear warheads are relatively small items having signatures that can be shielded from observation. The fissile material to make them is in great abundance already, with more being made all the time as a legitimate by-product of peaceful nuclear energy production, and there is considerable imprecision in the amount and fate of historical material known by the owner-state. With the construction of viable nuclear explosive devices being only truly limited by the acquisition of fissile material, complete confirmation of the overall number of warheads at the beginning of any reduction regime will likely be extremely difficult.

Ways have been and continue to be studied that could help reduce the uncertainty of fissile material inventories in a cooperative environment. Certainly production and retirement records could be made available for thorough inspection and consistency checks with known operations and declarations. Nuclear archeology procedures could in principle be used as a more independent check of the records.[14] Methods to validate graphite production reactor histories have been developed with considerable success, for example.[15] Devising new nuclear archeology procedures for other elements of the nuclear warhead production cycle would be very helpful in this regard.

Some would argue that because of the supposed impossibility of truly confirming baseline inventories, the whole endeavor of *going to zero* is quixotic. Accurately verifying the numbers of warheads dismantled can certainly help reduce the margin of error, and when combined with all other technical measures and changing political conditions, may help make the remaining uncertainties in baseline determinations less of an issue.

Needing Extensive On-Site Inspections and Reliable New Tools

Perhaps the most notable conclusion of the 1991 Robinson Committee study was the reduced efficacy of NTM in monitoring a nuclear warhead dismantlement regime. It is notable because this issue was discussed and debated at the appropriate levels of classification and similarly peer reviewed by one of the leading U.S. scientific bodies, the JASONs. Because the sources and methods the United States uses are extremely sensitive, it is impossible here to explore the thinking behind this conclusion. Intuitively it makes sense, given that direct observation of small, relatively nondescript objects is certainly more difficult than for very large objects like ballistic missiles. But, too, the Iraq War and other experiences suggest the need for an extensive on-site presence. Such a presence is consistent with the IAEA NPT regime, as well as some of the U.S.-Russia bilateral agreements.

While many types and variations of devices have been proposed for use in directly monitoring nuclear warhead dismantlement, very few of these have ever been taken beyond the prototype stage and thus remain unproven. Very few have ever been subjected to the extensive vulnerability analyses required. Even fewer have ever been subjected to the (security) certification process by any of the countries that have been working together. Many technical issues have been overcome, but many still remain. But even so, it is safe to say that specialists in the United States, United Kingdom, and Russia are on the same track and those technology problems that need to be overcome are fairly well defined. So much so, it is possible to envision a plausible dismantlement verification process and describe several of the important areas for further work.

Assuring the Protection of State Secrets in Cooperative Regimes

The protection of nuclear weapons information by individual governments can be both a hindrance and an aid to worldwide elimination. It is a hindrance because it greatly reduces the ability of technical specialists and negotiators to more quickly solve verification problems. But the protection of weapons design information is also necessary to minimize the ability of others to develop illicit arsenals, no matter how small, more quickly and cheaply. Such protection is the basis of the legal requirement under Article I of the Nuclear Nonproliferation Treaty. Whether one agrees that governments go too far in being secretive about nuclear weapons matters or not, if the means to solve the technical issues of warhead dismantlement verification can be found that do not require the compromise of sensitive information, policymakers and security specialists would likely find them more acceptable and the process could proceed with fewer objections.

The breadth of classified information associated with the nuclear arsenals of any of the nuclear weapon states is, unfortunately, extremely wide and varies from state to state. In the United States, for example, all information about nuclear weapons is *born classified*, requiring a specific review by an authorized person for release to the public domain. Such information is called *Restricted Data*. Such data may be released to a foreign power such as Russia only through an agreement of cooperation (*123 Agreement)* or an amendment to the U.S. Atomic Energy Act. (The situation in Russia is evidently different: while much more of the information about their warheads is kept classified, its release to a treaty partner is evidently allowed if the treaty requiring it is signed and ratified by the federal government.) It takes seasoned and experienced experts knowledgeable in the protection of often-arcane nuclear weapons information to sort things out to the degree that policymakers can be advised about the sensitivity of this or that fact. Studies on technical methods to protect classified information during hypothetical nuclear warhead inspection measurements are well advanced in the United States and Russia, and the remaining problems are well defined. Not so well studied are methods of information protection under hypothetical inspection regimes associated with locations of deployed warheads, maintenance and repair schedules, and so forth. Also, if host weapon-state monitoring equipment certification authorities rule the day and require that any instrumentation used by an inspectorate on host warheads must be supplied by the host (must have been in their private possession prior to use) and must remain in the host country once used, then the problem of equipment trustworthiness (authentication) by an inspectorate becomes a critical issue. The difficulties associated with authentication in this context are becoming more and more apparent to researchers.

Assuring Irreversibility

Assuring irreversibility of the dismantlement of individual warheads and/or the illicit reconstitution of a smaller secret stockpile of weapons-usable material is beyond the scope of this chapter and will not be discussed in detail. It is the subject of chapter 6 in this book. Certainly it would be important to chemically, isotopically, and physically alter the special fissile material items that constituted the warhead once they have been removed. Methods and processes to render special nuclear material unsuitable for use in a warhead have been reviewed in some detail by the National Academy of Science Committee on International Security and Arms Control.[16] A high level of assurance of irreversibility can only come with a robust regime controlling all fissile material as well as swift and decisive enforcement action by the international community against any new and illicit warhead production effort.

Options and Consequences

A construct for the verification of nuclear warhead dismantlement would include (1) verifying that an item presented for dismantlement is actually a nuclear warhead, (2) accurately counting and maintaining a continuity of knowledge about all warheads until they are dismantled, and (3) verifying the physical dismantlement of the warheads. These three elements are a slight simplification of the nine dismantlement activities offered by the U.S. Dismantlement Study Group more than a decade ago. The technical measures of warhead signature determination, unique identification, and sensitive information protection impact all of these dismantlement elements and activities.

Warhead Signatures

The term *warhead signature* refers to the physically observed properties that are useful to determine that an item is a nuclear warhead or warhead component and in principle may be detailed enough to determine the particular type-class or even the particular individual item. Two basic types of warhead signatures have been studied over the past several years: nuclear signatures and non-nuclear signatures. Very good overviews are provided elsewhere and need not be rehashed in detail here.[17]

It is particularly interesting that non-nuclear approaches have been investigated in the hope of finding a signature that is both very unique and also inherently protecting of weapons design information. Approaches such as eddy current hysteresis plots and Fourier transformed acoustic response plots have yielded promising results, with the data from a prototype eddy current system on actual warheads being cleared for presentation in a public forum.[18] Considerably more study is required on the sensitivity and uniqueness of such signatures, their reproducibility, and so forth.

If it is the presence of the fissile nuclear material that defines a nuclear warhead, then the most conclusive validation comes from making use of the most revealing physical property measurements associated with this material. There are many candidate properties with many well-developed instruments to measure them. The most useful are based on radiation detection and characterization.

Gamma-ray spectrometric measurements resulting from the warhead nuclear material itself are altered according to the specific design of the complete system. A full-energy-range high-resolution gamma-ray spectrum is very defining. The emanations are not only very sensitive to the overall configuration of device design, but are also altered by any container into which a warhead or its dismantled nuclear components are placed. The methods proposed and studied for dismantlement monitoring are based on highly developed and widely applied technology. In some situations, the inherent emissions from normal radioactive decay of the fissile material can be measured in a *passive* application of the radiation detection hardware. This is particularly true for plutonium-239. The detection and characterization of emanations directly from uranium-235 are considerably more problematic due to the relatively low energy at which they occur. The detection of other isotopes of uranium that might be seen with the uranium-235 has shown some promise.[19] In some situations, a neutron or high-energy photon source can be used to induce more and higher-energy emissions in fissile material that needs to be characterized. This is referred to as *active* interrogation. In some cases it is also very useful to measure intrinsic neutron emissions, although neutron spectrometric information from spontaneous or induced fission lacks uniqueness. Its value lies in measuring total neutron emissions in coincidence with gamma ray emissions. Such an approach can be very useful in determining the mass of fissile material present, for example.

Probably the defining set of experiments to date on the efficacy of radiation-based measurements for solving warhead identification and direct dismantlement verification issues was conducted by DoE as an adjunct to the work of its Dismantlement Study Group as an extensive measurement campaign at the U.S. Pantex facility in 1997. An oversight group comprised of technical specialists from across the national laboratory complex selected three measurement approaches after a series of presentations by various measurement system developers. These three approaches were utilized in a measurement campaign devised by the oversight group using 33 actual warheads and nuclear components. The three measurement systems selected were the Radiation Inspection System (RIS) developed by Sandia National Laboratories, the Controlled Intrusiveness Verification Technology (CIVET) developed by Brookhaven National Laboratory, and the *Nuclear Material Inspection System* (NMIS) developed by the Oak Ridge National Laboratory.[20] These systems are pictured in figure 4.1 and represent radiation measurement approaches well-known in the scientific community.

RIS was a system already used in the U.S. weapons complex for a variety of safeguards and security purposes. It consisted of a relatively simple low-resolution sodium-iodide scintillator gamma-ray spectrometer, coupled to a laptop computer data acquisition and analysis system. Conclusions about the authenticity of an item declared to be or to contain a nuclear warhead were made based on a comparison of the measured

Figure 4.1
Radiation Signature
Systems Experiments.
Source: Lawrence
Livermore National
Laboratory (LLNL),
photos-439292.

spectrum to spectra from a library of similar signature templates from previous measurements of known weapons systems. All the measured data were classified, and RIS directly associated each spectrum in the library with a particular U.S. warhead type. The specific measurement system configuration used would be virtually impossible to authenticate as producing believable results as would be required under a cooperative inspection regime. CIVET was a high-resolution germanium gamma-ray spectrometer coupled to a digital data acquisition system that was designed both to protect the classified data and be authenticatable. Both RIS and CIVET were only used in the passive mode. NMIS was a very sophisticated time-domain radiation characterization system based on measuring and analyzing the coincidence timing relationships between a wide variety of nuclear signals. This system was developed primarily for inspection of the uranium-containing canned subassemblies (thermonuclear warhead secondaries) at the Y12 facility in Oak Ridge, Tennessee, for which it has proved very effective. NMIS was used in both the passive and active mode. A particularly significant feature of the NMIS measurements, therefore, was the approval by the Pantex Nuclear Explosives Safety Department to use an active californium-252 neutron source to interrogate fully operational warheads (see figure 4.1). The NMIS data acquisition system, like RIS, was assembled using commercial hardware and a commercial software operating system and thus would be virtually impossible to authenticate as providing believable results in a verification regime context. But that was not an objective of this measurement campaign. Similarly, other equipment or software shortcomings were not viewed as significantly detracting from the potential usefulness of the basic measurement approaches.

The 33 items consisted of the operational nuclear warheads of various types, the nuclear components from other nuclear warheads of various types, and in certain cases the nuclear components taken from warheads that had been examined earlier and then dismantled. The measurement system selection committee was tasked to peer review the reports on the measurement campaign provided by the three laboratories involved.

While the data from this campaign remain classified, the basic results were declassified and then presented to Russian specialists at the

Russian Federal Nuclear Center for Technical Physics in Sarov, Russia, in 2001. In summary, consistent with the initial objectives for conducting the measurement campaign, these results were as follows:

1. Effective discrimination by type of warheads, pits, and secondaries was demonstrated.
   - Radiation signatures of different warhead types were clearly distinguishable (five types examined).
   - Signatures of different secondary types were distinguished, but only limited data were available (two types examined).
   - Signatures of different pit types were easily distinguished except for two very similar all-Pu pits (seven types examined).
2. Individual (serial number) identification is a very difficult problem due to the very close tolerances employed when constructing warheads of the same type.
   - One team provided evidence that such distinctions may be possible using minor-isotope information.
   - Study of a larger population of components will be necessary to definitively determine the utility of minor isotopes.

As alluded to earlier, about the time that this work was being completed, the United States entered into an agreement with the Russian Federation to build a state-of-the-art Fissile Material Storage facility (FMSF) to consolidate fissile material excess from dismantled weapons to make this material more secure. The U.S. Congress put as a condition of this assistance that the material be of *weapons origin.* This prompted considerable discussion and debate among measurement specialists in the United States about the best solution to this problem. In distilled form, the debate centered on the relative efficacy of the two basic measurement approaches using radiation emanations from objects declared to be weapons or weapons components: *templates* and *attributes.*

For the FMSF agreement, the attribute approach was chosen because it was, quite simply, judged to be adequate as well as much easier to negotiate and implement. Attributes are generally thought of as unclassified properties that taken as a group strongly suggest that an item is a nuclear warhead or warhead component, or in the case of FMSF, nuclear material that came from a warhead. Consider the most likely case of an item such as these that is sealed inside a special nuclear material container. Useable attributes might include the following:

- Presence of Plutonium-239 and/or uranium-235
- Nuclear material is in metal (not oxide) form
- Nuclear material is arranged in a symmetric configuration (is not rubble)
- Mass of the nuclear material is greater than X kilograms
- Isotopics of the fissile material are consistent with that used in a warhead (e.g., Pu240/Pu239 mass ratio <0.10)
- Age of the nuclear material is consistent with that of the warhead or warhead component provenance
- Presence of high explosive.[21]

The fact that these attributes are characteristic of certain nuclear warhead items is not sensitive. Their use can be discussed openly. The actual measured values of most of these attributes are classified but bounds can be carefully discussed in an unclassified manner. Unclassified nuclear calibration sources can be used to check to see that the measurement system is operating properly, and if not, the data can be discussed more openly to correct the problem. The main shortcoming of unclassified attributes is that they are not normally defining enough for warhead or component type differentiation, and they are likely to be at greater risk of spoofing. Also, in practice, the measurements themselves can take considerable time (order of hours). But in a regime of going to zero, at least eventually, attributes could prove quite adequate and confirmatory if the simple definition of what constitutes a nuclear warhead that was offered earlier is accepted.

Gamma-ray spectral templates offer a very high degree of uniqueness and in practice have shown that they can be acquired relatively quickly (minutes). The fact that a warhead type has a unique radiation signature is not sensitive. The problem arises from the fact that a full gamma-ray signature from a nuclear warhead or warhead component contains a vast amount of classified weapons design information. It does not seem particularly problematic for nuclear specialists party to a dismantlement agreement to agree on the type and design of a good comparative spectrometer system based on well-understood instruments and data-fitting (comparison) algorithms. But once constructed, it could prove very difficult to calibrate and otherwise unequivocally validate the instrument's function or to address anomalies that might come up during an actual inspection. The most appropriate calibration sources would very likely need to be actual warheads or components that are owned by the inspected party. Confirmation of the drawdown would depend on the long-term protection of the classified calibration sources and templates while they remain on host soil, but, also, much about the data could not be discussed if the system fails to function properly either during validation or use during an actual inspection. Because templates offer so much promise in other regards, these are very important issues for further study and solution.

Unique Identification

In the early 1990s as the Soviet Union was disintegrating, Senator Richard Lugar wrote in an op-ed article for the *Washington Post* that a critical action the United States should take was to *count* the nuclear weapons in such states as Ukraine.[22] To accomplish this feat, a very unique intrinsic signature or some extremely secure method of tagging with a unique identifier would be needed. Anything less could lead to a false sense of security. Even though there was a considerable research and development base from which to draw from the run-up to START I and the development of highly secure tagging methods for ICBM first-stage rocket motors, the problem was judged to be more challenging when associated with nuclear warheads. Questions that would need to be answered included (1) what part of an operational weapon system do we use, (2) what security metric do we use against which to judge proposed approaches, and (3) what are the applicable safety and security constraints?

Why not use manufacturers' (serial) numbers like we do under START and New START? The answer, of course, is that such numbers can only offer very low security. They are usually applied by the inspected country and could be duplicated at will on duplicate or counterfeit items. As part of the run-up to START I in the late 1980s, the United States formed an interagency Tagging Laboratory Advisory Group (the TAGLAG) which invested in excess of $30 million to develop very high-security unique identification devices for the first-stage ICBM rocket motors that were the treaty-limited items (TLIs). This group not only included the researchers from the DoE national laboratories, but also specialists from other U.S. government agencies who had experience involving other very high-security applications. The results of this effort were overseen by an interagency Verification Technology R&D Working Group led by flag officers from the Department of Defense and included representatives from other U.S. security organizations. For each approach that was proposed and funded by a national laboratory, another national laboratory was funded to conduct vulnerability studies and actually defeat prototypes. Much was learned from this effort, especially about seemingly very good approaches and how clever people could defeat them. Once START I was implemented, this effort wound down, though studies on high-security unique identifiers has limped along during the years hence as part of various other efforts.

Unique identifiers used in a going-to-zero context would also need to be designed to the same or even higher security and reliability standards. In effect, limited by the risk of spoofing detection afforded through random thorough item examination, the unique identifier becomes a surrogate for a warhead.

The Monitoring and Implementation Agreement associated with the U.S. assistance in constructing the Russian Fissile Material Storage Facility provided an opportunity to present ideas based on past work to U.S policymakers, the Russian policy and facility operations communities, as well as Russian technical advisers. At the time, negotiations focused on the scenario where the facility would be used to secure about 40 percent of the total Russian weapons plutonium inventory as ingots in the form of precision-machined 2-kilogram spheres. The strategic importance of securing this material was considered quite high by the United States.

Other applications for very high-security tagging and sealing are important to the United States; and there is a body of work, especially in regard to vulnerability assessment, from which to draw. Security limitations do not make full access to and use of this work very easy, however.

There are basically two ways to defeat a unique identifier, whether it is used to inventory automobile parts or nuclear weapons: to counterfeit it (or the answer from its reader), or to remove and replace it in a way that goes unnoticed. Only two technologies passed muster for use to uniquely identify rocket motors for START I: (1) the reflective particle tag (RPT)—based on recording a highly unique optical signal from a random mixture of micaeous hematite embedded in a clear coating that could only be removed intact from the rocket motors by undercutting (thus ruining) the motor skins; and (2) the ultrasonic intrinsic tag (UIT)—based on the recording of a highly unique, spatially gated intrinsic ultrasonic reflection signal from a small area 1 to 2 millimeters into the rocket motor skin (using technology not unlike that used for fetal or cardiovascular medical scans, but at a much higher ultrasound frequency). Development of the UIT for applications related to nuclear weapons has continued up to the present day.

Figure 4.2 shows the UIT under study at the U.S. Pantex facility being used on a B61 gravity bomb trainer (does not contain actual high explosive). These efforts are awaiting Pantex Nuclear Explosive Safety

Figure 4.2 Ultrasonic Intrinsic Tag.
Source: LLNL, photo-439292.

Department review and approval for use on actual warheads. The most suitable location to record the ultrasonic signature is also subject to study and approval.

While some of the lessons from the extensive START-era work remain valid today, particularly related to approaches that were thought secure at first but that were defeated even with 20-year-old technology, new studies using newer technology are truly needed. One area of particular promise is the use of battery-powered, active tags and seals employing cryptographic uniqueness and miniature tamper detection sensors. The Russian-developed Smart Bolt is such a system and is shown in figure 4.3. It is a unique seal that was under development for such applications as the FMSF fissile material containers. More robust versions of this type of electronic seal would be required, however.

The other big issue associated with nuclear weapon item unique identification, besides the availability of technology, is the issue of what part of the item to tag. Focusing on warheads and the nuclear components from warheads, in the United States it is only the B61 and B83 gravity bombs that are not secured in separate containers. Based on both safety and security reasons, there are very tight restrictions on

Figure 4.3 Russian Federation Smart Bolt Unique Seal.

where loaded nuclear warhead containers may be opened. There is a question of whether tagging and sealing just the warhead containers provides the required level of security, or whether critical components of the warhead itself must be uniquely identified. This is a fundamental issue requiring study and resolution, including the possibility that new types of highly impervious containers may need to be developed. The use of such special containers might eliminate the need to directly tag warheads and components, and thus be quite helpful due to the sensitive nature of these items.

This discussion begs yet another. Knowing that the gamma-ray emanations from a warhead or nuclear component can form a signature, why not use this signature as a unique identifier? Based on the Pantex measurement campaign of 1997, the answer is clear. Due to the close manufacturing tolerances of U.S. warheads, and presumably those of the other weapon states, the radiation signatures from warheads of the same type are probably not individually unique enough. Additional study that should be undertaken in this regard is the possibility of inducing a unique intrinsic signature in a nuclear component using an external neutron source. In principle, this might prove feasible in either the time domain or energy (gamma-ray spectrum) domain, though initial studies suggest that the size of the source required would be too large and too many safety concerns would arise.[23]

In summary, while there is much to be considered if we wish to very accurately *count* warheads and their nuclear parts after dismantlement, considerable prior work that has already taken place for other applications is applicable. This suggests various solutions.

Information Protection and Information Barriers

Solutions to problems of protecting nuclear weapons information under any sort of warhead dismantlement cooperative monitoring regime would greatly improve the regime's acceptability and therefore help hasten its implementation. It would also allow for broader participation by the inspectors from the non-weapon states. Arguments are sometimes made that the protection of weapons information is secondary to their elimination; and thus if secrets are to be lost in the process, it may be a reasonable price to pay, especially if an inspectorate is only comprised of weapons-state specialists. There would be legal issues to resolve, and the debate would likely be very contentious. The release of weapons information to hasten monitored dismantlement could adversely affect worldwide irreversibility and proliferation prevention efforts. Occasionally the argument is made that greater credibility be given to the exchange of weapons information between weapon states as a way to help overcome inspection issues. The implication, of course, is that such an exchange is somehow different and less harmful than a more general release. In this chapter, at least, no such differentiation is taken between the concepts of *exchange* and *release.* Significant differences of opinion and debate on the primacy of nuclear weapons–related information protection exist within the arms control and nonproliferation community. It may indeed be found that certain monitoring and verification problems cannot be adequately solved without considering the real need to divulge some sensitive information.

The good news is that a considerable amount of research and development has been undertaken in the United States and elsewhere to solve monitored dismantlement information protection problems. These efforts have been shared by the United States in great detail and with excellent cooperation with knowledgeable government weapons specialists from both, but separately, the Russian Federation and the United Kingdom. The procedures and technology that would be used in tandem to protect nuclear weapons information during cooperative regimes involving these systems and their components have been referred to as *information barriers.*

Late in 1998, the U.S. Departments of Defense and Energy established the Joint DoE-DoD Information Barrier Working Group (IBWG). The task of this group was *to devise optimal approaches to protect classified nuclear weapons design information when utilizing radiation signature monitoring methods.* The impetus for the work at that time was the U.S.-Russian Mayak FMSF, START-type agreements, and the U.S.-Russian-IAEA Trilateral Agreement. The group began its efforts by defining the fundamental functional requirements of an information barrier:

The host must be assured that his classified warhead design infor-
mation is protected from disclosure to the monitoring party, and

The monitoring party must be confident that the integrated
inspection system measures, processes, and presents the radia-
tion signature based measurement conclusion in an accurate and
reproducible manner.[24]

The IBWG was able to enumerate ten critical design elements
defining information barriers. After considerable technical work in later
years, these have evolved as follows:

- The host country would be the party that had last sole possession of the measurement equipment and on whose soil it would
  remain once classified measurements began (this criterion is
  often referred to as that of *host supply,* though there would certainly be cooperation in the area of design and fabrication of
  such equipment).
- The digital central processing unit (CPU) data acquisition and
  analysis subsystem that is usually a key part of a modern radiation characterization system would be based on a dedicated,
  trusted processor architecture.
- The non-CPU equipment such as the actual detector and associated analog signal preprocessing electronics would need to be of
  a design that could readily be inspected and authenticated.
- The overall system would need to be enclosed and otherwise
  designed to preclude any radio frequency emanations associated
  with the classified data, and similarly protected against host sur-
  reptitious control (the *hidden switch* problem).
- All CPU operating system code, firmware, and software should not
  contain extraneous elements, and must be completely inspectable.
- All hardware and software functional modules must have well-
  understood and dedicated functions, and there must be no
  extraneous inputs and outputs, with point-to-point direct inter-
  connections being preferred.
- If intermediate barriers can be employed without compromising
  inspection system authentication, then it is desirable to do so.

- For attribute-based inspection systems, no provisions for non-volatile data storage should be made whatsoever; but for template-based approaches, a solution must be found for the storage, authentication, and disposition of the reference data.
- Procedural limitations to augment the measurement system will play a critical role in any inspection where information protection is required.[25]

Subsequent to this initial IBWG report, several prototype radiation characterization systems that include many of these elements of design have been demonstrated in both the United States and Russia using classified material and actual weapons components. Pictured in figure 4.4 is a warhead component attribute measurement system jointly developed by the U.S. Livermore and Los Alamos national laboratories and demonstrated to a large contingent of Russian weapons specialists in August 2000.[26] A classified object was used for the actual demonstration. In addition to the successful use of a set of realistic attributes (basically the ones listed previously, less high-explosive [HE] detection), the fact that the U.S. security community certified such a system for use in the presence of uncleared visitors was a major accomplishment. It took about a year to obtain this certification. A major failing of this demonstration and the others that have followed in both the United States and Russia is that there have been

Figure 4.4 U.S. Attribute Measurement System with Info Barrier.
Source: LLNL, photo-439292.

no fully demonstrable provisions for inspector authentication of the systems function and trustworthiness.

It is generally acknowledged that because of the work on information barriers that has occurred over the last 10 years, realistic and useful attribute measurements on classified objects can be made without revealing classified information. (The same cannot be said yet about template-based measurements, with little work in that area for cooperative inspection of classified objects having been undertaken to date). The major unresolved issue associated with information barriers is that of authentication. *Authentication* refers to the process of assurance of the inspectorate that the measurement system works as advertised and does not contain any hidden feature that would allow the inspected party to surreptitiously alter the results during an inspection (e.g., providing a result that suggests the item under inspection is actually a metal object made with 90 percent or greater plutonium-239). This is the specific area that demands further attention if a truly useful radiation-based measurement system is ever to be successfully developed for use on nuclear warheads, their nuclear components and associated sensitive nuclear materials.[27] Cooperative work between the United States and Russia on these issues pretty much ceased with the demise of the WSSX Agreement in early 2008, though as early as 2005 it had become a sensitive topic. But as of today, there is good agreement between U.S. and Russian physicists on how, in principle, to solve the information barrier and the associated authentication problems. It would be a huge step forward to demonstrate a viable warhead measurement system authentication process. Because of the highly technical nature of making accurate and reliable warhead measurements, heads of state may eventually need to establish national authentication authorities to advise them about the trustworthiness of the associated information—this, in order to draw down arsenals to very low levels or to eliminate them completely.

Upon reaching *zero*, the broad need to protect nuclear weapons secrets during inspection measurements would essentially end. In fact, an unwillingness to allow just about any type of measurement on a suspect item would result in concern by the inspectorate and require significant explanation by the inspected party. There would be instances, of course, where the protection of non-nuclear defense or trade secrets might be warranted. In such cases, using information barrier principles, it should not prove prohibitive to develop a special measurement system that both confirms the item is not associated with nuclear weaponry and protects detailed design knowledge from disclosure.

Verification Solutions

Given the state of development of cooperative monitoring technology, the solutions suggested here are useful in the sense that they illustrate positive possibilities and list some additional problems that need to be solved. The basis for many of these recommendations is the intensive work performed early after the dissolution of the Soviet Union and the end of the Cold War. A revitalization of these activities is critical to support deep reduction and going-to-zero monitoring. Also, all of the methods and associated implementation procedures would need to successfully be reviewed for spoofing vulnerabilities.

Warhead Authentication

In a going-to-zero regime that defines a *nuclear warhead* as *any compact configuration containing a significant amount of fissile material*, warhead authentication would not be particularly difficult. An attribute-based measurement for such cases is straightforward, though the development of the required information barriers has not yet occurred. This definition best serves its purpose when we are very close to zero, or after all warheads have been declared to be eliminated.

As has been noted, since it is very likely that a massive drawdown will take significant time, the real difficulty lies in knowing more precisely how many warheads of a particular type are being eliminated during any given time period in the overall process. This knowledge would be required in order to maintain nuclear stability and deterrence parity until the time of total elimination.

Unclassified attribute measurements are probably not adequate for warhead type differentiation. This will almost assuredly require the use of full-spectrum templates, as was successfully demonstrated during the 1997 Pantex measurement campaign. The problem quickly reduces to authenticating and securing template *golden copies* for use with gamma-ray spectroscopic systems or more sophisticated technologies such as an NMIS time-domain system. In the context of a reference template, the term *golden copy* is defined as a signature template data taken directly from an item that has been independently authenticated as being that which it has been declared to be, and the data itself can be authenticated at a later time as having never been altered. Such templates would exist on nonvolatile computer storage media from which other reference copies could be made for use during actual and repeated inspections.

To obtain golden copy radiation templates for specific types of warheads that are still deployed as part of weapons systems, using the extensive information from START RVOSI and supplemented by NTM, the inspectorate would begin by selecting multiple items at random. Inspectors would witness the removal of the warheads from the delivery vehicle and its placement inside a container especially designed to help secure and minimize spectral signature deviations (the same type of container would be used to protect all the other items declared to be of the same type and slated for elimination). The warhead itself should be uniquely identified before it is inserted into the container using an intrinsic tag such as the UIT or an applied tag of very high security. This container would be sealed with another high-security mechanism such as an active, cryptographically protected electronic seal. Then using a gamma-ray spectroscopic measurement system, a radiation signature template would be acquired, protected by an information barrier, for the particular type warhead. Each of these initial templates would be checked for consistency with each other using unclassified statistical fitting algorithms. These containerized items would be set aside for the purpose of reaffirming the reference signature template. They would have to remain on inspected country soil, but they would be subject to highly secure continuous monitoring. The reference template itself would be stored on a nonvolatile memory device(s) and include a robust cryptographic tag for repeated authentication. The measurement systems used on a host country's classified items will very likely need to remain on host soil as well and be secured in a manner very similar to the templates.

For warheads or components that may have already been totally removed from deployment as a whole type class, where the RVOSI authentication approach breaks down, the inspecting country would have to judge for itself if it has enough independent information for verification, perhaps as a result of more extensive confirmatory declarations. If not, there would need to be a determination if it was important. Certainly a golden copy template could be made using random selections from a population of these warheads as a new type. This new type could be given an arbitrary class designation and thereafter tracked through dismantlement and final disposition.

Use of a template approach is not possible without some form of independently authenticated reference signature, and at the least is very difficult if the spectral variations due to manufacturing variations or any other comparison differences could be great enough to repeatedly yield no-match conditions. It might prove impossible for an inspectorate and a host to cooperate to solve legitimate inspection problems without discussing these spectral variations, thus classified information, in some detail. Further study of template-matching approaches is therefore needed. How are the matching limits set to assure good functionality as well as acceptance? How are no-match conditions rectified with the inspectorate? Many such conditions would be understood by the host knowing the classified spectral data, but could not be shared because they might reveal a warhead design feature that had to be protected from disclosure.

Warhead Counting and Continuity of Knowledge

For nuclear warheads that are declared excess, for warheads that may be kept in a ready reserve at a known location, or for unclassified partially sanitized nuclear objects or raw materials in storage awaiting final disposition (such as at the Russian Mayak Fissile Materials Storage Facility), maintaining an accurate item inventory is a straightforward process drawing from international safeguard containment and surveillance approaches. So too would be the occasional reauthentication of randomly selected items or raw material batches to validate the containment and surveillance technology and procedures. It would still be very important for all parties to understand the vulnerabilities of the unique identification devices and high-security seals used, and the surveillance technology employed in order to reduce the risk of diversion to effectively zero.

If there is to be an airtight inventory that includes warheads that remain part of the deployed deterrent at undeclared locations, the problem is more difficult. Certainly the delivery system inspection approaches agreed to under START I and New START are a good place to begin. These are quite intrusive but are accepted in the United States and Russia, and there are many years of experience in their implementation. If high-security unique identification of warheads is added to RVOSI procedures, then by employing random sampling against an encrypted declaration, considerably more confidence may be gained in the initial quantity declaration.

Such an approach involves the exchange of encrypted lists of locations of deployed warheads. During an RVOSI, through decryption, the presence of specific items on the numbered list would be confirmed. The observed warheads would then be tagged using a suitable very high-security method and the unencrypted identifier added to the appropriate item on the list. In the future, when the warhead entered the dismantlement process and the chain of custody was established, the tag would be reread and the identity confirmed. Such lists would need to be updated periodically. The inspectorate might find that certain unique identifiers are associated with newly encrypted locations—locations at which another random RVOSI might occur and the tag re-confirmed.

Accounting for undeclared warheads at undeclared locations is basically the same seemingly intractable problem of confirming baseline inventories. There is no ready solution given the ease with which such items could be hidden. NTM has been judged to be unreliable in this situation.[28] Other policy accommodations would have to offset this issue, but as insight and trust builds during deep reductions, given the continued will of all parties to go to zero, the day may come when these accommodations are possible.

Verifying Dismantlement

The actual physical dismantlement of a warhead would probably be the least difficult process to verify. In the United States, a warhead is considered fully dismantled once the high explosive has been removed from the fissionable material configuration from which the warhead is constructed.[29] This step is the result of other steps that come earlier that also contribute to the dismantlement. The end result for a two-stage thermonuclear warhead is the separation and individual containerization of two nuclear components, the pit and the canned subassembly. For a single-stage warhead, just a pit remains. These items are placed in storage for eventual disposition or reuse.

The United States and others have even conducted dismantlement cooperative monitoring technology demonstrations, albeit mostly in a transparency context, to help focus on the specific problems that can arise. In part, this work forms the basis for the verification process suggested here. Probably the best, though not the least expensive, approach to monitored dismantlement in any of the nuclear weapon states is to build (or have built by an international organization) a special new, aboveground dismantlement facility of a design that is acceptable to the other weapon states and to all involved in monitoring or having a stake in monitoring.

The only warheads located at the special facility would be those destined for monitored dismantlement. It probably would be less intrusive and more conducive to maintaining the continuity of knowledge required to assure irreversibility that the separated nuclear components remain in storage at the special facility until just before their final disposition. In this way, the collateral security concerns with other defense and security operations would be significantly reduced, and the design of the facility could include features that enhance verification instead of impede it. Such a facility, given the level of assurance that is necessary, should have a completely nonsensitive design (except perhaps for the protective security features) that could be shared with all involved, and the site should be permanently manned and monitored from the beginning of construction. Additional assurance would be provided that no hidden features were included that could be used to spoof the monitoring process. The site should be located away from allowed military or commercial operations and thus designed as well to maximize the effectiveness of additional monitoring by national technical means.

All items and personnel entering and leaving the site would be subjected to stringent portal perimeter monitoring inspections, consistent as a minimum with the manner in which nuclear weapons and warhead components are secured and protected in the United States today. Items brought to the special facility for dismantlement, having been authenticated on-site against a signature template and inventoried using unique identifier technology, would be taken by the host without any inspectors to the actual cell or bay for disassembly. Once the physical disassembly was accomplished, the disassembly cell could be swept by the inspectorate to make sure it is indeed empty. Template measurements employing information barrier technology and procedures would be made on the containers declared to hold the nuclear components, and the containers would be sealed by the inspectorate. Other agreed-to, more intrusive inspections, including visual examinations, would be made on the non-nuclear weapons components. For any of these non-nuclear components that are sight-sensitive, provisions for their conversion to a nonsensitive form (e.g., shredding or chopping) would be included within the disassembly facility (in a manner exactly analogous to current nuclear warhead retirements and dismantlements used today in the United States).

In conclusion, from the studies undertaken by the United States and others, options do indeed exist to confirm warhead dismantlement, though inspection technology authentication is a critical area requiring further study. The one seemingly intractable problem is that of assuring that there are no clandestine stockpiles of warheads as a result of incomplete initial declarations or illicit diversion of warhead items or nuclear materials.

Notes

1. "Nuclear Weapons and Deterrence in the 21st Century," speech by Secretary of Defense Robert M. Gates, Carnegie Endowment for International Peace, October 28, 2008.

2. Ivo Daalder and Jan Lodal, "The Logic of Zero," *Foreign Affairs,* November–December 2008, 80–95; George Perkovich and James M. Acton, "Verifying the Transition to Zero," *Adelphi Papers* 48, no. 396 (March 2008): 41–68.

3. James F. Morgan, chair, U.S. Department of Energy Dismantlement Study Group, "Transparency and Verification Options: An Initial Analysis of

Approaches for Monitoring Warhead Dismantlement," in *Proceedings of the Institute of Nuclear Materials Management 38th Annual Meeting*, July 1997.

4. Liu Su-Ping, Gong Jian, Hao Fan-Hua, and Hu Guang-Chun, "Template Identification Technology of Nuclear Warheads and Components," *Chinese Physics B* 17 (February 2008): 363–369.

5. Perkovich and Acton, "Verifying the Transition to Zero."

6. *Final Report—Field Test 34: Demonstrated Destruction of Nuclear Weapons (U),* United States Arms Control and Disarmament Agency, January 1969, declassified 30 March 1999, available at www.fas.org/nuke/guide/usa/cloudgap/index.html.

7. *Verification of Nuclear Warhead Dismantlement and Special Nuclear Material Control,* unclassified Executive Summary, President's Advisory Committee on Verification of Fissile Material and Nuclear Warhead Controls, Ambassador C. Paul Robinson, chair, Report to Congress, October 1991, available as a reprint as PNNL 18034, Pacific Northwest National Laboratory, November 2008.

8. *Verification Technology: Unclassified Version,* MITRE JASONs, Sydney Drell study group chair, JSR-89-100A, October 1990.

9. *Dismantling the Bomb and Managing Nuclear Materials*, Office of Technology Assessment, United States Congress, OTA-O-572, September 1993.

10. Liu et al., "Template Identification."

11. Christine Comley, Mike Comley, Peter Eggins, Garry George, Steve Holloway, Martin Ley, Paul Thompson, and Keith Warburton, *Confidence, Security and Verification: The Challenge of Global Nuclear Weapons Arms Control*, AWE/TR/2000/001 (London: United Kingdom Ministry of Defense Atomic Weapons Establishment—Aldermaston, 2000).

12. Committee on International Security and Arms Control, United States National Academy of Sciences, *Monitoring Nuclear Weapons and Nuclear-Explosive Materials* (Washington, DC: National Academy Press, 2005).

13. Ibid.

14. Steve Fetter, "Nuclear Archaeology: Verifying Declarations of Fissile-Material Production," *Science and Global Security* 3 (1993): 237–259.

15. T. W. Wood, D. C. Gerlach, B. D. Reid, and W. C. Morgan, *Feasibility of Isotopic Measurements: Graphite Isotopic Ratio Method*, PNNL-13488 (Richland, WA: Pacific Northwest National Laboratory, April 2001).

16. See, for example, *Management and Disposition of Excess Weapons Plutonium: Reactor Related Options*, Panel on Reactor-Related Options for the Disposition of Excess Weapons Plutonium, John P. Holdren, chair (Washington, DC: National Academy Press, 1995).

17. See Comley et al., *Confidence, Security, and Verification*; *Monitoring Nuclear Weapons*; Committee on International Security and Arms Control, United States National Academy of Sciences, *Monitoring Nuclear Weapons*; and David Spears, ed., *Technology R&D for Arms Control*, NNSA/NN/ACNT-SP01 (Washington, DC: U.S. National Nuclear Security Administration Office of Nonproliferation Research and Engineering, Spring 2001).

18. Ronald L. Hockey, *Electromagnetic Coil Technology for Arms Control Applications*, 42nd Annual Meeting of the Institute of Nuclear Material Managers, Indian Wells, CA, July 2001.

19. Spears, ed., *Technology R&D for Arms Control*.

20. Ibid.

21. Ibid.

22. Senator Richard M. Lugar, "A Crucial New Year's Resolution," *Washington Post*, December 23, 1991, p. A19.

23. Spears, ed., *Technology R&D for Arms Control*.

24. *The Functional Requirements and Basis for Information Barriers*, the Joint DoE-DoD Information Barrier Working Group, James Fuller, chair, PNNL-13285 (Richland, WA: Pacific Northwest National Laboratory, May 1999).

25. Ibid.

26. See *Management and Disposition of Excess Weapons Plutonium*.

27. Richard Kouzes and James Fuller, *Authentication of Monitoring Systems for Nonproliferation and Arms Control*, PNNL-SA-35296 (Richland, WA: Pacific Northwest National Laboratory, October 2001); and James Fuller and James Wolford, *Information Barrier R&D Progress and Recommendations for Future Directions*, PNNL-15567 (Richland, WA: Pacific Northwest National Laboratory and Livermore National Laboratory, December 2005).

28. See *Verification of Nuclear Warhead Dismantlement and Special Nuclear Material Control*.

29. See "Transparency and Verification Options," in *Proceedings of the Institute of Nuclear Materials Management 38th Annual Meeting*.

5. Establishing Non–Nuclear Weapon States' Confidence in Verification

STEINAR HØIBRÅTEN AND HALVOR KIPPE

All states, both nuclear weapons states (NWS) and non-nuclear weapon states (NNWS), are responsible for fulfilling the nuclear disarmament obligations of Article VI of the Nuclear Non-Proliferation Treaty (NPT). The major hurdles when cooperating on fulfilling these obligations are of both a legal and a technological nature. Nuclear weapons programs are typically of vast complexity. Verification of complete nuclear disarmament is for that reason a matter of gaining sufficient confidence in the genuineness of the disarmament process, more than about achieving total certainty that all weapons-usable material is rendered useless for military purposes. However, just embarking on the difficult path of exploring means of NNWS verification of an NWS carrying out nuclear disarmament (or even just limited reductions in its nuclear arsenal) will in itself be a way of building confidence. Nevertheless, such an exploration may shed light on issues that have been considered as impediments to verification, and may suggest methods of overcoming these impediments.

The formal obstacles to NNWS inspections are mainly the nonproliferation commitments under the NPT and national security concerns of the NWS. The constraints of the NPT are absolute and nonnegotiable, while national security concerns are somewhat negotiable in situations where both parties see an advantage to making certain compromises.

Furthermore, we recognize the need for addressing emerging concerns of preserving national security on the part of the NWS as nuclear reductions are conducted, and the balance of power is somewhat altered. NNWS should seek to play a constructive role in providing the appropriate security climate that will still make nuclear reductions possible— for example, by offering negative security assurances.[1]

We realize that taking the final steps toward zero nuclear weapons is much more demanding than achieving limited reductions. These final steps should be taken as simultaneously as possible by the remaining NWS, although reductions toward "near zero" may be realized at an individual pace.

NNWS can play a crucial role during several phases. Initially, we recommend that NNWS communicate to the NWS a common understanding of which physical attributes must be identifiable in order to authenticate a nuclear weapon and to maintain a verifiable chain of custody in a nuclear weapons dismantlement process. The nuclear weapons complex of the NWS in question may be of a scope that enables high-confidence verification of nuclear disarmament. For many NWS, however, the uncertainties in the produced amounts of special nuclear materials are such that one must rely on indirect and contextual confidence-building measures instead of strict verification. This will be easier to do at a point in time when limited, but concerted, reductions to "near zero" have first created, then significantly consolidated a norm *against* the possession of nuclear weapons. Such a norm is judged as a fundamental prerequisite for the NWS to take the final steps toward zero nuclear weapons.

This chapter shows that there are a number of ways in which NNWS can not only gain confidence in the verification of nuclear disarmament, but also participate in this verification. It is obvious that the opposite situation, in which the NWS refused to let any NNWS participate in the verification, would lead to great suspicion and therefore be unacceptable. It would also contradict the requirement of the NPT to negotiate "a treaty on general and complete disarmament under strict and effective international control." Our chapter explores in more detail the possible involvement of NNWS.

Background

In this chapter, we mainly examine what role the NNWS should assume during the process leading toward a nuclear weapons–free world so as to develop and maintain confidence in the verification process that will have to accompany nuclear reductions. We also briefly discusses the role of the NNWS in a world free of nuclear weapons.

The cornerstone for all work on nonproliferation and disarmament in the world is the NPT, which entered into force in 1970. This treaty has been signed and ratified by almost all states in the world, with the notable exceptions of India, Israel, and Pakistan. North Korea claimed its withdrawal from the NPT in 2003. The treaty "temporarily" acknowledges China, France, Russia, the United Kingdom and the United States as nuclear weapon states and all other signatories as non-nuclear weapon states. In short, by signing the NPT, the NWS promise not to share their nuclear weapons and/or related know-how with any NNWS, and the NNWS promise not to acquire such weapons. The status as an NWS is "temporary" because in the treaty's Article VI, all parties to the treaty undertake to "pursue negotiations in good faith on effective measures relating to cessation of the nuclear arms race at an early date and to nuclear disarmament, and on a treaty on general and complete disarmament under strict and effective international control." The responsibility to strive for complete nuclear disarmament rests on *all parties to the treaty*. This implies that the NNWS should proactively seek dialogue and cooperation with the NWS on the paramount goal of reaching zero nuclear weapons rather than just demand that the NWS on their own initiative initiate and implement their Article VI disarmament commitments.

Today, there are still on the order of 25,000 nuclear warheads in the world, and about 95 percent of them are in Russia and the United States. This is down from a total of about 70,000 warheads at the end of the Cold War, but still a long way from "complete disarmament."

It should be added that some nuclear weapons exist outside the parties to the NPT; they are in the arsenals of the de facto nuclear weapon states India, Pakistan, and North Korea and most likely also in Israel. A number of other states are capable of developing nuclear weapons should they decide to do so. The 1996 Comprehensive Nuclear Test Ban Treaty (CTBT) identifies 44 nuclear-capable states (states with nuclear power reactors or nuclear research reactors) whose ratification is required for the treaty to enter into force.[2] With the increasing interest in nuclear power in the world, the number of states that could enter the nuclear weapons race on relatively short notice is likely to increase in the future.

The disarmament that does take place today is mainly carried out without any international verification procedures having been established. That is not satisfactory for "a treaty on general and complete disarmament under strict and effective international control." Verification measures are an absolute prerequisite for achieving the level of confidence and trust that is needed to be able to approach the long-term goal of no nuclear weapons. A first step that is fully compliant with the NPT would be to allow the NWS to inspect one another's disarmament processes, but at some point both the NNWS and the NWS may find that to be an insufficient solution that does not meet the standard of "strict and effective international control." A way must be found in which to eventually include NNWS in the verification process. Otherwise, there would be no way for the NNWS to rest assured that the NWS, for example, have not kept a number of clandestine nuclear weapons under the guise of total disarmament. Furthermore, it is not sufficient to include only selected NNWS in a verification process; many NNWS still benefit from a "nuclear umbrella" controlled by one of the NWS, and this dependency may constitute a motive for providing false testimony regarding an apparent disarmament process. There is no reason to expect that all NNWS would want to participate in the nuclear disarmament process, but nobody should deny any state the opportunity to participate should it want to. Such participation is the core question addressed in this chapter.

It may be worthwhile to briefly review two real-world disarmament cases. The first case regards South Africa, which secretly established a nuclear weapons program during the 1970s and 1980s and eventually built a total of six quite simple nuclear weapons.[3] The weapons were of a design similar to the one that was dropped over Hiroshima in

August 1945, yet the South African weapons were in fact even simpler as they all lacked a neutron initiator. The program was ended in 1989, and by 1993, all bombs and all production facilities had been dismantled. During this process, South Africa became party to the NPT as an NNWS (1991), and the International Atomic Energy Agency (IAEA) was eventually given the opportunity to verify that the former weapons plants were no longer in use and that all weapons-grade uranium was accounted for.

The second case is North Korea. Since the fall of 2003, China, Japan, Russia, South Korea, and the United States have pursued a difficult path of negotiations with the North Korean regime with the aim of total denuclearization of this isolated state. Although ridden with frequent setbacks and apparent breakdowns, made most evident by the North Korean nuclear tests in October 2006 and May 2009, the so-called Six-Party Talks have since 2007 made substantial progress toward the goal of nuclear disarmament. This sometimes promising effort, led and facilitated by China, may turn out to be a historic feasibility study on how to eliminate stockpiles of weapons-grade plutonium and assembled nuclear weapons under (presumably) rigorous international verification. North Korea's plutonium-producing infrastructure in Yongbyon is partly disabled under agreements reached through the Six-Party Process, but there are still many bumps in the road to actually ridding the enigmatic state of its nuclear weapons and small stockpile of plutonium. Most observers point to China as a probable key player when the time comes to consider how to dispose of North Korea's plutonium and dismantled weapons. An important consideration is that nonproliferation concerns should be avoided by involving an NWS. Another consideration is of course China's relatively close relationship with the regime in Pyongyang.

Even if no NNWS were to be directly involved in a future North Korean denuclearization verification process, lessons would necessarily be learned along the way with respect to developing practical and acceptable verification procedures in an adverse and confidence-demanding context. Thus far, the world has not yet seen any nuclear disarmament verification process featuring a degree of transparency comparable to that which will most likely be demanded in North Korea. In this case, it will be necessary to ensure that the disarmament is in fact complete, as opposed to the more limited scope of various strategic nuclear reduction initiatives pursued by the Soviet Union (or Russian Federation) and the United States in the past. The North Korean nuclear program is undoubtedly of a more limited nature than these states' programs. It is therefore in fact technically feasible to perform material accounting verification in North Korea of a complete disarmament process within an acceptable level of uncertainty.[4] The main hurdles are of a political rather than a technical nature.

The next section addresses the role of NNWS in a world free of nuclear weapons—that is, when the goal of complete disarmament spelled out in the NPT is achieved. This is followed by a broader discussion of key issues and questions concerning verification of nuclear disarmament, options for the way ahead on some of the challenges discussed, and our conclusions regarding the way ahead.

The Role of Non-nuclear Weapon States in a World Free of Nuclear Weapons

In a nuclear weapons–free world, all states are NNWS, but some of them, the former NWS, possess nuclear weapons know-how that the original NNWS never had. Assuming that the disarmament process was satisfactorily verified, this is truly a state of zero nuclear weapons. The main challenge is therefore to ensure that none of the former NWS uses their knowledge to once again design and build nuclear weapons. Another challenge is to ensure that none of the states that have never possessed nuclear weapons sets out to acquire them; of course, any NNWS that ventured on such a course would have a less advanced starting point than would the former NWS.

In other words, the crucial task for all states is to ensure that the world remains free of nuclear weapons. Since there will presumably still be numerous facilities working on the nuclear fuel cycle and producing nuclear power, a regime for safeguards and verification must be in place in this ultimate stage. However, since a very similar regime would have been in place during the process of achieving zero nuclear weapons, the establishment of a safeguards and verification regime in a world completely free of nuclear weapons ought to be rather straight-forward. This regime would presumably also be able to ensure that any remaining stocks of weapons-grade fissile materials are not diverted back into weapons use. The fairly high degree of transparency required to maintain the state of zero nuclear weapons must already have been achieved during the verification processes that led to this state. The existing IAEA Model Additional Protocol (INFCIRC/540) and the pro-spective, verifiable Fissile Materials Cut-off Treaty (FMCT) are good starting points today for future verification norms to guarantee the nondiversion of and freeze in the production of weapons-grade fissile materials.

A world free of nuclear weapons constitutes the ultimate state of "de-alerting." Today, much effort has already been invested to reduce the hair-trigger alert on which many Soviet and American nuclear weap-ons used to be placed during the Cold War. The idea behind the work for de-alerting is that the longer it takes to launch a nuclear weapon, the lower the likelihood that the weapon will be used accidentally or with-out proper permission. In a world free of nuclear weapons, there will be a number of "virtual nuclear weapons states"—that is, the former NWS plus the technologically most sophisticated original NNWS, which could acquire nuclear weapons in a relatively short time. Their "alert time" to launch a nuclear weapon will still be at least many months. With this kind of a terror balance, there is no danger of any impulsive, erroneous firing of a nuclear weapon. This is illustrated by the sketch in figure 5.1 that shows a conceptual comparison of various nuclear weapons alert levels.

Once a world free of nuclear weapons is actually achieved, there is reason to believe that even though reintroducing nuclear weapons would carry a very high political cost, the former NWS would nev-ertheless wish to preserve not only their nuclear weapons know-how, but also their capability to develop and build such weapons. Nuclear weapons cannot be "un-invented," but as time passes and the politi-cal clout of nuclear weapons diminishes, one would expect that fewer

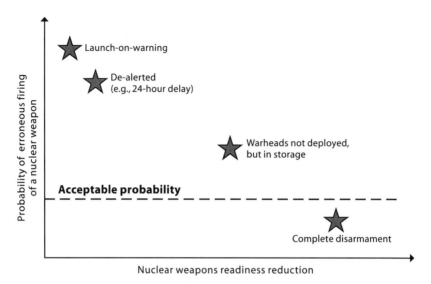

Figure 5.1 Conceptual Comparison of Nuclear Weapons De-alerting and Disarmament.

people would be employed in the nuclear weapons complex. It has already been a challenge in today's world to employ excess person-nel from the nuclear weapons complex in other lines of work (to help them fight any temptation to work for or sell their know-how to another state's clandestine nuclear weapons program). The NNWS may assist here and, for example, hire former nuclear weapons experts to work on non–nuclear weapons projects that these highly qualified people would still find interesting and rewarding. Such international efforts have been supported by both NWS and NNWS.[5]

The regime for safeguards and verification must be maintained for the long-term future because even in a world free of nuclear weapons, peaceful applications of nuclear technology will still be taking place. However, as the generations go by, technical and detailed know-how about the engineering and the manufacturing of nuclear weapons will most likely erode, thus slowly raising the threshold for any state or non-state actor to employ nuclear weapons in its arsenals.

Verification of Nuclear Disarmament

The rest of this chapter focuses on the role of the NNWS during the process of taking steps leading toward a nuclear weapon–free world so as to develop and maintain confidence in the verification process. We have gained some hands-on experience from an ongoing cooperation project of this kind between the United Kingdom and Norway, and this background necessarily influences the presentations and discussions below. The Anglo-Norwegian cooperation is described in the addendum at the end of this chapter.

According to Article VI of the NPT ("general and complete disarmament under strict and effective international control"), disarmament without verification is unacceptable. The importance of trust in the verification process will increase as the number of nuclear weapons approaches zero. Whether the actual number of remaining warheads is 10,000 or 10,001 is of little practical relevance, but the significance of the difference between zero nuclear weapons and one nuclear weapon is enormous.

The verification regime must necessarily be somewhat intrusive. In the case of an NNWS inspecting an NWS, there are two main complicating factors:

1. The NPT: Articles I and II of the NPT, which prohibit international exchange of "proliferative" information to an NNWS, are firm and clear and do not provide for exceptions.
2. National security of the inspected party (the NWS): Some classified information (e.g., the number of weapons, how and where they have been deployed, etc.) is not proliferative, and an exchange of this kind of information as well as access to some of the relevant facilities may be negotiated if both parties find it sufficiently important to the verification process.

These complicating factors demonstrate clearly that there is no way an NNWS can observe in detail the dismantling of a nuclear weapon. At the same time, the verifying NNWS must witness enough to be fully convinced that total dismantlement of the weapon has indeed taken place. How much information can the NWS give to the NNWS without compromising either the NPT or its national security?

The goal of the NPT is "complete disarmament." This is clearly very difficult to achieve in today's political climate; it is also extremely difficult, if even possible at all, to verify. The process of disarming to zero nuclear weapons must necessarily take place step by step, starting out with what is politically and practically doable at any given time. Particularly the beginning state and the end state (zero nuclear weapons) are very difficult to verify.

At the time when the process of verified disarmament begins, the NWS have typically been in possession of nuclear weapons and the corresponding nuclear infrastructure for a long time, generally for many decades. It will be very difficult, maybe impossible, to establish exactly how many warheads actually exist and where all the weapons-grade fissile materials in that state are to be found. If one of the NWS should desire to hide any of its nuclear weapons or weapons materials at this point in the process, the likelihood of getting away with such a deception appears to be quite high.

Similar difficulties exist for the end point of the disarmament process. How is it possible to verify that a state is completely free of nuclear weapons and weapons-grade fissile materials? Various items may have been kept hidden throughout the entire disarmament process or even diverted during the process. However, the example of South Africa discussed earlier shows that for a relatively simple nuclear weapons program, it is possible to verify with a high degree of confidence that the state is indeed free of all its nuclear weapons.

Based on these lines of thought, a reasonable first step for the process of verified disarmament must be to verify the destruction of one or several nuclear weapons without attempting to establish the total number of nuclear warheads. Success on this level will in itself constitute a major confidence-building measure, and it will be an excellent starting point for the more complicated and intrusive verification processes that eventually will be required in order to reach a world free of nuclear weapons.

Particular Restrictions between a Nuclear Weapon State and a Non-nuclear Weapon State

The general attitude among NWS and NNWS alike has been to consider essentially any information about nuclear warheads to be too sensitive for international discussion. Clearly, such an attitude effectively blocks all disarmament verification efforts by NNWS. It would be useful to reach a broader agreement between NWS and NNWS about which features of nuclear weapons one may share internationally. Furthermore, in case of a particular inspection, the parties involved must be allowed to negotiate the dissemination of at least some weapons-related information.

In principle, all information revealing nuclear weapons design details, including configuration of conventional high explosives, neutron initiator, fuze, securing and firing mechanisms, in addition to information concerning mass, shape, and isotopic composition of the fissile component and the tamper, can in general be regarded as proliferative. That means that the NPT prohibits NWS from sharing such information with NNWS, as well as prohibiting NNWS from seeking to acquire it from other states.

In a nuclear weapons disarmament verification context, it is paramount that the inspecting party is confident that the object to be dismantled is in fact the genuine and complete nuclear warhead or other "treaty-accountable item"[6] set forth in the agreement that governs the inspection. Such "authentication" of the warhead, its nuclear component or other vital and sensitive parts of the weapon, is obviously quite complicated to perform without breaching the NPT nonproliferation obligations.

What is needed is an authoritative interpretation and application of the NPT that would clarify that the NPT's nonproliferation requirements are not being compromised by such a verification process. Any modern-day application of the NPT must take into account the fact that a lot of nuclear weapons information has been made generally available in books, articles, declassified documents, and so forth, and also that generally available technology and computer tools have become much more advanced over the years since the NPT entered into force in 1970.

Materials, Equipment, and Other Items That Can Be Verified by a Non-nuclear Weapon State

As an example of the restrictions outlined earlier, several NWS today consider revealing a detailed gamma-ray energy spectrum from a nuclear warhead too sensitive to be allowed in an NNWS verification context. The notion that the isotopic composition of the nuclear component should still be a hurdle for an actor seeking to produce nuclear weapons is an anachronism. Not since the 1940s has there been any reason to pretend that states seeking nuclear weapons would not be aware of the composition of weapons-usable plutonium and uranium. Of course, an energy spectrum analyzed together with information about counting time and shielding materials would in principle enable the inspecting party to estimate the amount of fissile material in the weapon. That piece of information is also considered both proliferative and national security sensitive; it may, however, be circumvented by relatively straightforward means (in a technical sense). For instance, in the previously mentioned cooperation between the United Kingdom and Norway on verifiable nuclear disarmament, the development of an "information barrier" system for gamma spectroscopy takes this problem into account. The principle is to let the information barrier electronics look for a small set of predefined features in the spectrum and simply return a "yes" or "no" after a given amount of counting time. The physical discrimination criteria would typically be the presence and relative heights of any number of peaks in the spectrum of weapons-grade fissile material.

Such a method requires negotiations between the NWS and the inspecting NNWS to establish which features the system should look for, as well as the minimum amount of fissile material that will provide a yes within the given time limit. If the amount of fissile materials sufficient to provide a yes is set too low, it would allow for the possibility that the NWS could get away with taking a considerably smaller amount of weapons-grade materials out of service than what was agreed on. It would then appear that a larger amount of the total stock of weapons-grade fissile materials had been eliminated than was actually the case.

To avoid NWS "cheating" by either removing only parts of the nuclear material of a real nuclear weapon or by using a "spoof" warhead with only small amounts of weapons-grade material, while in both cases being able to pass the information barrier warhead authentication check, a combination of two strategies may be pursued. First, the NWS should permit the minimum mass necessary for a yes to be relatively close to the actual mass of the warhead component in question. The smaller this difference is, the less weapons-usable material could be diverted to later use. Still, when it comes to the dismantling of a large number of nuclear warheads, even a small diversion for each warhead will accumulate into amounts sufficient to build several new nuclear weapons. For that reason, one should also consider the parallel strategy of allowing partial verification by another NWS (or former NWS). The other NWS would be able to verify the integrity and completeness of the warhead undergoing dismantling without breaching any NPT obligations.

One could readily argue that the complete gamma-ray spectrum should in fact be considered nonsensitive to proliferation even without the use of an information barrier system to conceal the details. The reason dates back to 1989, and the so-called Black Sea Experiment.[7] In this historical experiment, American scientists were allowed to obtain a complete gamma-ray energy spectrum from a Soviet nuclear warhead deployed in a cruise missile. Even at a distance of more than three meters from the warhead, and in only ten minutes of counting time, it was demonstrated that it was indeed possible to perform meaningful measurements of the spectrum, thus allowing for warhead authentication without peeking inside the warhead. And perhaps of greater importance: the experiment set a precedent for all the other NWS in terms of allowing the revelation for verification purposes of a detailed energy spectrum of what presumably was an advanced nuclear warhead. Neither the Soviet commanding officers nor the Americans who later published the results have been accused of proliferation. This indicates that if the political context is unambiguous, and not just a cover for deliberate proliferation, one could probe relatively deeply into the gray zone of detailed nuclear weapons information without being perceived as an NPT violator. Given the fact that the NWS inspectors in this case actually published the spectrum afterward, the Soviet Union might just as well have allowed an NNWS to perform the measurements directly.

Nuclear warheads consist of much more than the fissile materials alone. In order to authenticate a nuclear warhead, one may wish to verify also the presence of certain non-nuclear materials. In this regard it is useful to differentiate between parts that are nonsensitive to proliferation, but still necessary constituents of a nuclear warhead, and those parts that are considered sensitive to the NPT and/or national security. If one worries about spoofing during the dismantlement process, it is generally considered that the non-nuclear materials are by far the easiest to replicate in a spoof warhead. In that perspective, it is undoubtedly most important to be able to verify the presence of sufficient amounts of weapons-grade fissile materials, but allowing verification of other parts in addition would add further layers of confidence in the warhead authentication process.

Several techniques may be useful in order to confirm the presence of certain nonradioactive materials, depending on the level of intrusiveness allowed. Of course, visual inspection would in any case be very convincing, but this may not be possible at every stage of the dismantlement process. Active interrogation methods, such as X-ray or ultrasound screening and neutron activation techniques, may help reveal shapes and compositions, but may very well be viewed as too intrusive and potentially hazardous to the integrity and safety of the warhead.

Some of the relevant non-nuclear features of modern, implosion-type nuclear warheads (including multistage thermonuclear devices) include:

- Shaped high-explosive charges, either in a spherical configuration or in a two-point initiation configuration, and typically applying two different types of high explosives
- Exploding bridge wire detonators
- Accelerator-type external neutron sources
- Tritium gas reservoirs and pump systems
- Beryllium reflectors
- Compact radar altimeters.

These features are widely accepted as typical attributes of modern nuclear weapons. If the presence of several such features is proven in a nuclear warhead set for dismantlement (in addition to weapons-grade fissile materials), this would clearly increase the inspectors' confidence that the object in question is the real nuclear warhead it is claimed to be.

Even though the verification of these and other weapons attributes may prove feasible and may contribute to the overall confidence-building, nuclear warhead authentication is in essence about confirming the presence and dismantling of the treaty-accountable items, which are likely to be the weapons-grade fissile materials.

Verification of Disarmament without Violating National Security or the NPT

Two principles must generally be applied in a multistep process of verified nuclear weapons dismantlement:

- *Authentication* of the warhead or other treaty-accountable item (see the earlier section "Particular Restrictions").
- Establishing and maintaining a well-defined *chain of custody* for the warhead or other treaty-accountable item throughout the dismantling process.

Authentication is an obvious challenge to both the NPT commitments and to the inspected state's national security concerns, while measures to ensure chain of custody mainly presents a challenge to the latter. The use of unique tags and seals that are trusted by both parties and applied to the transport containers for warheads or other treaty-accountable items may be helpful in terms of gaining confidence in the integrity of the chain of custody whenever continuous visual contact with the treaty-accountable item is impossible.

As suggested earlier, another NWS may play a role in providing additional assurances of the authenticity of the warhead or other treaty-accountable item. This may be helpful in the initial authentication, but also during the actual disassembly of the warhead, at which point any inspecting NNWS necessarily must lose visual contact with the item. The main obstacle to the participation of another NWS is national security concerns, not the NPT, as explained earlier.

Since authentication performed by NNWS cannot involve a visual inspection of the inside of the warhead, this "authentication" must instead be based upon various confidence-building measures. For example, the NNWS may be given access to documents showing the whereabouts of the warhead in question during its entire lifetime. The sharing of such information is not a proliferative act, but it may be a challenge to the national security of the inspected state. However, sharing information about nuclear weapons *that are to be dismantled anyway* should not be by far as challenging as sharing information about operational nuclear weapons.

Exercises in which an inspection team is tasked to track and monitor a fictitious dismantlement process taking place in a controlled and sensitive area is a very effective way of studying techniques for maintaining trust in the chain of custody. The host and the inspecting party will have to negotiate the degree of "managed access" to buildings, sites, and personnel in order to provide sufficient confidence in the genuineness of the dismantlement process without compromising the NPT or national security. The authentication of the warhead or other treaty-accountable item may in such cases be performed in a notional way, for the sake of the exercise.

In an optimal process of verified dismantlement, the host state may have to provide a customized, dedicated facility for the most sensitive steps. Such a facility would be constructed with verification in mind, so that managed access to the facility can be straightforward and not in conflict with other, out-of-scope activities that the host may have to maintain during the inspection period.

Provided the inspectors are allowed to authenticate the warhead or other treaty-accountable item by external, nondestructive means (possibly applying one or more information barrier systems), it should be feasible to assure the inspectors that no fissile materials are diverted during the dismantlement in a dedicated facility. The inspectors must be able to survey the facility, and it must be of sufficiently modest complexity to convince the inspectors that there are no hidden entrances or suspicious neighboring rooms in which fissile materials or spoof warheads may be diverted or exchanged. In the case of warhead dismantlement, the process should take place in a dedicated room within the facility, into which the inspectors are allowed access before and after the dismantlement of the warhead and the repackaging of its parts. Thus, the inspectors may be convinced that there has been no diversion during the dismantling, despite the fact that they have not actually been able to observe the process. See figure 5.2 for a sketch of a possible nuclear warhead dismantlement verification scheme.

One may argue that the security concerns in question in fact generally lose their relevance in case of a complete and genuine disarmament process. Why would location, inventory, and other security—but not NPT-sensitive information matter—if the inspected state is really planning to abandon its nuclear weapons as a whole? Surely, this argument will probably not work so well in an early phase with limited reductions in the number of nuclear weapons, but it may very well be brought out when the ultimate goal of no nuclear weapons is closer at hand.

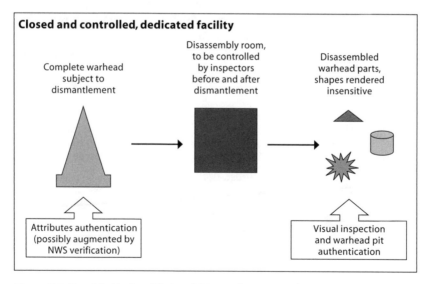

Figure 5.2 Possible Nuclear Warhead Dismantlement Verification Scheme.

Key Challenges

Security Deficit

The previous sections of this chapter address mainly technical disarmament issues. However, the disarmament of all nuclear weapons will most likely (but unintentionally) lead to a change in the global and regional balance of power. Especially the smaller NWS may find that their influence in the world as well as their ability to fight a war with their most likely enemies is reduced when they no longer have nuclear weapons.

How can this situation be remedied? It is somewhat related to the experiences of states that join the so-called Nuclear Weapons Free Zones in various parts of the world. In both cases, it is necessary that other states provide negative security assurances—that is, promise that they will not attack the state in question unless that state attacks them first. It is likely that complete nuclear disarmament will have to be accompanied by one or more international treaties that compensate for the immediate loss of power and capabilities that will accompany the disarmament of all nuclear weapons of a given state. (The necessary treaties may have to be initiated by some of the NNWS to function as a "carrot" for the process of complete nuclear disarmament.) Stabilizing treaties may prove instrumental to create a climate necessary for total nuclear disarmament.

NPT and National Security Issues

The constraints imposed by the NPT are nonnegotiable. However, it may be timely to revisit the way these constraints are generally understood and applied. As already pointed out, not all aspects and parameters of nuclear weapons need to be kept formally secret anymore because they are now widely known anyway and therefore do not add to today's risk for further nuclear proliferation. There may therefore be some space for negotiation between the inspecting NNWS and the inspected NWS in regard to issues that traditionally were considered completely nonnegotiable due to the NPT.

The national security of the inspected NWS is not rooted in any international treaties; it is a concern of that particular state and possibly its allies. Therefore, whenever there is a risk that verification of nuclear disarmament could come to a halt because of national security concerns (as opposed to the NPT), there is room for negotiation. The goal of the cooperation between the NWS and the NNWS must be to achieve confidence in the disarmament verification without challenging national security more than is absolutely necessary. It should be possible to accomplish this, for example, by applying various information barriers (see the previous subsection "Particular Restrictions").

Verifiable Items and Processes

Having established that there is indeed room for compromises and negotiation in the verification process, the next step is to define exactly what should be verified, what information is necessary to do it, and how the verification should be carried out.

This is the topic of the joint exercise in verifiable disarmament between the United Kingdom and Norway mentioned earlier. The exercise investigates the use of information barriers and managed access. The term *managed access* refers to the controlled circumstances under which the NNWS inspectors are granted access to the sensitive facilities of the NWS to perform their inspections. What level of access should the inspectors be given, and how should their inspections be conducted? Information barriers are used to make available some information about the warhead or other treaty-accountable item without revealing any proliferative information or unnecessarily compromising national security. More specific information about the aforementioned exercise is provided in the addendum at the end of this chapter.

In general, the goal of NNWS verified disarmament is to be able to state with confidence that a given disarmament process, such as the dismantlement of a certain number of nuclear warheads, has been completed. The actual items and processes to verify will depend crucially on the specific task at hand. It should be sufficient to note that there are no reasons, in principle, that one should not be able to negotiate a satisfactory way to carry out the required inspections.

A Possible Approach to a Process Leading toward a World Free of Nuclear Weapons

This section lists some thoughts on a possible step-by-step process to achieve a world free of nuclear weapons. Each of the steps is in itself a large process that in turn will call for further evaluation and analysis.

1. **NNWS consensus:** The NNWS interested in the verification of nuclear disarmament need to reach a certain point of agreement as to which attributes must be verified in order to authenticate—with sufficient confidence and without breaching the NPT—the presence of a nuclear weapon subject to dismantlement, or weapons-grade fissile materials subject to monitored storage or destruction.

2. **NWS consensus:** In an iterative fashion, the NNWS consensus on warhead attributes would be presented to the group of established and de facto NWS, which in turn would probably counter-propose a much shorter list. In case the differences between the NNWS demands and the NWS acceptances turn out to be significant and insurmountable, the two groups should seek to agree on a two-way split of the warhead attributes in question, so that the attributes that are too sensitive with respect to the NPT could be verified by other NWS in the dismantlement process, while the less sensitive attributes could be verified by an NNWS. This approach would probably constitute a less-than-perfect solution to the warhead authentication problem, but it would still provide more confidence than completely avoiding verification of some of the crucial features of a nuclear weapon.

3. **Declarations and assessments:** The NWS would have to declare its total stocks of weapons-grade fissile materials to the world at large or, at the very least, to the NNWS verifying its disarmament. The NWS and the inspecting NNWS would then need to perform an assessment of the verifiability of the declared stock of weapons materials.

   a. Specifically, if verification of zero weapons-grade fissile material in that particular NWS is not technically achievable within uncertainties on the order of one "significant quantity" of weapons-usable material (that is, 8 kilograms of plutonium or

25 kilograms of uranium-235 in highly enriched uranium), the NWS and the NNWS should focus on verifying limited reductions until the political conditions and the general level of confidence are considered appropriate for taking the final step toward zero. With a presumably strong global norm against the possession of nuclear weapons, the considerable political consequences of being caught trying to conceal one or more nuclear weapons would help to offset the lack of actual verification.

b. However, if the extent of the weapons-grade fissile materials production in the NWS is limited such that verification of zero weapons materials is considered feasible, the focus should of course be on just that. (In this case, the completed South African and prospective North Korean nuclear disarmament processes may act as feasibility tests, as described in Ifft's Chapter 1 of this volume.)

4. **Limited reductions:** Both substrategies in the previous point refer to limited reductions, in a sense, since the complete disarmament of a limited, well-defined nuclear program can be verified with about the same means and the same degree of uncertainty as limited reductions of an otherwise opaque and complex nuclear program. The methods should therefore be similar in these two cases, with a similar degree of confidence. Politically, limited reductions would be crucial for the process of establishing an anti–nuclear weapons norm, as pointed out earlier. NWS and NNWS alike should also during this phase work for the universalization of the Additional Protocol or even more sophisticated safeguards regimes, and a verifiable FMCT, to prevent clandestine revitalization of nuclear facilities and ensure irreversibility of reductions.

5. **Strengthening the norm:** When at some point it seems evident that most NWS are approaching the goal of zero nuclear weapons and no stocks of weapons-usable fissile materials, one may seek to introduce additional political disincentives to secretly keeping a small nuclear arsenal or stock of weapons-usable materials. One measure could be to revisit the idea of a convention against nuclear weapons, as the political climate at that point probably would be much more hospitable to adopting such a convention after years

of a concerted worldwide reduction of the nuclear weapons arsenals. The context should be clear, however, that this should only
be viewed as a further strengthening of the obligations already
imposed on the temporarily acknowledged NWS under the NPT. A
convention against nuclear weapons would of course not discrimi-
nate between established and de facto NWS. And it would certainly
not render the NPT redundant.

Conclusions

It is recommended that NPT states-parties during the NPT Review
Conference process seek an overall strategy for medium-term nuclear
reductions, with a long-term goal of zero nuclear weapons. States
should endeavor to implement such a strategy at a level comparable to
that of the step-by-step process just outlined, because the specifics and
timelines would necessarily have to be customized for each NWS. A
useful approach in achieving any such strategy might be to use future
NPT Review Conferences as milestones for the steps outlined in the
strategy. More specifically, an assessment should be provided outlin-
ing how far each of the NWS seems to be from arriving at the last
stage of disarmament in which the final few, but most demanding, steps
toward zero nuclear weapons are all that remain. While the highly vari-
able security conditions that exist among the NWS, as well as the differences in the size of their respective nuclear arsenals, make it hard to
demand simultaneous and one-for-one reductions for all the NWS, the
final step toward zero should be performed in a concerted fashion, so
that no state could discern an opportunity to stop short and become a
nuclear weapons monopolist.

Any NNWS should in principle be welcome to take part in
the disarmament verification process of an NWS fulfilling its NPT
Article VI commitments. In reality, the vast number of NNWS, and
also the huge differences between them in the level of technological
sophistication, make it impractical to invite "any NNWS" to take
part in a given disarmament verification process. For that reason,
the NNWS should agree on a number of "trusted agents" for each

individual case. The trusted agents would most likely be appointed from among the 44 nuclear-capable states, but there are no formal reasons to exclude any interested state from the process. Thus, in any disarmament verification process, there should be inspectors present from a small selection of "trusted agent states" acting on behalf of the NNWS as a whole, such that every NNWS may be convinced by the testimony of a like-minded, and technologically capable, state present during the process.

Conversely, also the NWS, though there are fewer of them, may need to agree on which of them should be represented during another NWS disarmament process, so that verification of proliferation-sensitive features is performed in a way that is satisfactory for the other NWS as well as for the NNWS, and of course, for the NPT.

Addendum: Cooperation on Verifiable Nuclear Disarmament between the United Kingdom and Norway

In these times of great uncertainty and concern about the future of the NPT, mainly due to the complete failure of progress at the NPT Review Conference in 2005 as well as the proliferation challenges posed by several states in recent years, positive engagement in the field of nuclear nonproliferation and disarmament is much sought after. Some countries have recently explored new paths in their efforts to revive the NPT process. In particular, Norway has taken the lead in the so-called Seven-Nation Initiative, together with Australia, Chile, Indonesia, Romania, South Africa, and the United Kingdom, in which experts in many areas have joined ranks to produce constructive ideas to forward the nuclear nonproliferation and disarmament agenda.

In a separate initiative in 2007, experts on nuclear weapons disarmament from the United Kingdom and Norway agreed on an unprecedented and ambitious research cooperation project: How may an NNWS play a constructive role in gaining confidence in the nuclear disarmament process of an NWS?[9] Exploring such a sensitive issue between two states-parties to the NPT is obviously a challenging task, and the political downfall in case of a failure of adherence to the NPT and/or a national security breach would most likely be substantial. Nevertheless, the two sides agreed on a two-track approach to the task: One was to explore possible *verification procedures* that may be applied in the context of a hypothetical NNWS inspecting a voluntary dismantlement process of a limited number of nuclear warheads in a hypothetical NWS. The two countries agreed to carry out a mock disarmament verification exercise involving *managed access* of a hypothetical NNWS (played by the United Kingdom) to the relevant nuclear facilities of a hypothetical NWS (played by Norway). The other track was the mutual development of a simple *information barrier* to be applied for the authentication of the nuclear component of the weapon (the *treaty-accountable item* in this exercise). The objective of the second track was to prove the feasibility of doing this in a transparent and realistic way.

Along both tracks, substantial sensitivity hurdles arose from the nature of the problem at hand: How could the inspecting party achieve and maintain confidence that the object undergoing dismantlement really was the nuclear warhead it was declared to be? How could one even discuss in detail ways of authenticating nuclear warheads between two states parties without breaching the NPT and/or violating national security concerns? What kind of measurements and visual access would be required for the inspecting party to be assured that no significant amounts of weapons-usable materials were clandestinely diverted for later use? Could such measurements and visual access be allowed? Further, what indirect confidence-building measures could be applied to bridge some of the confidence gaps that might still be lingering even after the agreed-on measures had been carried through? And how could one discuss aspects of the security regime at a real nuclear weapons facility without compromising it?

For this first cooperation project, two simplifying measures were agreed on. First, as mentioned, there was a total switch of roles. The British side took on the role of the NNWS of "Luvania," while the Norwegian side assumed the role of the friendly, regionally dominating NWS of "Torland." This fundamental switch allowed both sides to discuss fictional nuclear weapons in a fictional nuclear weapons laboratory (based on two of the participating Norwegian research institutions, the Institute for Energy Technology and the Norwegian Defence Research Establishment). The mock disarmament verification exercise was carried out in this "Nuclear Weapons Laboratory" of Torland.

Second, to avoid potential complications involved in discussing the physical attributes of a plutonium or uranium nuclear weapon component, another substitution was made: for exercise purposes, the mock weapon manufactured to be the subject of the measurement campaign contained cobalt-60 instead of plutonium or uranium. The reason for this choice of material was twofold: cobalt is obviously not usable for nuclear weapons purposes in real life and is thus irrelevant to the NPT, and this readily available material is one of the easiest elements to identify by gamma spectroscopy due to the distinct, high-energy gamma rays it emits. This introduction of cobalt-60 into the measurement campaign circumvented a number of legal and technical challenges for the sake of the exercise. Obviously, at a later point in time one will need to address the problem assuming more realistic attributes of a nuclear weapon, but the choice of cobalt as a first stage allowed for rapid progress in the technical development of a prototype information barrier.

The first Luvanian inspection of the Torian "nuclear weapons facilities" took place in December 2008 with the intention of familiarizing the Luvanian inspectors with notional Torian weapons dismantlement procedures and the facilities in which the later mock dismantlement would be played out. This successful mock inspection gave the participating teams experience in areas such as managed access, addressing sensitive topics, and negotiating terms for future inspections. (Figure 5.3 shows a picture taken during the exercise.) Some early information about the exercise was published by the British Foreign and Commonwealth Office.[10] The follow-up inspections of the dismantlement of a mock "nuclear weapon" took place in June 2009. The results of the complete exercise were reported to the 2010 NPT Review Conference.[11]

Figure 5.3 Luvanian inspectors visiting the Torian facility for monitored storage of "nuclear weapons components." The people wearing vests are observers and planners, while Torian officials are nonuniformed. Military guards were present but are not visible in the picture. The picture shows the entrance to the Norwegian combined storage and repository for low- and intermediate-level radioactive waste at Himdalen, Norway, which is operated by the Institute for Energy Technology.

Notes

1. By *negative security assurances*, we mean guarantees of nonaggression against the disarming NWS.

2. These 44 states are identified in Annex 2 to the treaty.

3. See, for example, Elin Enger, "South Africa's Nuclear Weapons Programme," FFI Report no. 2008/00696, Norwegian Defence Research Establishment, 2008, rapporter.ffi.no/rapporter/2008/00696.pdf.

4. Here we assume that the alleged research and development efforts into gas centrifuge enrichment in North Korea never reached a point of maturity that would call for extensive verification with potentially significant discrepancies between declarations and verification measurements.

5. The International Science and Technology Center (ISTC) in Moscow connects scientists in the Commonwealth of Independent States with their

peers and research organizations in Canada, the EU, Japan, Norway, South Korea, and the United States.

6. Presumably, any disarmament verification inspections will be based on a bilateral or multilateral treaty between the states involved. Such a treaty must also define exactly what objects and/or features are to be verified. These constitute the "treaty-accountable items."

7. See, for instance, Steve Fetter, Valery A. Frolov, Marvin Miller, Robert Mozley, Oleg F. Prilutsky, Stanislav N. Rodionov, and Roald Z. Sagdeev, "Detecting Nuclear Warheads," in *Science & Global Security* 1 (1990): 225–253; and especially Steve Fetter and Frank von Hippel, "The Black Sea Experiment – US and Soviet Reports from a Cooperative Verification Experiment," *Science & Global Security* 1 (1990): 323–327.

8. See, for example, Linda Mari Holøien, "Weapons of Mass Destruction Free Zones in the Middle East," FFI Report no. 2006/02488, Norwegian Defence Research Establishment, 2006,; rapporter.ffi.no/rapporter/2006/02488.pdf.

9. The Ministry of Defence and the Atomic Weapons Establishment (AWE) participate from the United Kingdom; the Norwegian Radiation Protection Authority, the Institute for Energy Technology, NORSAR, and the Norwegian Defence Research Establishment participate from Norway. The Norwegian participation is supported by the Norwegian Ministry of Foreign Affairs. The London-based nongovernmental organization VERTIC is involved as a facilitator of and rapporteur from the process.

10. British Foreign and Commonwealth Office, "Lifting the Nuclear Shadow: Creating the Conditions for Abolishing Nuclear Weapons," Policy Paper, February 4, 2009, www.fco.gov.uk/resources/en/pdf/pdf1/nuclear-paper.

11. The Kingdom of Norway and the United Kingdom of Great Britain and Northern Ireland, "The United Kingdom-Norway Initiative: Research into the Verification of Nuclear Warhead Dismantlement," The 2010 Review Conference of the Parties to the Treaty on the Non-Proliferation of Nuclear Weapons, NPT/CONF. 2010/WP.41.

6. Verifying the Nonproduction of New Nuclear Weapons

EVERET H. BECKNER

Verifying the nonproduction of new nuclear weapons requires that three major manufacturing activities be monitored and their null outputs verified: (1) manufacture (or purchase) of fissile materials, either plutonium or enriched uranium; (2) manufacture of specialized nuclear components from those fissile materials; and (3) assembly of those nuclear components together with a number of non-nuclear components to produce a nuclear weapon. These are the necessary activities to produce a nuclear weapon, whether the production of new nuclear weapons is being done by an established nuclear weapon state or by a state that is embarking on a program to become a new nuclear weapon state.

Production of new nuclear weapons can result in either qualitative or quantitative changes in the weapon status of nuclear or (previously) non-nuclear states. The verification strategies for the two cases would need to be somewhat different.

A qualitative change would be the following. For a nuclear weapon state, production of a new nuclear weapon for its stockpile could occur when one of two things happened: (1) an existing weapon type aged to the point where it became either unreliable, or unsafe, and needed to be replaced; or (2) the weapon state decided to upgrade or change some features in certain weapons in its stockpile. While the primary verification strategy in this case would be to concentrate on verifying that the net nuclear weapon count had not gone up and thereby violated

the agreed stockpile level, there could also be agreed verification protocols that imposed significant barriers to upgrading the output features
of weapons during refurbishment. This will be discussed further in the
"Background" section on refurbishment later in this chapter.

A quantitative change in nuclear weapon status would occur when
(1) a nuclear weapon state decided to increase (or decrease) the size
of its stockpile or (2) a nonweapon state moved to become a nuclear
weapon state as a result of its nuclear weapon program having advanced
to the point where an actual nuclear weapon could be produced. In this
case, the verification strategy would need to focus on identifying any
new production that resulted in an unauthorized increase in nuclear
stockpiles and that, thereby, would trigger an inspection.

In seeking to control the production of nuclear weapons through
a treaty verification regime, it is also necessary to understand the
many stockpile-sustaining activities that a nuclear weapon state must
be allowed to conduct in order to maintain a safe, secure, and reliable
stockpile. The primary activities of interest are weapon maintenance,[1]
weapon surveillance,[2] weapon refurbishment,[3] and production of new-
build[4] weapons to replace aged weapons in the nation's stockpile.

While stockpile "maintenance" and "surveillance" activities can
probably be accommodated without undue stress on protocols employed
to verify stockpile numbers, there is probably no way—short of extremely
intrusive processes—to assure that the weapon that flows from the
stockpile refurbishment production line does not have improved
nuclear characteristics compared with the original weapon. This will
be discussed later.

For a variety of reasons, mostly having to do with weapon carriers becoming obsolete, it seems likely that several (perhaps all) nuclear
weapon states will wish occasionally to replace existing weapons in their
stockpile with new-build weapons, while controlling the total number of
weapons in their stockpile. In that case, it will be extremely difficult to
know whether the nuclear characteristics of the new-build weapons have
been improved compared with the weapons that were replaced.

In the next few years, it appears that it might be possible for the
United States and Russia to agree to a more ambitious stockpile reduction and verification plan: (1) to reduce their stockpiles to 1,000, more
or less, and (2) to agree to a robust, bilateral verification protocol. If

achieved, this "minimum starting" condition (1 + 2) could potentially set the stage for reductions by other countries, as well as for further reductions by the United States and Russia. At that point it would be important (some would say necessary) to incorporate into the verification agreements the role of an international body to be responsible for all elements of the verification processes, rather than trying to accomplish this end state while relying on bilateral agreements.

Since there are presently nine nations with nuclear stockpiles of varying sizes, ranging from a few tens to a few thousand, the path to "zero nuclear weapons" would need to contain intermediate waypoints that would probably need to be at different stockpile levels for the large stockpile states compared with the small stockpile states.

Attempting to use a verification regime to restrict the progress of any new state toward becoming a nuclear weapon state will probably require that a verification protocol be adopted *worldwide* that includes accurate accounting of *all* the fissile material inventories of each country, including the civilian nuclear reactor inventories.

Stated differently: Unless controls are in place to account worldwide for all fissile materials, both civilian and military, it seems very unlikely that any of the nuclear weapon states will agree to approach "zero" with their stockpile, since there would be no assurance that some adversary would not be able to break out with nuclear weapons at a future date to threaten other countries.

The pathway to substantially smaller nuclear weapon stockpiles worldwide will encounter a special, and somewhat arcane, challenge based on the argument that it may be impossible to maintain a competent nuclear design and production workforce if, in fact, there is very little nuclear weapons work for those people to do. This argument will not be easily sidestepped, since modern nuclear weapons are exceedingly complex and, in the absence of full-scale testing, require a highly trained and motivated workforce to assure their reliable performance and safety.

Background

This chapter will examine the technical details of all the activities normally accompanying the maintenance, surveillance, refurbishment, and production of nuclear weapons. In other words, I will outline the activities required to produce and sustain a reliable nuclear weapon stockpile.

The actual production of a new nuclear weapon entails three principal activities: (1) production (or acquisition) of fissile material in the form of weapons-grade plutonium[5] and/or highly enriched uranium (HEU, usually at least 70 percent U-235); (2) fabrication of specialized nuclear components made from this Pu or HEU; and (3) assembly of those nuclear components together with a number of non-nuclear components (like high-explosive charges) to form the nuclear weapon. Generally speaking, those activities are independent of weapon production rates.

Thus, the first step in verifying the nonproduction of new nuclear weapons is to control the production of new fissile materials (plutonium from reactors and HEU from enrichment facilities) and to tightly control worldwide existing stocks of fissile materials. This means that a worldwide, verifiable inventory system would have to be put in place for all stocks of fissile materials, including those associated with both civilian and defense nuclear reactors, their fuels (both fresh and spent), and reprocessing facilities. The second step would be to identify and verifiably monitor the production of all components fabricated from fissile materials involving quantities approximating a critical mass, or larger, of either Pu or HEU. The third step would be to identify and verifiably monitor the assembly and disassembly of all nuclear weapons assembled or disassembled from those nuclear components. It is far easier to monitor and verifiably control step 1 in this process than either steps 2 or 3, due to the large physical scale of the activities and the identifying physical markers that accompany step 1.

These manufacturing activities apply both to an extant nuclear weapon state and to a state attempting to become a new nuclear weapon state. Step 1 tends to be of primary interest when the objective is to prevent or observe a non–nuclear weapon state attempting to become a nuclear weapon state. Steps 2 and 3 tend to be of primary interest when the objective is to prevent a nuclear weapon state from clandestinely inserting new nuclear weapons into its stockpile.

There is not much new we can say about the processes required to verifiably monitor the production of fissile materials of quantities that might become a critical mass of either Pu or HEU. A reactor of 50 to 100 megawatts is adequate to produce kilogram quantities of plutonium in periods of months. If frequent refueling can be accomplished, the plutonium extracted chemically from the fuel rods can be "weapons-grade" plutonium, meaning that it will not have an excessive population of plutonium isotopes higher than Pu-239. Similarly, kilogram quantities of HEU can be produced from a modest-sized centrifuge enrichment plant, using technology that is now more available than we would wish. Historically, it has been relatively easy to hide the production of weapons-grade plutonium within the operations of either a large research reactor or a small power reactor and its associated reprocessing facilities. Examples to date are Israel, India, Pakistan, and North Korea. Similarly, South Africa produced enough HEU from its enrichment plant to manufacture more than a half dozen HEU weapons, although not without arousing a lot of suspicion that they were doing so. So, the evidence is quite clear that production of weapons-quantities of fissile materials can only be controlled through a comprehensive, worldwide inventory and verification regime of nuclear weapons facilities, nuclear power facilities, and all relevant nuclear laboratories.

Let's now move to discussion of steps 2 and 3 in the production of new nuclear weapons, with emphasis on production activities associated with maintenance, surveillance, and other ongoing activities of nuclear weapon states. First, for these states (which obviously includes the United States), we must look at the ongoing stockpile activities that are necessary to maintain a safe and secure stockpile of nuclear weapons. Hence, we must look at the restrictions and other potentially intrusive activities that might be necessary in order to verify that, within those activities, new nuclear weapons were not being clandestinely produced and inserted into a country's stockpile.

The first scenario explored applies to declared nuclear weapon states that are continuing to maintain and refurbish their stockpiles, but that have agreed to not produce any new nuclear weapons for their stockpile. The second scenario is one in which a declared nuclear weapon state has agreed to only produce new nuclear weapons for its stockpile if it simultaneously destroys an equal number of weapons presently in its stockpile. The rationale for allowing such activities might be that the "upgraded, new weapon" would contain improved safety and security features. Such arguments have been used, for instance, by the U.S. National Nuclear Security Agency (NNSA) and the Department of Defense (DoD) in attempting to convince Congress that they should be funded to go forward with a program called "Reliable Replacement Warhead" (RRW) to upgrade the U.S. stockpile.

Finally, I will explore the realities of attempting to control the clandestine development and production of new nuclear weapons by states that do not presently possess any nuclear weapons.

Normal Activities Required to Maintain a Reliable Nuclear Weapon Stockpile

The description of weapon stockpile activities described in this chapter will be within the context of the way things are done in the U.S. nuclear weapon program. They cannot be expected to represent exactly the way things are done in the programs of all the nuclear weapon states. Among other reasons, of course, is the fact that we do not know how they are done in all the other states. Nonetheless, it is not unreasonable to expect that most of the things that are done in the U.S. nuclear weapons program must also be done in the programs of other weapon states. In other words, we can be reasonably confident we know what they have to do to sustain their stockpile—we just do not know the details. A necessary part of agreeing to future, low stockpile limits would have to be agreement by all the participants on how to deal with those unknown details.

In seeking to control the production of nuclear weapons via a treaty verification regime, it is necessary to understand the many activities that must be allowed because, in fact, they are necessary in order for any nuclear state to maintain its nuclear stockpile in a safe and reliable configuration. If that condition cannot reasonably be expected to obtain, then no nuclear weapon state will be willing to enter into a treaty designed to limit, let alone reduce, its stockpile.

Though designers and military custodians of nuclear weapons would wish it not to be so, nuclear weapons are far from being "wooden bombs," and as such require considerable care, maintenance, and refurbishment. They have components that age with time, like the high-explosive chemical components, which must be replaced at predictable intervals. They have critical components that oxidize and thereby change their mechanical behavior. They contain several radioactive materials, some with long half-lives and some with relatively short half-lives, like tritium, with a half-life of only 12.5 years. Since several components in modern weapons may contain tritium in precise amounts, it is predictable that certain components must be replaced at intervals of 5 to 20 years. All these features are unavoidably designed into modern nuclear weapons, thereby setting the requirement that such weapons receive frequent maintenance and occasional replacement of major components.

Therefore, we must look carefully at the routine and relatively predictable operations that must be performed on nuclear weapons, in order to understand fully how those processes may impact any verification regime designed to assure the nonproduction of new nuclear weapons.

Maintenance

Maintenance activities are generally less intrusive than either surveillance activities or refurbishment activities. They involve either repairing superficial damage that may have occurred to the weapon or, more normally, replacing limited life components (LLCs, those components that are routinely replaced when their normal life expectance is reached). The activities most likely to warrant consideration within the context of nonproduction of new nuclear weapons would be the LLC replacements. Since modern weapon systems have to be designed to accommodate LLC replacements, those activities are generally not very complicated or intrusive into the body of the nuclear weapon. This might not be true in the case of states with small stockpiles or states that are late entries as nuclear weapon states. For instance, whereas some of the LLC replacements in U.S. weapons involve replacement of tritium gas reservoirs (resulting from the decay of tritium), or the neutron generators (again, due to the decay of tritium in the generator tube), or batteries, it is unknown how other states' weapon designs may deal with such requirements.

Also, if the weapon is not "boosted,"[6] it would not need tritium gas to be replaced at regular intervals. Similarly, many of the early U.S.

designs did not have external neutron generators to assure performance. As they say, "the devil is in the details," and each country's details will doubtless be different.

Surveillance

For a nuclear weapon state, there is a recognized requirement to provide information to the political and military leadership of that country, stating that the nuclear weapons are in good condition and could be expected to perform as designed, in terms of yield and ability to survive normal delivery environments. These routine laboratory/plant measurement activities generally are called "surveillance activities." In the United States, they occasionally call for partial dismantlement and removal of certain critical weapon components for inspection. These components are then either tested or examined, nondestructively if possible, or destructively if necessary. The design laboratories issue surveillance reports on each warhead type in the stockpile. The original weapon is then rebuilt with some old parts and some new parts, as necessary, and returned to the stockpile. In some cases, new primaries or secondaries[7] may have to be used to build the replacement weapon. In other cases, the weapon may not be rebuilt at all if the original stockpile of this weapon type was large enough to support loss of such surveillance units. Obviously, as the stockpiles of nuclear weapon states become smaller, one would expect that in most cases it would be necessary to rebuild the original weapon, and that might require fabrication of a new pit or a new secondary, among other components that might require replacement, like explosively actuated components.

Refurbishment

Refurbishment is the term used in the United States to describe a "major overhaul" of a nuclear weapon, sometimes including substantial work on either or both the primary and the secondary. Hence, the weapon may be completely torn down and major work performed on the nuclear components, including the high-explosive system, in some cases. In the U.S. program, the intent of a weapon refurbishment program is generally to cure a problem in a particular set of weapons, which has been discovered via the surveillance program. It might involve only replacing the high-explosive component surrounding the pit. It might involve only replacing nuclear components that have been found to have experienced unacceptable levels of corrosion. In any case, the process begins by tearing down the existing weapon and possibly replacing major functional parts of the nuclear system, and then building up the weapon into its original form. In U.S. terminology, "refurbishment" activities are not performed to provide new capabilities to the original weapon. They only restore the weapon to its original form and functional capability.

Within the context of this chapter, however, there is no way—short of extremely intrusive processes—to assure that the weapon that flows from the "refurbishment" assembly line does not have improved nuclear output characteristics compared with the characteristics of the original weapon. To be meaningful, those "intrusive processes" might require that the declaration by the host country include the following information regarding the design features of each weapon type in the stockpile: (1) single-stage or two-stage weapon; (2) boosted or not boosted; (3) plutonium or uranium primary; and (4) length, diameter, and total weight of nuclear package (primary, secondary, interstage materials, and radiation case). Then, the verification protocol would be to compare the "before" and "after" versions of this information for each weapon that was refurbished. Having this much detail in a verification agreement would cause it to be very difficult to negotiate, especially if the inspection and challenge protocols were intended to eliminate upgrading of weapon features during refurbishment.

New Builds of New Nuclear Weapons

Depending on the details of the agreements reached between the declared nuclear states, it seems likely that the parties would agree to specific conditions regarding introduction of new weapons into the stockpile. As mentioned, this chapter will cover the possibility that such agreements might allow the introduction of new weapons into a stockpile if an equal number of older weapons were removed and destroyed. This scenario would be very similar to the refurbishment program just described, except that instead of tearing down an old weapon and replacing it with a refurbished weapon (with many, but not all, new components), the new-build program would first build the new weapon (presumably with all new parts) and then destroy an old weapon before introducing the new weapon into the stockpile.

This approach (new build) obviously invites continual upgrading of capabilities of the stockpile of the declared state. This may, or may not, be viewed as acceptable. Unfortunately, though, it appears inevitable that it will have to be considered during the course of negotiating the contemplated treaty. From a verification perspective, it would be impossible to know with any degree of certainty whether improved weapon features were being inserted into new builds unless something like the "intrusive inspection features" described in the previous section were incorporated into the agreements.

Realities of the Stockpiles of the Nuclear Weapon States

The following sections describe the present-day stockpiles of nuclear weapons of the weapon states of the world.

United States and Russia

The nuclear weapon stockpiles of the United States (thought to be more than 5,000 total weapons today) and Russia (thought to be more than 7,000)[8] are regarded to be rather similar today in terms of their design features, with the exception that Russia is thought to have considerably more tactical weapons than the United States. This difference in the number of tactical weapons is connected with the fact that the nuclear weapon treaties to date have not attempted to include counting of tactical weapons in the same way that they count the number of strategic weapons. Otherwise, both countries are thought to have developed similar designs with similar carriers (air delivered by bombers, fighter aircraft, and cruise missiles; ICBM- (intercontinental ballistic missile) carried reentry vehicles and SLBM carried reentry bodies).

The tactical weapon stockpiles were once dominated by artillery-delivered nuclear devices, but many, if not all, of those weapons have been retired as the military threats to the two countries have changed. However, due to the threats that Russia perceives from neighboring countries following the breakup of the USSR, the Russian government places a higher value today on tactical weapons than does the United States, and it continues to retain larger numbers of them. The majority, if not all, of the nuclear weapons in the stockpiles of the United States and Russia contain plutonium primaries. Most of the weapons have secondaries to provide thermonuclear yield from highly enriched uranium components associated with components made of a compound of lithium and deuterium (LiD). It is quite possible that both the United States and Russia will over time wish to replace some elements of their existing stockpiles with weapons of a different design.

United Kingdom

The United Kingdom is thought to have approximately 200 weapons today.[9] Though considerably smaller in numbers, the U.K. nuclear weapons are generally thought to be quite similar to some of the weapons in the U.S. stockpile, particularly since their only nuclear weapon carrier at present is the Trident missile, purchased from the U.S. government. This could change in the future, since one day they will have to replace their fleet of Trident submarines. This impending event makes it quite possible that someday the United Kingdom may wish to replace its existing stockpile with weapons of a different design, consistent with a new carrier.

France

Thought to be approximately 350 weapons today,[10] the French nuclear weapon stockpile has been developed quite independently from the U.S., U.K., and Russian programs. Nonetheless, by virtue of the unavoidable realities of nuclear physics and engineering limitations, French weapons are thought to be quite similar to the modern weapon designs of those countries. Thus, they are thought to be built around tritium-boosted plutonium primaries coupled to thermonuclear secondaries containing HEU and LiD fuel. Like the United Kingdom, it is quite possible that someday the French will wish to replace the weapons in their present stockpile with new designs, consistent with new carriers.

China

China is thought to have approximately 300 weapons today.[11] It is believed that the evolution of the Chinese nuclear weapon program has been rather different from any of the previously described programs, in that it first appeared as an HEU-oriented program for the designs of their primaries, rather than plutonium as the pit fissile material. Presumably, this choice was dictated by the early-on availability of stocks of HEU rather than plutonium. In any case, the Chinese have apparently in later years also developed plutonium-based primaries for the weapons now thought to be in their stockpile. These realities, however, would leave the Chinese program possibly in a position to benefit from upgrading their stockpile (from HEU primaries to Pu primaries, if any HEU primaries are still in their stockpile) while still limiting the total number of weapons. Beyond these considerations, the Chinese are thought to have a mix of tactical weapons in their stockpile, consistent with delivery systems that are relatively short range.

As time goes on, it would not be surprising to see the Chinese program shift its stockpile mix to increase the number of strategic weapons at the expense of tactical weapons. If at that time they had joined in a treaty limiting the number of weapons in their stockpile, they could presumably want to do a one-for-one replacement of new weapons for some of their older weapons.

Israel

Although not a declared nuclear weapon state, Israel is generally thought to have built a stockpile of around 200 nuclear weapons of modern design, meaning boosted-plutonium primaries and thermonuclear secondaries containing HEU and LiD.[12] The Israeli government has never stated that it has developed nuclear weapons capability. However, it can be hoped that a more forthcoming position on Israel's weapons program will occur in the future since it would seem unavoidable that Israel would have to be included in any future treaty designed to limit the numbers of weapons in the stockpiles of all the nations of the world. On that basis, the nuclear weapons of Israel would probably look much like the weapons found in other modern stockpiles.

India

India is estimated to have perhaps 50 weapons in its stockpile.[13] After testing in 1974 and again in 1998, India has demonstrated a nuclear weapon capability. Based on the plutonium that it may have produced and on various possible sources for HEU, it appears that India has focused on a plutonium primary design, but with a questionable ability in its designs to drive a thermonuclear secondary. The Indian program is definitely one that should be expected to develop improved designs over time, and as such to seek to upgrade its stockpile as newer designs become available to replace lower-performance warheads.

Pakistan

Pakistan has perhaps 50 weapons in its stockpile,[14] but the quantity and quality of weapons of Pakistan is highly questionable. However, Pakistan tested a design successfully in 1998. Its sources of material are uncertain. The government does have a master spy and technology thief in A. Q. Kahn, who previously headed the Pakistani program. He also appears to be eager to sell nuclear weapon technology secrets to the highest bidder. The fact that the Pakistani government has done so little to control his activities leaves Pakistan's nuclear reputation in tatters. It is very uncertain what the government intends to do to maintain or improve its stockpile.

North Korea

North Korea has perhaps 5 to 10 weapons in the stockpile.[15] The North Korean nuclear weapons program is a bad example of a rogue nation whose leadership is determined to develop and manufacture a few nuclear weapons in order to gain military respect at all costs. This demonstrated recklessness toward the opinion of most of the rest of the world makes it especially troublesome. It is unknown what would be required for the nation's leaders to ever allow its nuclear weapon program and stockpile to come under any verification regime, but this chapter assumes that such would be possible. Its present weapons are thought to be plutonium based and probably fission-only primaries with no thermonuclear secondary yet demonstrated.

Issues

Assessing the Links between Nuclear Stockpiles, Treaty Objectives, and the Nonproduction of New Nuclear Weapons

Inspection of the sizes and details of the nuclear stockpiles of countries today yields several objectives that might be incorporated into future arms control treaties. I begin by recognizing the overarching objective already stated in this book: explore and analyze the objective of elimination of all nuclear weapons from the face of the Earth—"the zero nuclear weapons objective."

Since there are presently nine nations with nuclear stockpiles of varying sizes, ranging from a few tens to a few thousand, the path to zero would have to (1) contain logical intermediate waypoints to allow all the nuclear participating nations to sign on to the strategy. Also, it needs to (2) make it economically and strategically uninviting for nations that are presently non–nuclear weapon states to develop a nuclear weapon capability.

The next logical objective for stockpile reductions worldwide would seem to be a limitation on the total nuclear stockpile of any country to around 1,000 (deployed) weapons. The "1,000" limit would impact only the United States and Russia, and as such require only those two states to agree on the time to achieve those reductions and the verification regime. We will assume that might be three years and a verification regime agreed not unlike that employed today (self-inspection and self-verification). However, to make further reductions intended to begin to impact the stockpiles of other nations, it would seem to be necessary at the 1,000-weapon limit to do two things: (1) agree on a process and timescale to eliminate the nondeployed stockpiles of both countries, and (2) bring in an outside body to perform verification: perhaps the International Atomic Energy Agency (IAEA).

So, by 2015–2020, it might be possible to have established a verification regime under the auspices of IAEA that has concluded that the United States and Russia have reduced their deployed stockpiles to 1,000 and have eliminated or otherwise put under control their nondeployed stockpiles.

The next round of reductions would be expected to be hard ones. At this point, it is likely that further reductions on the part of the United States and Russia would have to be accompanied by commensurate reductions (in some sense) and verification regimes applied to the stockpiles of all the other nuclear states: China, United Kingdom, France, Israel, India, Pakistan, North Korea, and any other states that may have developed a nuclear weapons capability by that time. The reason to engage in this much speculative thinking is to recognize that realistically, by 2015–2020 it is likely that the path to zero would encounter the difficult task of multilateral negotiation of a treaty to limit the stockpiles of all the nuclear states and to also install a verification regime in all those programs. It is at this point that difficult realities would arise that are associated with this postulated verification regime.

Using the aforementioned verification regime to also impede the progress of any new states toward becoming nuclear weapon states will require that the inspection protocols include accurate accounting of *all* the fissile material inventories of each country. There is no other way to get control over the ambitions of countries which have set their sights on acquiring nuclear weapons. From studies of the history of the development of such programs in all the counties known to have embarked on a nuclear weapon objective, the dominant motivator is fear of a rival country's nuclear capability. It is unrealistic to expect that motivation to disappear in the multipolar world we must anticipate in the future, so this verification regime will have to extend to all countries with any fissile material, irrespective of the apparent attitude of that country toward development of nuclear weapons for that country. Since the quantities of fissile material required to develop a modest nuclear weapon capability (one weapon, or more) are no more than a few tens of kilograms, this verification regime will potentially be quite intrusive into the civilian nuclear power programs of the world.

Relevant Historical Reminders from the Past

History shows that for every country that has developed nuclear weapons since the first three (the United States, the Soviet Union, and the United Kingdom), all have used a civilian nuclear energy R&D or civilian nuclear power program to hide their program to develop nuclear weapons until it was ready to be unveiled.[16] Bluntly put, they all cheated on their sworn statement that they were only conducting peaceful nuclear energy activities. This "cheating" strategy also extended to South Africa and Taiwan, although they later abandoned their aspirations to become nuclear weapon states.[17]

Two other lessons from the past must also be remembered as we contemplate the realities of nuclear weapons development by a non-weapon state:

- Obtaining a source of fissile material for the contemplated nuclear weapons, whether it be plutonium or HEU, is the most time-consuming and expensive part of the program. By contrast, while nuclear design is not a trivial scientific challenge, much design information is now available on the Internet and in other public forms. Also, high-performance computers are now available for a few thousand dollars that are more capable than the largest computers used to design and develop all the weapons in the present stockpiles of the world. On the other hand, building an enrichment plant to produce HEU, or a good-sized reactor and fuel-reprocessing plant to produce plutonium, is a time-consuming and expensive proposition. Also, these fuel-manufacturing operations tend to be the best way to detect a clandestine nuclear weapon program, which means that a lot of care and money must be expended to hide them if that is your objective.
- The time to produce a few nuclear weapons following production of the requisite fissile material is relatively short—generally no more than a year or two. This compares with a period of at

least five years to build the necessary plant (reactor) and to produce the requisite fissile material.

So, the devil has just come out of the details.

A verification regime designed to preclude entry of new states into the list of nuclear weapon states would potentially have a very serious impact on the world's nuclear power industry, since it must verify very small holdings of fissile materials (kilogram quantities of fissile material in a material accounting system that normally deals with metric ton levels). It would push all aspects of civilian nuclear power—from uranium mining, to material preparation, to enrichment, to fuel loading and unloading, to spent fuel storage and/or reprocessing—to install material monitoring and inventory systems that would be viewed as a serious impediment to progress of that entire industry. This is clearly asking a lot of an industry already struggling to make a difference worldwide in the looming energy shortage.

It appears we have identified a potential impasse. Since all the recent nuclear weapon states have used a strategy best described as "riding a peaceful nuclear energy Trojan horse" as a means of developing clandestinely a nuclear weapons capability, it is obvious that future aspiring entrants into the nuclear weapon club are likely to do the same. One must control the inventory of fissile material available to aspiring nuclear weapon builders if one is to have a chance of "going to zero" with world nuclear stockpiles. Otherwise, the risks will be too high for any leader of a major nuclear power to approach the zero level while having no assurance that some adversary would not be able to break out at any time with several nuclear weapons to threaten his country.

Key Verification Strategies and Identification of the Limitations to Verifying the Nonproduction of New Nuclear Weapons

As outlined in the previous section, it appears to be extremely difficult to use verification to reach the broad goal of moving toward zero nuclear weapons in the world, unless the worldwide inventory of fissile materials can be brought under verifiable control. However, even in the absence of such a sweeping development, several steps in that direction are possible.

For Non-weapon States

As a minimum, the effort to prevent nonweapon states from developing nuclear weapons should focus on two key requirements of an aspiring nuclear weapon program: (1) key technical people and (2) purchases of specialized nuclear equipment.

The key technical people have to be highly trained in nuclear chemistry, nuclear engineering, nuclear operations, nuclear physics, hydrodynamics, computer science, high-speed diagnostics, health physics, and materials science, among other disciplines. They require access to nuclear processing laboratories, nuclear manufacturing facilities, specialized facilities to protect workers from radiation exposure, specialized experimental facilities to conduct explosives research and hydrodynamics experiments (firing sites), high-performance computing equipment, and facilities to manage and dispose of nuclear waste. The verification strategies should, therefore, focus on identifying such people and such equipment being assembled where they had not heretofore been present—for instance, a new nuclear engineering or nuclear physics laboratory being staffed and equipped.

Similarly, the verification strategies should monitor sales of specialized equipment that could constitute the foundation of a program to acquire fissile materials and the equipment to produce plutonium or HEU weapon parts. This starts with either a nuclear reactor to produce plutonium or a uranium enrichment facility. These are very expensive undertakings, requiring time, money, and people. In the past, such technology has often been purchased from an established nuclear/chemical supplier, ostensibly for the purpose of furthering a civil nuclear program.

For Weapon States

For established nuclear weapon states with "countable" stockpiles of weapons, it appears to be possible to monitor those programs in such a way as to verify that *additional* weapons are not entering the stockpile as a result of normal stockpile operations: surveillance, maintenance, and refurbishment. The techniques used would probably be approximately the same for all three of these functions, although the details would be different: (1) a weapon would be withdrawn from the stockpile and inserted into a room (building) for processing, (2) the weapon would be processed with no intrusion from the verification controls, and (3) the weapon would leave the room (building) and be returned to the stockpile. The limitation to this process would be that there would be no way, short of broad declarations and potential inspection of the nuclear design features, discussed in the "Background" section, to know whether the weapon exiting the process had been upgraded in some way relative to the weapon that entered the process.

For established nuclear weapon states with "countable" stockpiles of weapons, which also desire to upgrade their stockpile while not expanding the numbers in the stockpile (a circumstance that might have to be accommodated in order to move toward zero, as mentioned earlier), it appears to be possible for a new nuclear weapon (a new build) to be put into the stockpile while controlling the total number of weapons in the stockpile, if the verification regime allowed such potential stockpile improvements to occur. In this case, the new-build weapon would only be allowed to enter the stockpile if an existing weapon was withdrawn and dismantled. This latter action (dismantlement) would be monitored by observing that the weapon entered the processing room and that the necessary number of fissile components and other structural members exited the processing room.

The boundary between maintenance and new production would appear to be readily defined and managed. Maintenance does not normally involve removal and replacement of major nuclear components. New production by definition does involve removal and replacement of major nuclear components. If maintenance were conducted as described previously, in a room for which all material movements in and out are completely monitored, then there would seem to be no way for new nuclear components to get into the "maintenance room" for purposes of transforming the output to new-build production.

Distinguishing nonintrusively between new production and refurbishment is much more difficult, if not impossible. Since refurbishment by its very nature may involve replacement of many, if not most, of the major components in a weapon (including the nuclear components), the weapon that comes off the refurbishment assembly line can easily look identical to, but be quite different in its military characteristics from, the one that entered the line. At this point, we encounter directly the need to evaluate intent. It would seem that evaluating and managing intent is well beyond the scope of any verification treaty that could be expected to be negotiated in the real world.

Distinguishing between new production and surveillance activities is midway between the two previous examples of maintenance and refurbishment activities. Most surveillance activities look a lot like maintenance activities and could be accommodated in much the same way by the verification protocols. However, some surveillance activities might involve destructive evaluation of the pit or the secondary, and they could potentially require monitoring pit production and secondary production to assure that the weapon that emerged from these surveillance activities did not have improved military characteristics.

Problems Potentially Associated with Verification Violations

For Nuclear Weapon States

Obviously, the verification strategies discussed in this chapter have been constructed around the premise that all the nuclear weapon states of the world would have a common desire to (1) limit the number of nuclear weapon states, (2) verify the number of nuclear weapons held by each nuclear weapon state, and (3) reduce the number of weapons held by each nuclear weapon state in such a way as to move toward smaller world stockpiles. An important question is obvious: how would violators be managed or punished? The answer would seem to be "If a state violates those objectives it could be exposed as a violator of the agreements and potentially expelled from the operative treaty." Such sanctions might, or might not, be adequate measures to keep the multiple parties working toward the common goal.

In the event of a violation of the verification protocols, and especially in view of the potential military dangers associated with such violations, one would expect that the original agreement documents (the treaties) would state the processes that would be followed if military action appeared to be necessary of consideration. If all the agreements were conducted under auspices of the United Nations, it would be logical that the UN would take action (military, if necessary) against violators. If the agreements were done outside UN auspices, it is not at all obvious what form of military action would be contemplated by the language of the agreements. However, it is obvious that failure to incorporate appropriate sanctioning language into the agreements would invite violations and lead eventually to discrediting and destruction of the agreements. Presumably, unilateral or multilateral military force would be the ultimate sanction that might be employed.

For Non–Nuclear Weapon States

A new, or modified, nonproliferation treaty would seem to be the structure that could be most easily used to cover all the potential, new nuclear weapon states. As stated previously, all states with nuclear operations would have to agree to a rigorous inventory verification and inspection regime. The key to success would be the manner whereby inspections were required following suspected violations of the verification protocols. History has shown that suspect countries do not readily submit to intrusive inspections of suspect facilities.

Key Areas for Research or Further Analysis

It will be necessary to seek and obtain better methods to detect and identify fissile materials, at high resolution, in remote and nonintrusive ways.

An additional, difficult task will be to develop new ideas to help maintain technically competent nuclear weapons scientists, engineers, and production workers when, in the future, the stockpiles of the major nuclear powers become relatively small and there is little challenging design or production work for the key technical personnel to do. However, the "road to zero" and the challenge of protecting the world from nuclear terror involves technical challenges that call for the same skills as needed for the enterprise of nuclear weapon development and production, but oriented along a different national mission. The device used by a nuclear terrorist will not necessarily look like a design in the U.S. stockpile, but the sophisticated capability for science-based prediction that was developed for the U.S. Stockpile Stewardship Program can be adapted to this new mission, which would be focused on the national security goals of nonproliferation, nuclear energy development, and nuclear security.

The problems described in this chapter of approaching the goal of zero nuclear weapons are indeed formidable. We can only call for yet more study of this very fundamental problem of devising the world verification and inspection systems and authorities for a world seeking to eliminate, with confidence, nuclear weapons from its future.

Notes

1. Weapon *maintenance* is the activity to repair superficial problems with deployed weapons, or to replace limited life components.

2. Weapon *surveillance* is scheduled activity designed to examine many of the components in a nuclear weapon and check their functionality and overall condition.

3. Weapon *refurbishment* is a general overhaul operation conducted on a particular set of weapons to restore their condition to that of a new production weapon.

4. *New-build weapons* are those that have recently been manufactured.

5. Weapons-grade plutonium is plutonium that has had limited irradiation of the uranium fuel so that not too many of the higher isotopes of plutonium have been generated.

6. Boosting is a modern weapon design feature whereby the addition of a small amount of deuterium-tritium gas to the primary results in fusion yield during the functioning of the primary, to boost the yield.

7. The *primary* (consisting of the Pu or HEU pit plus its explosive system) is the fission stage of a weapon, where fission yield is achieved by implosion of the Pu or HEU component. The *secondary* is the second stage of a two-stage modern weapon, in which HEU components in combination with lithium-deuterium components are imploded by the functioning of the primary, thereby producing thermonuclear fusion yield.

8. Stephen M. Younger, *Wall Street Journal,* "Taming the Nuclear Dragon," January 10, 2009; J. T. Richelson, *Spying on the Bomb* (New York: Norton, 2007), 35–96 and 195–218.

9. Ibid.

10. Ibid.

11. Younger, "Taming the Nuclear Dragon"; Richelson, *Spying on the Bomb*, 136–194.

12. Younger, "Taming the Nuclear Dragon"; Richelson, *Spying on the Bomb*, 236–265; M. Vanunu, in Richelson, *Spying on the Bomb*, 360–370.

13.. Younger, "Taming the Nuclear Dragon"; Richelson, *Spying on the Bomb*, 218–235, 427–435.

14. Younger, "Taming the Nuclear Dragon"; Richelson, *Spying on the Bomb*, 327–333.

15. Younger, "Taming the Nuclear Dragon"; Richelson, *Spying on the Bomb*, 317–359; Choe Sang-Hun, "North Korea Says It Has 'Weaponized' Plutonium," *New York Times,* January 18, 2009.

16. See Sang-Hun, "North Korea Says It Has 'Weaponized' Plutonium"; and Richelson, *Spying on the Bomb*.

17. Richelson, *Spying on the Bomb*, 243–291.

7. Verifying Reductions and Elimination of Tactical Nuclear Weapons

STEVEN P. ANDREASEN

The Uncharted Nuclear Waters

With the exception of the U.S.-Soviet/Russian Presidential Nuclear Initiatives (PNIs) in 1991 and 1992 and—more tangentially—the 1987 Intermediate-Range Nuclear Forces (INF) Treaty, tactical (or nonstrategic) nuclear weapons have remained outside bilateral U.S.-Russian arms control discussions and agreements. Moreover, the PNIs and INF Treaty provided little in the way of monitoring or verification of U.S. and Russian tactical nuclear weapons inventories—though the PNIs led to perhaps 17,000 tactical nuclear weapons being withdrawn from service. There are no agreements regarding tactical nuclear weapons that apply to nations who possess them other than the United States and Russia.

In 1997, Presidents Clinton and Yeltsin agreed that in the context of START III negotiations, the United States and Russia would explore as separate issues possible measures relating to nuclear long-range sea-launched cruise missiles and tactical nuclear systems, to include appropriate confidence building and transparency measures.[1] However, consultations on a START III Treaty ended with the onset of the Bush administration in 2001. The 2002 Moscow Treaty applies only to operationally deployed strategic nuclear warheads.

Tactical nuclear weapons are considered to be the most likely targets for terrorist acquisition of a nuclear bomb. Their small size and uncertain use control mechanisms—in particular, in older weapons and weapons deployed by states other than the United States and Russia—contribute to their vulnerability to theft and unauthorized use.

In two op-eds published in the *Wall Street Journal* in 2007 and 2008, former secretaries of state George Shultz and Henry Kissinger, former secretary of defense William Perry, and former senator Sam Nunn argued for eliminating short-range nuclear weapons designed to be forward deployed. They also suggested starting a dialogue, including within NATO and with Russia, on consolidating the nuclear weapons designed for forward deployment to enhance their security and as a first step toward careful accounting for them and their eventual elimination. These steps relating to tactical nuclear weapons are a subset of a series of practical measures advocated by "the four" as part of an initiative to achieve a world free of nuclear weapons.[2]

This chapter examines issues and alternatives for monitoring and verifying reductions and elimination of tactical nuclear weapons consistent with achieving the vision of a world free of nuclear weapons through the pursuit of practical steps consistent with that goal.

For the purposes of this chapter, *tactical nuclear weapons* refers to all nuclear weapons intended for use with nonstrategic nuclear delivery systems—that is, any nuclear weapon not intended for use on a long-range ballistic missile (ICBM or SLBM) or Heavy Bomber. These nonstrategic nuclear weapons can be delivered by aircraft or missiles deployed on land or at sea, as well as by artillery, torpedoes, and mines.

It should be noted that other definitions of what constitutes a tactical nuclear weapon are possible. For example, one possible alternative would be to apply the term only to those nuclear weapons intended for use with delivery systems with a range less than 300 miles. This less inclusive definition would in practice mean that some nuclear weapon states other than the United States and Russia would have both tactical and strategic nuclear weapons, based on the range characteristics of various delivery systems (aircraft and missiles) in their respective inventories. While this may better reflect the reality of how these states view their nuclear weapons—that is, as a strategic versus tactical deterrent—it could also complicate any approach to monitoring and verification.[3]

Issues Associated with Verifying Reductions and Elimination of Tactical Nuclear Weapons

Prior to reviewing various alternatives for verifying reductions and elimination of tactical nuclear weapons, it will be useful for Washington to think carefully about the specific issues that are associated with this task.

The first issue pertains to what is known regarding the size and disposition of global inventories of tactical nuclear weapons. As is the case with overall global nuclear inventories (i.e., approximately 20,000 nuclear warheads—both strategic and tactical—worldwide),[4] there is significant uncertainty over the size and location of global inventories of tactical nuclear weapons.

To begin, it is important to note that tactical nuclear weapons constitute a large percentage of the arsenals of the nuclear weapon states— by one estimate, perhaps 30 to 40 percent of the American and Russian arsenals; nearly 100 percent of the Chinese and French arsenals; and all of the Israeli, Indian, and Pakistani arsenals (Great Britain no longer has tactical nuclear weapons).[5]

According to published estimates, Russia is thought to possess the largest stockpile of tactical nuclear weapons, numbering between 3,000 and 8,000 total.[6] These warheads are distributed throughout the Russian armed forces—ground, air defense, air, and naval—located at both operational bases and central storage.

The United States is thought to possess approximately 1,670 tactical nuclear weapons, including 320 submarine-launched cruise missiles and 1,350 air-delivered B-61 gravity bombs. Approximately 150 to 240 of the B-61 bombs are deployed in Europe at six bases in five NATO countries. The rest of the B-61 inventory along with the submarine-launched cruise missiles are stored in the United States.[7]

Outside the United States and Russia, France, China, Israel, India, Pakistan, and North Korea have approximately 800 tactical nuclear weapons—either air-delivered nuclear bombs or nuclear warheads for short-, medium-, and intermediate-range ballistic missiles.[8]

The second issue is to determine the key monitoring and verification tasks associated with the reduction and elimination of tactical nuclear weapons. To a large extent, the key monitoring and verification tasks associated with the reduction and elimination of tactical nuclear weapons mirror those for strategic nuclear weapons. In the context of creating an overall regime designed to support efforts to achieve a world free of nuclear weapons, five basic tasks are associated with monitoring and verifying the reduction and elimination of tactical nuclear weapons:

- **Task 1:** a historical account of tactical nuclear weapon production and pre-agreement elimination
- **Task 2:** a detailed exchange of data regarding existing tactical nuclear weapon stockpiles
- **Task 3:** verification of existing tactical nuclear weapon stockpiles
- **Task 4:** verification of tactical nuclear weapon destruction and fissile material storage and final disposition
- **Task 5:** Inspection of suspect sites

The third issue is whether monitoring and verifying reductions and elimination of tactical nuclear weapons can be divorced from monitoring and verification of the reduction and elimination of strategic nuclear weapons in the United States and Russia. While the basic verification tasks associated with monitoring and verification of reductions and elimination of tactical nuclear weapons mirror those for strategic nuclear weapons, one could design a monitoring and verification regime that purported to cover "only" tactical nuclear inventories. Specifically, the data exchanges regarding historical production and existing stockpiles and associated monitoring and verification tasks would be applied only to tactical nuclear weapons.

There may also be some benefit to a segregated approach. In the U.S.-Russia context, the PNIs provide a possible political template that could be expanded to include monitoring and verification of tactical nuclear weapons, perhaps initially as a manageable subcomponent of the overall problem (though it should be noted that questions over Russian compliance with their PNI commitments may undercut the validity of the PNI template). Moreover, disaggregated information exchanged and verified regarding tactical nuclear weapons would provide greater insight into a long-obscured aspect of U.S. and Russian nuclear inventories. Finally, focusing on monitoring and verification of tactical nuclear weapons in the United States and Russia may provide at least a rhetorical stepping stone into tactical nuclear inventories held by other nations.

That said, in practice, such a regime may be difficult to credibly segregate from strategic nuclear weapons. To begin, it will be difficult, if not impossible, to distinguish a "tactical" from a "strategic" nuclear weapon—complicating any attempt to monitor and verify data that purports to deal only with tactical nuclear weapons inventories. For example, both the United States and Russia reportedly co-locate strategic and tactical nuclear weapons at certain facilities, which complicates attempts to monitor or verify numbers of weapons or their disposition, including their absence or presence at any facility or location.

Finally, at some point in the process of getting to zero, monitoring and verification of all nuclear weapons, tactical and strategic, will need to be merged. It may be simpler and more effective—albeit potentially more time intensive—to construct a regime that takes this into account at the outset, rather than at some later point in the process.

The fourth issue is what extent do U.S. and Russian interests overlap or diverge with respect to tactical nuclear weapons—and similarly, to determine what are the interests of other states with tactical nuclear weapon inventories. Since 1991 and the imminent dissolution of the Soviet Union, the United States has been concerned over the disposition and security of Russian tactical nuclear inventories. The sheer size of Russia's tactical nuclear stockpile along with concerns over security and use control of these weapons continue to be a concern for the United States and a threat to American and global security. For these reasons, the United States has been focused—albeit intermittently—on consolidating and securing Russia's tactical nuclear inventory, along with encouraging reductions in Russia's tactical nuclear weapons stockpile.

Russia has made clear it does not share U.S. concerns over the security of Russia's tactical nuclear inventory; and since 1991, it has viewed these weapons and the threat of first-use as critical in offsetting Russia's reduced conventional capabilities vis-à-vis NATO and perhaps other nations—as well as one of the few marks on the nuclear ledger where Russia retains a perceived if not real advantage.

Russia continues to press for U.S. withdrawal of tactical nuclear weapons from Europe, noting that America is the only nation to deploy tactical nuclear weapons outside its own territory. Indeed, Russia may insist on the withdrawal of U.S. tactical nuclear weapons from Europe as a prerequisite to any discussion of reductions and elimination of tactical nuclear weapons, perhaps complicating any U.S. diplomatic nuclear initiative. Moreover, Russia has raised other concerns over various aspects of U.S. nuclear and military posture and is likely to raise these concerns in discussions over tactical nuclear weapons (e.g., conventional global strike capabilities and missile defense).

With respect to other nations, given their relative inexperience with and lack of participation in the process of nuclear arms control, as well as concerns over divulging sensitive information relating to their limited nuclear stockpile to a potential adversary (where lack of transparency is seen as a strategic asset and crucial to deterrence), they would seemingly be resistant to each and every one of the five verification tasks outlined in the discussion of the second issue (i.e., a historical account of production; data exchange regarding current inventories; verification of existing stockpiles and the destruction, storage, and disposition of those stockpiles; and inspection of suspect sites). While it is possible that a less inclusive definition of tactical nuclear weapons (e.g., one where the term applied only to those weapons intended for use with nonstrategic nuclear delivery systems with a range less than 300 miles) could alleviate some concerns regarding divulging sensitive information, the problem is likely to persist, no matter what the definition.

The fifth issue is to what extent the process of monitoring and verification of reductions and elimination of tactical nuclear weapons can and should be global in scope from the outset, as opposed to bilateral between the United States and Russia. The United States and Russia today possess nuclear stockpiles, strategic and tactical, that dwarf those of all other nations. Moreover, American and Russian leadership will be required to reinvigorate nuclear arms reductions. These two facts—combined with years of bilateral experience in nuclear arms talks—might argue for a bilateral U.S.-Russian approach to monitoring and verification of tactical nuclear weapons, at least at the outset.

For example, the United States and Russia could proceed bilaterally with monitoring and verification of tactical nuclear weapons until such time as the process of bilateral nuclear reductions in the United States and Russia resulted in nuclear force levels approaching the combined total of other nuclear weapon states (e.g., 1,000 nuclear warheads). At that time, other nations could be brought into the monitoring and verification regime.

That said, achieving a world without nuclear weapons will by definition involve all nuclear weapon states, as well as those states with the ability to produce nuclear material for weapons. Achieving buy-in from other nuclear weapon states regarding monitoring and verification of their own nuclear stockpiles might be best achieved through early involvement of these nations in designing a monitoring and verification regime.

In summary, a process that is U.S.-Russia centric at the outset might facilitate early progress on devising a monitoring and verification regime applied only to United States and Russian tactical nuclear weapons. However, not involving other nuclear weapon states might undermine the potential for devising a truly global monitoring and verification regime for nuclear arms, as well as a global prohibition. Alternatively, a process that envisions the early involvement of other nations—many of which have little incentive for transparency in their nuclear weapons programs or experience in arms control—risks bogging down.

Alternatives for Verifying Reductions and Elimination of Tactical Nuclear Weapons

Examining and ultimately choosing among alternative approaches for verifying reductions and elimination of tactical nuclear weapons requires an assessment based on a set of uniform evaluative criteria. The preceding discussion suggests at least three criteria that are relevant to this problem. First, will the approach allow the United States to effectively monitor and verify reductions and elimination of tactical nuclear weapons? Second, will the approach create early momentum behind both the vision and the steps? Third, will the approach be inclusive enough to prevent an "outsider dynamic" where states that are not equally involved at the outset refuse to take part at a later date?

Alternative 1: U.S.-Russia Pilot Program

One alternative would be a U.S.-Russia pilot program regarding reduction and elimination of tactical nuclear weapons. Under this approach, the United States and Russia would designate X number of tactical nuclear weapons for a pilot monitoring and verification program. These weapons would be monitored from their current deployment/storage location through the process of dismantlement, destruction, and final disposition. Lessons learned from this exercise would be used in constructing a monitoring and verification regime that could be applied to all tactical nuclear weapons.

In the near term, a pilot program would by definition not provide for effective monitoring and verification of reductions and elimination of tactical nuclear weapons. This approach could, however, provide a valuable set of lessons learned and—more ambitiously—a template for constructing an effective regime for monitoring and verification.

A U.S.-Russia agreement to pursue a pilot program relating to monitoring and verification of reductions and elimination of tactical nuclear weapons would be seen as a positive step toward the elimination of tactical nuclear weapons, consistent with both the vision and steps—and, in that sense, would create early momentum behind both the vision and the steps.

Finally, a pilot program relating to monitoring and verification of reductions and elimination of tactical nuclear weapons that included other nuclear weapon states and other nations from the outset (e.g., the United Kingdom, Norway, France, or China) could be the most opportune and ideal way to prevent an outsider dynamic from taking hold, without requiring a commitment from these nations to participate fully or even partially in a subsequent monitoring and verification regime.

That said, an exclusive U.S.-Russia pilot program that did not involve other nuclear weapon states from the outset could provide a political basis for excluded nations to opt out of any future regime for monitoring and verification of their own nuclear stockpiles. Moreover, a pilot program that did not involve other nuclear weapon states might develop certain measures that would not be adequate for or applicable to the task of monitoring and verification outside the United States and Russia, providing a substantive basis for nations to remain outside any future regime. These problems might be mitigated somewhat if the U.S.-Russia program were transparent in terms of what was being done and how, and if the lessons learned—albeit not in terms of the data itself—were made available to other nations as a way of providing all countries a basis for future decision making and for possible future multilateralization.

Alternative 2: Politically Binding Transparency and Confidence Building

A second alternative would be developing U.S.-Russia politically binding transparency and confidence building regarding reduction and elimination of tactical nuclear weapons. Under this approach, the United States and Russia would agree to apply to all tactical nuclear weapons any agreed measures relating to transparency and confidence building. These measures could include verification tasks 1 and 2 (i.e., a data exchange regarding historical production and preagreement elimination and existing stockpiles) and reciprocal visits to deployment, storage, destruction, and final disposition facilities—perhaps including measures relating to U.S./European bases where U.S. tactical nuclear weapons are or were previously stored.

Politically binding transparency and confidence-building measures involving data exchanges and site visits relating to tactical nuclear weapons inventories are likely to increase our understanding of Russian tactical nuclear weapons inventories, and would do so more than Alternative 1. Confidence-building and transparency measures applied only to tactical nuclear weapons would, however, not provide for effective monitoring and verification, in that it would not be a comprehensive regime applied to all five verification tasks identified earlier, including suspect sites, and it would not include strategic nuclear weapons, thus introducing significant uncertainties. That said, even more than alternative 1, this approach could provide a valuable set of lessons learned and—more ambitiously—a template for constructing an effective regime for monitoring and verification.

Even more than Alternative 1, a U.S.-Russia agreement in 2010 to apply transparency and confidence-building measures to all tactical nuclear weapons inventories would be seen as a positive step toward the elimination of tactical nuclear weapons, consistent with both the vision and steps. Reaching an agreement in 2010 on even a limited set of transparency and confidence-building measures would, however, require an intensive effort by both the United States and Russia and may not be possible.

Finally, even more than Alternative 1, an exclusive U.S.-Russia agreement on transparency and confidence-building measures covering tactical nuclear weapons that did not involve other nuclear weapon states from the outset could provide a political or substantive basis for excluded nations to opt out of any regime covering their own nuclear stockpiles.

Alternative 3: Legally Binding Monitoring and Verification

A third alternative would be U.S.-Russia legally binding monitoring and verification regarding reduction and elimination of tactical nuclear weapons. Under this approach, the United States and Russia would agree to consolidate, reduce, and eliminate their tactical nuclear weapons stockpiles on an agreed timetable, and they would apply all five of the basic monitoring and verification tasks outlined earlier (i.e., an exchange of data regarding historical production and preagreement elimination and existing stockpiles; verification of existing stockpiles and their destruction and final disposition; and inspection of suspect sites). An early step in this process might be the creation of a European Exclusion Zone, where U.S. and Russian tactical nuclear weapons were prohibited within a defined European geography, including monitoring and verification measures applied to U.S./European bases where U.S. tactical nuclear weapons were previously located as well as former Russian tactical nuclear weapon sites (where the initial focus would be to monitor and verify the absence of weapons, rather than their elimination per se).

A legally binding, comprehensive approach to monitoring and verifying reductions and elimination of tactical nuclear weapons would provide greater confidence than Alternatives 1 or 2, but still would be open to circumvention (e.g., by underdeclaring initial holdings, covert production, etc.). Confidence would also be undermined if the regime were not also applied to strategic nuclear weapons.

Initiating work on a legally binding comprehensive approach to monitoring and verifying reductions in tactical nuclear weapons could be seen as a positive development in 2010, consistent with the vision and steps, more than for Alternative 1 and perhaps to about the same extent as Alternative 2. That said, reaching an agreement in 2010 on a comprehensive approach—even one that applied just to tactical (as opposed to all) nuclear weapons—would seem unlikely.

Like Alternatives 1 and (especially) 2, an exclusive U.S.-Russia agreement on monitoring and verifying reductions and elimination of tactical nuclear weapons that did not involve other nuclear weapon states from the outset could provide a political or substantive basis for excluded nations to opt out of any regime covering their own nuclear stockpiles. Indeed, the risk presumably is greater in the context of developing a legally binding, comprehensive regime in the absence of input from other nations.

Alternative 4: A Legally Binding, Integrated Approach with Strategic Nuclear Weapons

A fourth alternative would be a U.S.-Russia legally binding, integrated approach with strategic nuclear weapons regarding reduction and elimination of tactical nuclear weapons. Under this approach, the United States and Russia would apply the approach specified in Alternatives 1, 2, or 3 to both strategic and tactical nuclear weapons.

A legally binding, comprehensive approach to monitoring and verifying reductions and elimination of tactical and strategic nuclear weapons would provide greater confidence than Alternatives 1, 2, or 3—at least with respect to Russia's nuclear stockpile, but still would be open to circumvention (e.g., by underdeclaring initial holdings, covert production, etc.).

Like Alternative 3, initiating work on a legally binding comprehensive approach to monitoring and verifying reductions in tactical and strategic nuclear weapons could be seen as a positive development in 2010, consistent with the vision and steps. But also like Alternative 3, reaching an agreement in 2010 on a comprehensive approach—this one involving both tactical and strategic nuclear weapons—would seem unlikely.

Like Alternatives 1, 2, and 3, an exclusive U.S.-Russia agreement on monitoring and verifying reductions and elimination of tactical and strategic nuclear weapons that did not involve other nuclear weapon states from the outset could provide a political or substantive basis for excluded nations to opt out of any regime covering their own nuclear stockpiles. Also like Alternative 3, the risk presumably would be greater in the context of developing a legally binding, comprehensive regime—this one involving both tactical and strategic nuclear weapons—in the absence of input from other nations.

Alternative 5: A Multilateral Approach

A fifth alternative would be a multilateral versus U.S.-Russia approach. Under this approach, the United States would seek to apply Alternatives 1, 2, 3, or 4 to all nuclear weapon states, not just itself and Russia.

In each option, the addition of other nuclear weapon states beyond the United States and Russia would be a net plus in terms of effective monitoring and verification (though it would require greater monitoring resources applied over a broader territory). The limitations of each alternative with respect to effective monitoring and verification as previously noted in Alternatives 1, 2, 3, and 4 would, however, still apply—and may be exacerbated if greater monitoring resources are not made available.

In each alternative, the addition of other nuclear weapon states beyond the United States and Russia could at least at the outset create a greater perception—if not reality—of early momentum behind the vision and the steps. It is also true, however, that the addition of other states beyond the United States and Russia could delay any agreements under Alternatives 1, 2, 3, or 4—perhaps leading to a real stalemate that would undermine momentum behind the vision and steps. This problem could be mitigated somewhat by a more restrictive definition of what is a "tactical" nuclear weapon (e.g., where the term applied only to those weapons intended for use with nonstrategic nuclear delivery systems with a range less than 300 miles).

Opening the door to the inclusion of all nuclear weapon states—and possibly other nations (e.g., Norway)—in the development and implementation of each option would potentially minimize any risk of an outsider dynamic. That said, it is unlikely that every nuclear weapon state would participate in the development and implementation of Alternatives 1, 2, 3, or 4; so the risk of an outsider dynamic providing either a political or substantive basis for "nonparticipating" nations to opt out of any future regime covering their own nuclear stockpiles would remain, which could render the resulting situation less effective and provide less momentum than full participation.

A Path Forward

This analysis highlights a number of trade-offs—both substantive and diplomatic—that will need to be considered in the context of monitoring and verifying reductions and elimination of tactical nuclear weapons. In particular, two basic considerations will need to be addressed:

- Whether to seek to work this problem separate from or in concert with the issue of monitoring and verifying reductions in strategic nuclear weapons
- Whether the United States should seek to work this problem from the outset as a U.S.-Russia issue, or whether to seek the involvement of other states

The approach taken regarding monitoring and verification of tactical nuclear weapons—in particular, with respect to these two points—may well be determined by what template is used by the Obama administration to achieve its stated goal of further nuclear reductions beyond the New START agreement.

One possible template would be to seek further reductions in U.S. and Russian nuclear stockpiles by simply amending downward the numerical ceilings in the 2010 New START agreement, assuming that treaty is approved in both countries and enters into force. Using the existing New START framework may be the fastest and the surest route to further reductions; but it would continue to leave tactical nuclear weapons outside the process—and therefore place a premium on doing "something separate" on tactical nuclear weapons, at least in a U.S.-Russia context.

Another possible approach would be to seek to move away from the New START framework without delay and to construct a new template for nuclear reductions, one whose limits were applied to nuclear warheads of all types and where monitoring and verification was applied to warheads not delivery vehicles—and seek to involve other nations in the process. While this approach may be inevitable in the context of moving toward a world free of nuclear weapons, adopting it now could significantly complicate nuclear diplomacy and extend the time for reaching any agreement on further nuclear reductions.

It might be possible—and even desirable—to defer a decision on those two basic considerations (that is, whether to work the problem of tactical nuclear weapons together or separate from strategic weapons; and whether to involve other nations), depending on the alternative chosen. For example, Alternative 1—a pilot program regarding reduction and elimination of nuclear weapons—could be proposed without prejudging whether the pilot program would be applied to tactical and strategic nuclear weapons (consistent with the intent of Alternative 4) and combined with Alternative 5 (a multilateral approach) to test the willingness of other states to participate in the process of monitoring and verifying reductions and elimination of nuclear weapons. One way to do this would be to make explicit that the assumptions guiding both the scope of and participation in any pilot program are not intended to prejudge the final scope or participation of any subsequent arrangements.

Similarly, an approach that does not prejudge the question of whether to include both tactical and strategic nuclear weapons and seeks the involvement of other nations at the outset could also be used with respect to Alternative 2—politically binding transparency and confidence-building measures. That said, those nuclear weapon states who decide not to participate in a multilateral pilot program (or transparency and confidence-building measures) would be conspicuous by their absence. This may work against their eventual participation in any regime.

Moving directly to Alternative 3 (legally-binding monitoring and verification regarding reduction and elimination of tactical nuclear weapons) or Alternative 4 (a legally-binding, integrated approach with strategic nuclear weapons regarding reduction and elimination of tactical nuclear weapons) may be more difficult to execute at the outset in a multilateral context (Alternative 5), as all other nuclear weapon states may be less likely to commit to participate in a legally-binding framework as opposed to Alternative 1 (Pilot Program) or 2 (politically binding transparency and confidence building measures).

Ascertaining Russian views regarding whether to include both tactical and strategic nuclear weapons and whether to involve other nations at the outset will be essential, if not determinative. There cannot be an effective approach to monitoring and verifying reductions and elimination of tactical nuclear weapons that does not involve Russia from the outset. In particular, while combining tactical and strategic nuclear weapons is both logically and practically inevitable, diplomatically, it may remain difficult in the near term vis-à-vis Russia.

Finally, it will be important to consider how the question of verifying reductions and elimination of tactical nuclear weapons—and other questions posed by the inclusion of tactical nuclear weapons in future arms control—fits into the broader fabric of U.S. arms control policy (e.g., whether to press for a global INF Treaty banning INF-range ballistic and cruise missiles in all states that possess them, where the focus would remain on delivery vehicles, not warheads); and the political viability, in both Washington and Moscow, of any subsequent U.S.-Russian agreement on further reductions in nuclear forces. One conclusion seems clear: tactical nuclear weapons can no longer remain the uncharted waters of arms control policy.

Notes

1. "Text: Joint Statement on Parameters of Future Nuclear Reductions," Clinton-Yeltsin Summit, Helsinki, March 21, 1997, www.nti.org/db/nisprofs/fulltext/statemen/helsinki/s3helsin.htm.

2. George P. Shultz, William J. Perry, Henry A. Kissinger, and Sam Nunn, "A World Free of Nuclear Weapons," *Wall Street Journal*, January 4, 2007; and "Toward a Nuclear Free World," *Wall Street Journal*, January 15, 2008.

3. Moreover, in a U.S.-Russia context, the "300-mile" definition would almost certainly have to include in practice any sea-launched nuclear cruise missile or air-delivered nuclear weapon intended for use with a submarine or non–heavy bomber. Otherwise, the United States and Russia could exclude all or part of their inventory of sea-launched nuclear cruise missiles or air-delivered bombs on the grounds they were intended for use with nonstrategic nuclear delivery systems with a range greater than 300 miles.

4. International Panel on Fissile Materials, "Global Nuclear Inventories," www.fissilematerials.org/ipfm/pages_us_en/fissile/inventories/inventories .php.

5. Nuclear Threat Initiative, "Issue Brief: Tactical Nuclear Weapons," www.nti.org/e_research/e3_10a.html.

6. Rose Gottemoeller, "Eliminating Short-Range Nuclear Weapons Designed to Be Forward Deployed," *Reykjavik Revisited: Steps toward a World Free of Nuclear Weapons* (San Francisco: Hoover Institution Press 2008), 157.

7. Nuclear Threat Initiative, "Issue Brief: Tactical Nuclear Weapons."

8. Ibid.

8. The Role of the IAEA in a World Reducing Stocks of Nuclear Weapons

THOMAS E. SHEA

The Fissile Material Agenda

Fissile materials remain essential for nuclear weapons. Therefore controls on fissile materials are fundamental to nonproliferation and will provide an important venue to encourage and support future arms reductions and complementary measures aimed at the eventual elimination of all nuclear weapons. Nuclear weapons were acquired by states facing existential security threats. If progress is to be made toward a nuclear weapon–free world, each nuclear-armed state—and every other state relying on nuclear security assurances from a nuclear-armed state—must assure its national security before, during, and after each successive step.

While individual states may opt out of nuclear weapons unilaterally, global nuclear disarmament is likely to proceed in stages with significant periods to digest each adjustment. International monitoring and verification offers a means to sustain and encourage additional progress. Appropriate monitoring and verification steps could confirm that nuclear-armed states are honoring the commitments associated with each phase, thereby creating a new baseline with each measured step and setting the stage for the next. International monitoring and verification could also play an important role in detecting noncompliance, providing all states threatened by such a step with means and opportunities to avert crises.

International participation is built into Article VI of the Non-Proliferation Treaty (NPT), so it isn't a question of whether there will be international participation, only when, what specific missions, and which particular organizations. Progress toward nuclear disarmament will likely involve unilateral, bilateral, and multilateral steps. While unilateral and bilateral agreements are steps in the right direction, multilateral negotiations will provide uniform terms and conditions, reduce costs, enhance transparency, provide a neutral platform, and connect to existing nonproliferation measures much more clearly than if limited disarmament steps are taken without international participation.

Fissile Material Controls

Eight technical missions could serve to lock in progress on the road to disarmament and stimulate additional activities (see table 8.1). These are (1) monitoring arms reductions and inventories; (2) monitoring the storage and conversion of classified forms of fissile material to remove its classified properties; (3) monitoring the disposition of fissile material surplus to a nuclear-armed state's defense requirements; (4) applying International Atomic Energy Agency (IAEA) safeguards to unclassified forms of fissile material; (5) verifying a fissile material cutoff treaty (FMCT); (6) analyzing the historical production of fissile material and its disposition to come up with best estimates of current inventories; (7) analyzing the history of nuclear weapons in a nuclear-armed state; and (8) implementing a system of controls on the production, storage, and use of one of the basic fusion materials used in nuclear weapons, tritium.

These eight should be seen as pieces of a puzzle that will eventually need to be completed. Opportunity and interest could determine the order in which they are added, and some nuclear-armed states may not follow others. Progress on several could be pursued simultaneously. Of the eight, item 2 may be an attractive first step: based on the work

Table 8.1 Potential Technical Nuclear Disarmament Monitoring/Verification Activities for International Organizations.

No.	Potential Task	Required Capabilities	Implementation Arrangements
1	• Monitor storage and dismantling of warheads, and storage of pits and secondaries and other classified forms of fissile material, either in the context of negotiated arms reductions, or of monitoring caps on nuclear weapons arsenals, or on strategic reserves, for example.	• Seals/tracking devices suitable for nuclear weapons/components. • Verification systems acceptable to states and international organization. • Monitoring systems acceptable for use in classified environment.	• Verification agreements, perhaps based on model Trilateral Initiative agreement. • Authentication arrangements for monitoring/ verification use. • Security certification to assure that inspection does not lead to divulging classified information. • Trial exercises to gain confidence in approach.
2	• Monitor conversion of classified forms of fissile material to unclassified forms. • Monitor input of classified forms into conversion facility. • Apply safeguards on converted unclassified fissile material.	• Common architectural designs of conversion facilities incorporating features that allow monitoring all inputs, assure no undeclared inputs, verify all outputs. • Verification/monitoring systems as for #1. • Safeguards on unclassified products according to standard IAEA equipment/procedures.	• Create organization, staff, train, and execute mission. • Develop reporting arrangements with states subject to monitoring/ verification, also to policymaking organs, public.
3	• Monitor the disposition of plutonium excess to a nuclear-armed state's nuclear weapon requirements, as foreseen in the U.S.-Russian Plutonium Management and Disposition Agreement (PMDA) of 2000.	• Depends on scope of monitoring requested of the IAEA.	• Create and conclude verification/monitoring agreements between the IAEA (specifically mentioned in the PMDA) and the Russian Federation and with the United States.
4	• Safeguard unclassified forms of fissile material from civil and military sources.	• Safeguards on unclassified forms of fissile material according to standard IAEA equipment/ procedures.	• Need protocol to NPT nuclear weapon state voluntary offer IAEA safeguards agreements to make this mission mandatory. • Non NPT nuclear-armed states need new safeguards agreement for this purpose.

(Continued)

Table 8.1 *(continued)* Potential Technical Nuclear Disarmament Monitoring/
Verification Activities for International Organizations.

No.	Potential Task	Required Capabilities	Implementation Arrangements
5	• Verify Fissile Material Production Cutoff Treaty (FMCT) according to specific provisions.	• Age-dating capability to detect production after entry into force. • Environmental sampling capability to detect undeclared production facilities/operations, in locations where standard methods would divulge classified information on design/manufacturing of nuclear weapons. • Verification approaches required according to treaty provisions, including trials.	• Create and conclude verification/monitoring agreements between international organization and parties to FMCT.
6	• Examine history of fissile material production and use.	• Further develop isotope ratio method for estimating plutonium production reactor yield. • Develop procedures for estimating plutonium reprocessing yields and accountancy methods. • Develop procedures for estimating historical enriched uranium production and disposition.	• Create and conclude protocols for estimating fissile material inventories, including interviews with relevant personnel, use of measurement methods, and use of corroborating information.
7	• Examine/confirm nuclear weapon histories to determine total production, disposition, remaining arsenal.	• No technological developments required.	• Create and conclude protocols for historical analysis of production of nuclear weapons and their disposition, including interviews with relevant personnel and use of corroborating information.
8	• Verify controls on tritium production, storage, use.	• Establish accountancy system taking into account production, radioactive decay, consumption (e.g., radioisotope use, fusion fuel), losses. • Establish monitoring systems for production and storage installations. • Establish capabilities for verifying tritium use in peaceful applications.	• Create and conclude agreements for monitoring tritium production, peaceful use, withdrawals for nuclear weapon use.

carried out under the Trilateral Initiative, it represents a way for an individual state, or a small number of nuclear-armed states, to set in place a formal undertaking addressing one of the essential steps on the road to disarmament.

Agreeing to a road map of successive actions focusing on fissile material controls will allow pressures to be applied to engage all nuclear-armed states and sustain progress. The road map could include the following five steps:

- **Step 1:** Conclude and implement new agreements pursuant to the Trilateral Initiative between the IAEA and each of the states possessing nuclear weapons for the verification of fissile material released from military use but remaining in classified forms.
- **Step 2:** Bring into force arrangements for the IAEA to safeguard unclassified forms of fissile material that would be determined by states possessing nuclear weapons to be in excess to their current arsenal requirements, including civil stocks and stocks of fissile materials not clearly removed from defense programs.
- **Step 3:** Conclude and implement the FMCT.
- **Step 4:** Conclude and implement a convention on the phased reduction of existing nuclear arsenals. If successfully implemented, this convention could lead the world to the point where the nations retaining nuclear weapons would come to a maximum inventory of an agreed, small number (e.g., 25), and then determine how and when to go to zero, and what conditions should be created to facilitate such a monumental step.
- **Step 5:** Conclude and implement a nuclear disarmament treaty, bringing about the final elimination of nuclear weapons, establishing mechanisms to preclude their reintroduction, removing the distinctions within the NPT for two categories of states-parties (i.e., non–nuclear weapon states and nuclear weapon states), and bringing the NPT to universal acceptance. Negotiating a nuclear disarmament treaty in the near term would raise the need to decide on issues that cannot now be predicted and in any case do not yet require resolution.

Selecting the IAEA for Disarmament-Related Assignments

The selection of a verification authority for each of the steps identified may affect their acceptability and may determine their success. An ideal international organization should have a formal legal foundation and be accepted by the international community. It should have recognized status in terms of international relations, the authority to enter into binding commitments, and the financial, human, and physical resources appropriate for the work. It should have demonstrated technical competence or a certain means to acquire them, and available mechanisms for research and development to improve continuously its capabilities, practices, and procedures. It should have mechanisms to resolve disputes and conflicts that are appropriate to interactions with sovereign states. It should have inspired and engaged leadership and competent and motivated staff. It should have the ability to support—as requested—unilateral actions undertaken by a single nuclear-armed state, bilateral actions resulting from two-party arms reductions, and multilateral actions undertaken by any larger grouping of states. If an existing organization is to be considered for a task, it can be appraised in terms of these characteristics; if a new organization is to be created, these considerations can be used to design its charter and to review its operation.

That said, no institution is ideal and if it performs in an exemplary manner at one point, there is no guarantee that its excellent performance will continue. There is much to be said for tasking the IAEA to carry out missions related to nuclear disarmament. The potential missions identified in table 8.1 could all be undertaken by the IAEA; the question, rather, is what considerations should be taken into account when deciding whether to assign it a specific task. Some of the tasks very closely resemble the agency's current nonproliferation safeguards activities. Those involving warheads are rather distant.

In any discussion of international participation of disarmament, the IAEA is the obvious reference point for monitoring and verification missions involving fissile material:

1. IAEA safeguards focus on the peaceful use of nuclear materials, including fissile materials suitable for use in nuclear weapons and

hence its capabilities and experience are directly relevant. The IAEA is a *technical* organization carrying out activities embedded in a political environment. Scientists and engineers dominate the professional staff.

2. Expanding the IAEA's existing missions in relation to reducing world stocks of nuclear weapons appears to be consistent with existing provisions of the IAEA Statute:[1]

   a. The objective of the agency encompasses disarmament: "The Agency shall seek to accelerate and enlarge the contribution of atomic energy to peace, health and prosperity throughout the world. It shall ensure, so far as it is able, that assistance provided by it or at its request or under its supervision or control is not used in such a way as to further any military purpose" (Article II).

   b. The statute provision defining its safeguards mission is sufficiently flexible as to allow "safeguards" to be aimed at disarmament: "The Agency is authorized: . . . To establish and administer safeguards designed to ensure that special fissionable and other materials, services, equipment, facilities, and information made available by the Agency or at its request or under its supervision or control are not used in such a way as to further any military purpose; and to apply safeguards, at the request of the parties, to any bilateral or multilateral arrangement, or at the request of a State, to any of that State's activities in the field of atomic energy" (Article III.A.5).

   c. The IAEA is expressly instructed to support disarmament in its statute. To paraphrase: In carrying out its functions, the IAEA shall conduct its activities in accordance with the purposes and principles of the United Nations to promote peace and international cooperation, and in conformity with policies of the United Nations furthering the establishment of safeguarded worldwide disarmament and in conformity with any international agreements entered into pursuant to such policies (paraphrasing of Article III.B.1).

3. The IAEA is entrusted with responsibilities under United Nations Security Council Resolutions and many treaties and conventions.[2] Negotiations of IAEA safeguards agreements and their subsidiary

arrangements are carried out by the agency and the member state(s) involved, and, in addition, a number of conventions have been negotiated at the IAEA with the participation of the secretariat.[3] Any new conventions or agreements impacting the IAEA should be negotiated under its auspices, taking into account the ready access to the technical missions maintained in Vienna by many IAEA member states. The negotiation of any new *treaty* in which the IAEA or a new international organization might be assigned new tasks related to nuclear disarmament would presumably be assigned by United Nations General Assembly resolution, presumably to the United Nations Conference on Disarmament.

4. IAEA safeguards are carried out in accordance with safeguards agreements concluded between the agency and member states. IAEA safeguards agreements have the status of treaties (ratification of the U.S. safeguards agreement required the Senate to give its advice and consent). IAEA safeguards agreements obligate the non–nuclear weapon states to submit their nuclear facilities and materials to inspection and obligate the agency to carry out the inspections and other activities included under the safeguards system;

5. The IAEA has been tasked to undertake the following missions that are in the nature of nuclear disarmament:

   a. The IAEA director-general was assigned the role of dismantling the Iraqi nuclear weapons program pursuant to UNSCR 687 and subsequent resolutions. The IAEA worked alongside UNSCOM and UNMOVIC in resolving the nuclear portfolio in Iraq, receiving praise for the manner in which it carried out its mission.

   b. As part of determining the completeness of the initial declaration by South Africa following its decision to scrap its arsenal, the IAEA board of governors requested the director-general to examine the steps that South Africa had taken in dismantling its nuclear weapons and the disposing of its highly enriched uranium (HEU) inventory.[4]

   c. Under voluntary offer safeguards agreements with nuclear weapon states, the IAEA has undertaken steps that would prepare it to assume broader responsibilities in connection with arms control agreements:

- The United States placed 10 tons of HEU and 2 tons of plutonium released from defense requirements under IAEA safeguards and also arranged for the IAEA to verify HEU down-blending operations under its Voluntary Offer Safeguards Agreement and provided extra-budgetary contributions enabling the IAEA to inspect the materials involved.

- The IAEA applies safeguards at enrichment plants under arrangements worked out in a "hexapartite" group, which includes a URENCO plant at Capenhurst in the United Kingdom; IAEA safeguards are planned at three new gaseous centrifuge enrichment plants in the United States and one in France, and a laser enrichment plant to be constructed in the United States. Under a future FMCT the safeguards experience gained will likely be directly applicable to this and other facilities.

- China placed two enrichment facilities equipped with Russian centrifuges on its list of facilities from which the IAEA can choose to carry out inspections. The IAEA continues inspections at one facility (at Shaanxi) as a means to acquire experience that could be directly relevant should an FMCT including verification requirements enter into force. China, Russia, and the IAEA cooperated in a "tripartite" project to develop a safeguards approach for centrifuge enrichment facilities equipped with Russian centrifuges.

- Advanced safeguards development work carried out under the Department of Energy Advanced Fuel Cycle Initiative and the National Nuclear Security Administration Next Generation Safeguards Initiative will improve the national and international safeguards technology available for spent fuel recycle and enrichment plants, and these developments will impact future verification in relation to a fissile material cutoff treaty.

d. The Russian Federation, the United States, and the IAEA cooperated in a Trilateral Initiative to establish a verification system for classified forms of weapon-origin fissile material released from defense requirements. The Initiative was launched in 1996 by then IAEA director-general Hans Blix and was completed in 2002 following 98 trilateral meetings. By then, political leadership had changed in both countries, and neither of the new governments was prepared to implement the arrangements. In the course of the six years, a model verification agreement was developed; verification systems were invented that would allow IAEA monitoring without divulging sensitive nuclear weapon design or manufacturing information; facility-specific verification approaches were developed for IAEA monitoring at the Fissile Material Storage Facility at Mayak in the Russian Federation and at the K-Area Material Storage Facility at Savannah River in the United States; and concepts were elaborated for perimeter verification of conversion operations that would remove the classified properties from the fissile materials, enabling normal quantitative safeguards verification measures to be employed thereafter. When the Initiative was concluded in 2002, both Russia and the United States committed to continue toward implementation, but to date, no such steps have been taken.[5]

e. Acting in accordance with successive UN General Assembly resolutions requesting the IAEA to provide assistance as required for examination of verification arrangements for a nondiscriminatory, multilateral, and internationally and effectively verifiable treaty banning the production of fissile material for nuclear weapons or other nuclear explosive devices, the secretariat organized a working group to consider verification arrangements in relation to a fissile material cutoff treaty, and made many invited presentations to the UN Conference on Disarmament.[6]

f. Taking these factors into consideration, the principal arguments *for* choosing the IAEA for nuclear disarmament-related assignments are that the agency is already up and operating and it is highly respected by the international community. The core competence of the IAEA relative to nuclear arms reductions relates directly to its nuclear material safeguards activities: the IAEA knows how to recruit and train experts, it knows how to carry out inspections, and it knows how to confront noncompliance in ways that generally get the job done. By virtue of its experience in applying safeguards, in dismantling the nuclear weapons program in Iraq in cooperation with UNSCOM and later UNMOVIC, in rolling back the programs in South Africa and Libya, and in addressing specific challenges in North Korea, assigning the IAEA appropriate disarmament-related roles makes eminent sense.

Moreover, certain disarmament-related roles could complement the IAEA's existing safeguards functions and the expanded capabilities could benefit both. Conversely, choosing a new organization to carry out activities that are similar to IAEA safeguards could undermine IAEA safeguards by forcing the IAEA to compete with a new organization for the resources essential to its success.

Choosing the IAEA for disarmament roles would avoid another discriminatory arrangement that would somehow advantage the "haves" versus the "have-nots."

The principal argument *against* choosing the IAEA is the possibility that it could become so large and so distracted that it could lose its focus on nonproliferation and thereby damage the nonproliferation regime.

When deciding on the verification authority for each of the eight missions identified, two guiding principles should be foremost:

1. The IAEA should be assigned new missions that complement its nonproliferation safeguards mission; no other organization should be assigned any task that will duplicate in any way the activities carried out under IAEA safeguards, or that place the IAEA in a position where it would have to compete for financial and human resources.

2. The IAEA should be assigned no task that will undermine its nonproliferation mission, in particular by embroiling it in political machinations on the political dimensions of nuclear disarmament at the expense of its focus on nonproliferation.

Developing the Requisite Technological Capabilities Could Expedite Progress

While much of the technical capability required to implement the eight activities identified already exists in some form or another, each activity will need to be examined by each state to determine whether the state is comfortable with the method being used on its territory by the IAEA or another body, to determine whether the method might compromise secrets it is not prepared to have discovered, and whether it might compromise national technical measures currently employed as part of its intelligence apparatus. For sensitive methods, consideration should be given to whether a method is suitable for the IAEA to have; or, following the arrangements established for sharing intelligence information related to proliferation with the IAEA, whether information resulting from the national application of the method could be shared, and if so, under which circumstances and governing arrangements.

When it is time to consider whether a specific step might be contemplated, having the methods in hand could help it gain acceptance. Hence, it would be prudent to embark on coordinated development and demonstration activities.[7]

The following examples suggest some of the technical measures that could be developed by the verification organization or on its behalf for its own use and perhaps for use by the nuclear-armed states. At present, there are 20 Member State Support Programs providing technical assistance to the IAEA safeguards mission. IAEA member states would likely welcome the opportunity to develop the technical means to enable the IAEA to verify nuclear disarmament and might be prepared to undertake work even before formal tasking is decided.

Safeguarding unclassified forms of fissile material would require no unique methods or techniques, as essentially identical fissile material is already subject to IAEA safeguards in non–nuclear weapon states. Efforts to improve existing safeguards capabilities to improve their sensitivity or the cost effectiveness continue. Unclassified forms of fissile material will expand the IAEA's workload, require higher budgets, and benefit from tailored solutions taking into account the physical circumstances existing where inspections will be applied. But this mission is a straightforward extension, rather than a new departure.

Under the Trilateral Initiative, a concept for verification was adopted that makes use of nondestructive assay systems to measure classified parameters (isotopic composition, mass). The results are compared to unclassified attributes, and the results are presented to inspectors in ways that do not reveal the classified data. For example, is plutonium present? If so, is the ratio of the measured isotopic concentrations of ^{240}Pu to ^{239}Pu less than 0.1? Is the mass of plutonium more than a specified amount? If yes, the only answer shown to the inspector is "true."

Further work is needed on the following three concerns before Trilateral Initiative–type verification systems could be used in practice:

- Completed prototype systems need to be certified through vulnerability testing by responsible authorities in each state, to confirm that their use would not risk divulging classified information, and by the IAEA (or a newly created organization, as appropriate) to assure that the results obtained are authentic.
- The IAEA accepted that the verification systems would be manufactured by each state according to agreed design drawings as a means to secure the state's approval.[8] Multiple copies of all systems would be manufactured, and the IAEA would then authenticate the use of the systems by selecting each component for use and select components from the approved inventory from time to time for off-site examination and testing, including destructive analysis, recognizing that once removed, the equipment could not be returned for use.
- A common approach is needed for how to design conversion facilities that would receive classified forms of fissile material and process those materials to remove their classified properties. The arrangements would follow a perimeter control arrangement, similar to that for monitoring warhead-dismantling operations, as described later.

Under an FMCT, three areas of work need to be investigated:

- Environmental sampling is an extremely powerful method when used for detecting undeclared fissile material production in non–nuclear weapon states. Use of the procedure as it stands for FMCT verification in nuclear-armed states could reveal secrets related to nuclear weapon design features and/or manufacturing methods. Modified equipment or procedures are needed that enable environmental sampling to be used for nuclear disarmament.
- Depending on how the FMCT is written, the verification activities may extend to complex facilities already in operation that were not designed to facilitate such measures. It would be useful to begin the process of examining how the verification needs might best be addressed through trial investigations at the actual facilities or at similar facilities, in the nuclear-armed states or elsewhere. This would also enable the verification organization to make accurate resource estimates and implementation planning to prepare for entry into force.
- If fissile material use for nonexplosive military applications is included within the FMCT, verification and monitoring provisions will be needed for all activities where visual analysis and/or measurements could compromise sensitive information.

Several capabilities would benefit the anticipated missions. Chain of custody technology is required for verifying demounting warheads from weapon delivery systems. Active systems that can be mounted permanently (i.e., cannot be removed without being destroyed) should incorporate secure/unique identification features, secure communications capabilities and monitoring of additional parameters—such as location (by GPS), motion, temperature, and radiation.

Architectural studies will be needed to design identical warhead-dismantling facilities that would be built in each nuclear-armed state, incorporating design features to facilitate IAEA verification under a three-dimensional perimeter verification approach (meaning that all surfaces through which ingress/egress might be achieved are in open view, facilitate inspector examination at any time, and are continuously monitored—requiring elevated structures resting on I-beam structural supports having no internal channels that could allow transfers of any nuclear material or equipment or other material that could compromise the verification mission), with occasional managed access into the dismantling areas.

The attribute verification[9] capability developed would need to be modified to verify receipts of warheads into dismantling facilities.

It might be technically possible to determine the identity of a given model nuclear weapon pit or a secondary, and thereby a means to confirm the demounting, storage, dismantling, or conversion of specific weapon systems. The challenges to provide meaningful confirmation without divulging classified information would be complex and difficult, however.

Confirmation of historical plutonium production can be accomplished through the use of isotope ratio methods as a means to improve confidence, especially in the final stages of reductions.[10] The isotope ratio method needs to be certified for use in all types of production reactors.

Controlling the production and use of tritium may be applicable as the remaining numbers of nuclear weapons decrease to hundreds.[11] Investigations into the practicality and benefit of methods to constrain arsenals need to be considered, taking into account the increasing use of tritium in peaceful applications.

Fitting the IAEA into a Multilayered Verification Scheme and Changes Needed on a Path to a Nuclear Weapon–Free World

A path to a nuclear weapon–free world might require efforts extending over decades and include diverse elements, such as the following:

- A road map that would engage the international community in a manner that would demonstrate a common commitment and early progress on actions that signify the change
- Accelerated bilateral reductions of deployed strategic warheads, tactical nuclear weapons, and strategic reserves of functional

warheads between the United States and the Russian Federation, evolving into phased reductions of nuclear arsenals of all nuclear-armed states
- Earnest negotiations on a treaty banning the production of fissile material for use in nuclear weapons or other nuclear explosives incorporating verification of former production facilities, existing stocks of weapon-usable fissile material, and new production of weapon-usable material in peaceful or military operations
- Monitoring and verification agreements on classified and unclassified forms of fissile material outside deployed nuclear weapons.

Steps on the path toward a nuclear weapon–free world could entail international verification. Requests to the IAEA (or to another organization) would likely be realized over time, and each mission would be planned and implemented as the legal arrangements and financial resources allow. The IAEA would need to staff up, develop the tools and procedures necessary, and secure the funding essential for it to perform its mission successfully. As the disarmament-related tasks grow, they will require the organizational structure to evolve to ensure that the new objectives are met without degrading the safeguards program. Eventually, it might be appropriate to create a separate department focused on disarmament matters.

If another organization is created to take on certain of the disarmament-related functions, it would have to interact with the IAEA and would, like the Organization for the Prohibition of Chemical Weapons, study the agency's processes and methods of operation in developing its capabilities.

Several of the disarmament missions may require the verification authority to carry out assessments of the inspected parties to determine whether they remain in compliance with their undertakings. This may require national assessments of motivations for cheating or abrogation, identification of plausible means through which they might act or develop latent capabilities in the event they decide to cheat or abrogate in the future, design and implementation of detection mechanisms through which the IAEA (or another organization) can reach conclusions regarding compliance, and steps it can take to resolve situations of material breach. Recall that cheating or abrogating any disarmament agreement would cast into doubt the validity of the assumptions on which national security estimates are made that enable participation in disarmament, thereby leaving few options besides collective suspension of the agreement and resumption of the nuclear arms race. The IAEA currently makes assessments of states in relation to the motivations and capabilities for acquiring nuclear weapons, using all information available to it, including the following:

- Information provided by the state in reports and design information
- Information obtained through examination and verification of design information; through inspections at declared facilities seeking to detect the diversion of safeguarded nuclear material or misuse of the declared facilities for undeclared production of weapon-usable fissile material; through open-source information reviews, transit matching; or through satellite imagery or environmental sampling or by information provided by third parties (intelligence information)
- Information on the acquisition of materials or equipment suitable for use in relation to weaponization activities

Presumably, corresponding efforts, as appropriate to each mission that is adopted, will become part of the modus operandi of the verification organization. The IAEA has a distinct advantage here; through its experience with sensitive investigations (Iraq, Iran, North Korea), it has developed a security infrastructure for dealing with sensitive information without leaks, and it has gained the trust of the national intelligence organizations.

What Might the IAEA Do to Encourage Progress?

Currently there are no standing programs or committees within the IAEA addressing these potential activities, and no new initiatives are under way. No General Conference Resolutions adopted in 2008 even include the terms *disarmament* or *arms reductions*.

The current absence of encouragement or support for such activities reflects the likely fact that the international community is not—at least not yet—engaged in the substance of nuclear disarmament. Some states—especially some with nuclear arsenals—will prefer to let the issue rest. If the anticipated reluctance to commence can be overcome, initial IAEA activities might be expected to be voluntary in nature and limited in scope. Funding start-up activities will help gain their acceptance by the board.

The IAEA Statute provides broad latitude for possible IAEA activities related to nuclear disarmament, and there is no competition (at present) for the practical steps the agency could best carry out. That being said, some IAEA member states may not support some roles for the IAEA, and hence there may be hurdles to overcome.

Slippery Slope

Some states possessing nuclear weapons are likely to oppose any concerted effort to stimulate nuclear arms reductions on the basis that they have no viable alternative means to protect their national security.[12] If the planning for nuclear disarmament allows some states to defer, that could allow substantive progress to proceed, and the framework created by the early participants could set the stage for latecomers. Starting in this way will create growing pressure on the holdouts to join in and address the underlying reasons that they may be hesitant initially. Hence, to the extent that the IAEA serves the purposes of disarmament, some of the states possessing nuclear weapons may attempt to prevent the steps needed for implementing even modest programs.

Effectiveness

IAEA safeguards have improved dramatically since their inception. Today, they are aimed at three objectives:

- Detection of diversion from declared flows and inventories of nuclear material
- Detection of undeclared nuclear materials and activities that may be part of a clandestine nuclear weapons program

- Detection of weaponization activities that may or may not involve nuclear material.

Today's safeguards are much better than in the 1980s, but they are not perfect. The greatest problems facing IAEA safeguards today are legal/political in nature: resolving the Iran crisis and regaining the viability of the NPT regime.

Some of the new tasks would involve applying the same methods and procedures to disarmament. Verifying declared unclassified fissile material under safeguards would raise the same problems as in nonproliferation. The verification goals might be different, taking into account the relevance of significant quantity values in nuclear-armed states.

Restrictions on verification involving nuclear weapons or components or other classified forms of fissile material, or sites where they are or have been stored or processed, will limit the information available. Environmental sampling and measurements of items that could reveal classified data will continue to be excluded.

The IAEA receives sensitive intelligence information relating to proliferation, and its performance depends to a considerable extent on the information provided to it. Presumably, similar information would be forthcoming regarding disarmament violations. It is not clear whether such information would be entrusted to an international organization, or what it would do with it, but "third-party" information is likely to be an essential part of verifying disarmament compliance.

Verifying declarations of past fissile material production and disposition is likely to encounter significant limitations. The best estimates are likely to have relatively large uncertainty limits.

Money

Should IAEA member states be required to finance IAEA activities related to nuclear disarmament? Or should financing be on a voluntary basis in the form of extra-budgetary funding? Should the entire international community support IAEA activities in pursuit of nuclear disarmament, or should the states possessing nuclear weapons pay?

IAEA activities are funded through a mechanism established in the IAEA Statute, in which national treasuries are taxed according to a formula reflecting the relative wealth of nations. A number (over 60) of extra-budgetary funds that have been established by the IAEA are supported through voluntary contributions, including the Technical Cooperation Fund and the Nuclear Security Fund.

Increasing the regular budget to implement a new formal mission, as might arise with an FMCT, for example, would be worked out during the negotiation of the treaty and hence would follow as a matter of course.[13] Significant increases to the existing budgets are difficult to realize; all national treasuries must agree to give additional funding, and forging a consensus requires a major effort. Starting a new IAEA activity involving staff while relying on extra-budgetary contributions is the simplest way to overcome the initial hurdles. However, the contributions must be in the bank rather than promised; the duration of expenditures planned must anticipate obligations to staff that might be employed through the proposed activities; and the board may wish to approve the activity and the funding arrangement.

Anticipating that the costs for IAEA participation in the process of disarmament may be significant, and that the cost to states of actions necessary for implementing disarmament may slow down the process or provide nuclear-armed states with reasons to refuse to engage or to delay their activities, consideration should be given to a funding process that will meet these needs. A surcharge on nuclear electricity could help to meet this and other worthy agency goals.[14]

Tradition

Some states may sense that the process of adopting steps should come about through multilateral negotiations through the UN Conference on Disarmament (CD). "The IAEA is not the lead agency or forum for nuclear disarmament; nuclear disarmament negotiations take place between nuclear weapons states, at the United Nations, and at the Conference on Disarmament."[15] "The nuclear powers should actively engage with other states on this issue at the Conference on Disarmament in Geneva, the world's single multilateral disarmament negotiating forum."[16] There is clearly a need for both the CD and the IAEA, reflecting the nature of the work to be carried out and their respective accomplishments and capabilities. The IAEA should emphasize its technical character and the diplomatic frameworks essential for encouraging progress toward disarmament and the steps necessary to lock in progress as it is made.

Getting Started

Two *Wall Street Journal* pieces by former secretary of state George Schultz, former secretary of defense William Perry, former secretary of state Henry Kissinger, and former senator Sam Nunn argue that now is the time to begin the immensely complex process of eliminating nuclear weapons.[17] As part of a project undertaken by the Nuclear Threat Initiative, this chapter has considered the strengths and potential challenges of engaging international organizations (especially the IAEA) in this pursuit.

The attitudes of the United States determine the outlook on progress in nuclear arms reductions and other steps aimed at the eventual elimination of nuclear weapons. With the election of Barack Obama as president of the United States, and his statements and actions, there is renewed optimism that meaningful progress can be made and locked into place.

Progress will require working with two basic considerations:

- The underlying motivation that drove each nuclear-armed state to acquire nuclear arms involved perceived threats to its existence; and while new circumstances may prevail, most nuclear-armed states and the states that they provide with nuclear security assurances are not eager to jeopardize the stability that their arsenals afford.
- The nuclear arsenals of the Russian Federation and the United States dwarf all others, making proportionate arms reductions difficult to comprehend, and hence emphasizing corollary activities until such time that the two major arsenals drop to the neighborhoods of the others.

International participation in multilateral negotiations on activities such as those described in this chapter are essential for progress to be made on the global dimensions of nuclear disarmament. International monitoring and verification will be critical to demonstrating compliance with new undertakings, thereby cementing progress and creating the conditions for the next logical step.

On the basis of its capabilities and experience, the IAEA would appear to be the logical choice for new missions related to fissile material. It would behoove the international community to invest in the IAEA to enable it to prepare for the missions ahead, and to engage with interested states in the development and demonstration of new arrangements, methods, equipment, and procedures, so as to be ready when called.

Notes

1. Statute of the International Atomic Energy Agency, initially adopted in 1957 and as amended up to December 28, 1989. The text of the statute is reprinted in a booklet available from the IAEA and accessible at www.iaea .org/About/statute_text.html.

2. Treaties including IAEA-related provisions: Treaty on the Non-Proliferation of Nuclear Weapons (NPT); Treaty for the Prohibition of Nuclear Weapons in Latin America (Tlatelolco Treaty); the African Nuclear-Weapon–Free Zone Treaty (Pelindaba Treaty) including Annexes and Protocols; and the Cairo Declaration; South Pacific Nuclear Free Zone Treaty (Rarotonga Treaty); Southeast Asia Nuclear Weapon–Free Zone Treaty (Treaty of Bangkok); Agreement between the Republic of Argentina, the Federative Republic of Brazil, the Brazilian-Argentine Agency for Accounting and Control of Nuclear Materials (ABACC) and the IAEA for the Application of Safeguards; Verification Agreement between the IAEA and the European Atomic Energy Community (EURATOM); Guidelines for Nuclear Transfers, 1993 Revision of NSG London Guidelines; Convention on the Prevention of Marine Pollution by Dumping of Wastes and Other Matter (London Dumping Convention); International Convention for the Safety of Life at Sea; Convention Relating to Civil Liability in the Field of Maritime Carriage of Nuclear Materials; Treaty Banning Nuclear Weapons Tests in the Atmosphere, in Outer Space and under Water; Partial Test Ban Treaty; Paris Convention on Third Party Liability in the Field of Nuclear Energy; Brussels Convention Supplementary to the Paris Convention; Code of Practice on the International Transboundary Movement of Radioactive Waste:

The IAEA Code of Practice; Code of Conduct on the Safety and Security of Radioactive Sources and the Supplementary Guidance on the Import and Export of Radioactive Sources; Comprehensive Test Ban Treaty; Convention for the Suppression of Acts of Nuclear Terrorism.

3. Conventions negotiated under IAEA auspices: Convention on Early Notification of a Nuclear Accident; Convention on Assistance in the Case of a Nuclear Accident or Radiological Emergency; Convention on Nuclear Safety; Joint Convention on the Safety of Spent Fuel Management and on the Safety of Radioactive Waste Management; Convention on Physical Protection of Nuclear Material; Vienna Convention on Civil Liability for Nuclear Damage; Protocol to Amend the 1963 Vienna Convention on Civil Liability for Nuclear Damage; Convention on Supplementary Compensation for Nuclear Damage Optional Protocol Concerning the Compulsory Settlement of Disputes to the Vienna Convention on Civil Liability for Nuclear Damage; Joint Protocol Relating to the Application of the Vienna Convention and the Paris Convention; Nordic Mutual Emergency Assistance Agreement in Connection with Radiation Accidents; and Convention on the Prevention of Marine Pollution by Dumping of Wastes and Other Matter.

4. Highly enriched uranium (HEU) is uranium in which the concentration of the isotope ^{235}U is increased from the level found in nature (0.712%) to 20% or more.

5. Thomas E. Shea, "The Trilateral Initiative: A Model for the Future?" *Arms Control Today*, May 2008; Thomas E. Shea, Third Annual report of the International Panel on Fissile Materials, Scope and Verification of a Fissile Material (Cutoff) Treaty, chapter 6: "Weapon-origin Fissile Material: The Trilateral Initiative, 2008," www.fissilematerials.org/ipfm/pages_us_en/about/about/about.php.

6. See, for example, United Nations General Assembly Resolution A/RES/48/75 of January 7, 1994.

7. The American Physical Society has recommended technical steps to support nuclear arsenal downsizing, which can be accessed at www.aps.org/policy/reports/popa-reports/upload/nucleardownsizing.

8. The only alternative would be for the IAEA (or a newly created organization, as appropriate) to provide the equipment to the nuclear-armed state, in which case, according to advice provided by the Russian Federation, the national security services would examine it over an 18-month period and determine whether it could be used. If not, no explanation would be given, and the IAEA would somehow have to convince itself that no modifications had been made that could affect the authenticity of the results obtained.

9. Attribute verification involves comparing a measurement result to a stated quantity and asking a simple question: is the measured amount greater than the stated quantity? Through this means, the results of measurements on classified objects can be made available to international inspectors.

10. C. J. Gesh, "A Graphite Isotope Ratio Method Primer: A Method for Estimating Plutonium Production in Graphite Moderated Reactors," PNNL-14568, February 2004.

11. M. B. Kalinowski, *International Control of Tritium for Nuclear Non-proliferation and Disarmament* (Boca Raton, FL: CRC Press, 2004).

12. See, for example, International Panel on Fissile Materials, "Banning the Production of Fissile Materials for Nuclear Weapons: Country Perspectives on the Challenges to a Fissile Material (Cutoff) Treaty," companion volume to *Global Fissile Material Report 2008*.

13. In a 1995 study, the IAEA estimated that the verification funding it would need would range from $40 million to $140 million a year, depending on the scope and intensity of the verification measures adopted. See "A Cut-off Treaty and Associated Costs," Workshop on a Cut-off Treaty, Toronto, January 1995.

14. See, for example, T. Shea, "Financing IAEA Verification of the NPT," PNNL-SA-52583, as published in *Falling Behind: International Scrutiny of the Peaceful Atom*, ed. Henry D. Sokolski, the Strategic Studies Institute Publications Office, February 2008, www.npec-web.org/Books/20080327 -FallingBehind.pdf.

15. "Reinforcing the Global Nuclear Order for Peace and Prosperity: The Role of the IAEA to 2020 and Beyond," report prepared by an independent commission at the request of the director-general of the IAEA, May 2008.

16. Secretary-General Ban Ki-moon of the United Nations, "The United Nations and Security in a Nuclear-Weapon-Free World," address to the East-West Institute, October 24, 2008, www.un.org/apps/news/infocus/sgspeeches/ statments_full.asp?statID=351.

17. George P. Shultz, William J. Perry, Henry A. Kissinger, and Sam Nunn, "A World Free of Nuclear Weapons," and "Toward a Nuclear-Free World," *Wall Street Journal*, January 4, 2007, and January 15, 2008, respectively. Both articles appear in appendix A of this volume.

9. Role and Responsibility of the Civil Sector in Managing Trade in Specialized Materials

RALF WIRTZ

In January 1982, I joined the German vacuum company Leybold, then named "Leybold Heraeus GmbH." The company had two major facilities, one in Cologne, producing all components that are required to generate, maintain, and measure vacuum; the other one in Hanau near Frankfurt, where huge systems were designed and assembled (e.g., coating machines, electron beam welders, crystal pulling machines) and later—after the merger with the German company Degussa—also various kinds of vacuum furnaces.

In the middle of the 1990s, Leybold was merged with its largest competitor, a company named Balzers, located in the city of Balzers in Liechtenstein. After a while, several business activities were divested, the group focused on information technology and was renamed UNAXIS, and later "Oerlikon" (see figure 9.1).

Currently, Oerlikon is a widely diversified high-tech group with approximately 19,000 employees that owns, in addition to the vacuum technology activities, manufacturers of textile machinery (Saurer group) and drive systems (Fairfield, IN, USA; and Graziano Trasmissioni, Italy).

Oerlikon Leybold Vacuum—one of the business segments of Oerlikon—has approximately 1,500 employees, worldwide, production

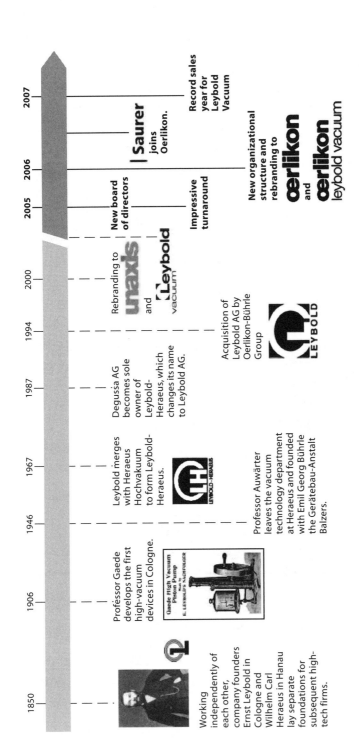

Figure 9.1 Company Overview: Historic Milestones.

in Germany, France, and China, subsidiaries in 17 countries, and a tight network of service centers and representative companies around the globe.

Oerlikon Leybold Vacuum has a very high export control risk exposure. This chapter will mainly focus on the experience and nonproliferation activities of this business segment.

Since 1992, I have been in charge of export compliance for this former division of Leybold and, since 2006, head of Global Trade Control of the Oerlikon group.

Background

This chapter seeks to shed light on the role which industry and trade can play in the prevention of proliferation of weapons of mass destruction (WMD) and missiles. Such proliferation is dependent on the ability to import large quantities of high-technology products that, by definition, would have to be exported from the countries where they are manufactured or stored.

Illicit procurement leaves visible traces that can be identified by industry, sometimes in cooperation with government agencies. As a matter of fact, industry is in the first line of defense when it comes to stopping procurement for nuclear enrichment, WMD, and missiles. Such traces, however, will hardly be available for governmental investigation and analysis unless the company, for whatever reason, chooses to forward the information to the authorities.

For instance, industry knew about the early stages of the Iranian nuclear program long before the IAEA was informed, as well as about the role of South African companies that later became the main proliferators and suppliers to the Libyan nuclear weapons program in the mid-1990s.

This chapter examines the question "Can companies help build an effective early warning system through information sharing?" and answers that question with an unambiguous "yes." It touches on export controls only where necessary. Endless criticism of the export control process will not lead us anywhere. Such laws are made by humans and hence can never be perfect. However, what separates the human race from other species is the free will to decide to do "good," and a decision to do good does not require any laws or regulations. For instance, do we really have to make deals in the gray area, where the laws do not work effectively enough? Who or what entitles us to reduce the stakeholder value to the fiscal bottom line? Don't we deprive our stakeholders of moral and business ethics when we do so?

After embarrassing IAEA discoveries in Iraq of items that Leybold had delivered, Leybold introduced a voluntary program of self-restraint in export matters that, despite several management changes, remains fully intact. The forwarding by our company of inquiries that we identify as "suspicious" is perceived by government officials as extremely valuable and helpful.

This chapter does not seek to persuade other companies to follow this example; industrial leaders have to come to their own conclusions regarding their ultimate responsibility. Only they can decide whether they wish to help reduce the threat caused by the world's most dangerous weapons.

Where Do We Come From?

Oerlikon Leybold Vacuum: A Short Glimpse at the Company History

With a 157-year history, Leybold was the unrivaled leader in vacuum technology for decades. Whenever somebody needed a vacuum pump, Leybold was what he wanted to buy. The company's products had and still have a very good reputation; Leybold had long experience, the leading scientists to develop new products, and an excellent "made in Germany" quality. I have seen letters in the company archives dating back to the mid-1960s, written by famous German researchers of that time, requesting Leybold to reserve—if possible—one pump for their institute, for which they would be willing to wait for years and to pay any price.

This may help explain why scientists from all over the world sent their inquiries to Leybold. This includes researchers from Middle Eastern countries, who wanted to make some first steps in nuclear research. Communication was not what it is today; neither e-mail nor fax existed back then. The state-of-the-art way to communicate was by airmail letters. It was a good time for stamp collectors, and even better for exporting companies, since there were hardly any export controls.

The business grew, and with it grew staff and staff turnover. In the mid-1980s, Leybold Heraeus in Cologne employed approximately 2,500 people and had three large divisions—Vacuum Technology, Physics Teaching Equipment (later separated under the name Leybold Didactic), and Surface Analysis (ESCA, SIMS, Auger, etc.).

Export controls at that time consisted of two more or less simple principles (see figure 9.2):

- Export was basically "free" to occur, with the only exception being for "controlled technology."
- There was a list of controlled technologies, the export of which required an individual license.

The world was divided into two parts: the Western countries and the so-called Eastern Bloc. Export controls at that time were designed to prevent goods of strategic importance from finding their way through and behind the Iron Curtain.

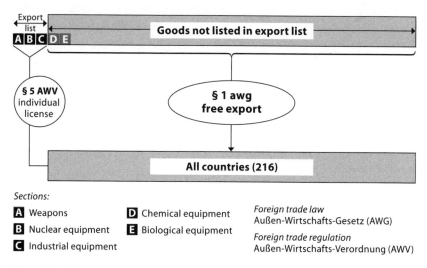

Figure 9.2 German Foreign Trade: Law and Regulation 1961–1991. From ALD Vaccuum Technologies AG, Central Export Control.

There was, however, little or no industry awareness of other potential problems, such as the ambitions of several states to acquire weapons of mass destruction and related delivery technology.

The "nonpapers" which the German government received almost on a daily basis, primarily from the United States, had the exports of companies such as Siemens, Degussa, its daughter company Leybold, and several others as targets.

"Jurassic" Business

When I joined Leybold Heraeus (Cologne) in 1982 as part of the commercial sales team, I saw old invoices documenting significant component shipments to organizations in Pakistan that were later said to be "fronts" for the nuclear weapons program (e.g., the "Special Works Organization," and contracts concluded with the embassies of Pakistan in both France and Germany). The paper trail pointed back to the mid-1970s, presumably the time when Dr. A. Q. Khan returned to Pakistan to help his country develop a nuclear weapon.

The component business with Pakistan was sizable, and after a while there were also projects in other countries in the Middle East and Far East. The supplies may have been destined for nuclear applications, but other end uses were also plausible. Owing to the wide range of possible applications, a final judgment based only on the shipped goods is not possible.

In retrospect, taking into account all facts such as names of involved individuals, purchasing organization, and shipped components, it is highly likely that the end use was the beginning of nuclear programs in the respective countries.

The business with Iraq was different: there was not a single hint of a nuclear program. Iraq was buying other pumps in larger quantities, and there were assumptions that the components were for vacuum furnaces, and that the country was perhaps building up its conventional military infrastructure, but no one in the company in Cologne had a clue that Iraq was trying to enrich uranium by means of the EMIS (electromagnetic isotope separation) principle (see figure 9.3).

Today, we may find it hard to believe that these deliveries were legal and did not even require a license. But, even today, only a very

The EM Method of Separating the Components of Tuballoy

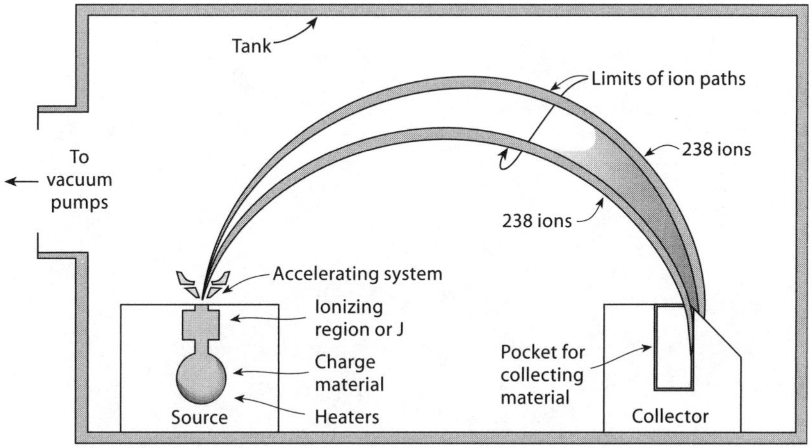

Figure 9.3 EMIS: Electromagnetic Isotope Separation in a Vacuum Chamber.

few vacuum components that Oerlikon Leybold Vacuum produces are controlled by international regimes and require a license. One should also not forget that when these export shipments took place, there were no awareness-related export control regulations, or so-called catch-all clauses. They did simply not exist. The first catch-all regulation was put into force by the German government in spring 1991.

Nevertheless, Leybold's supplies to Middle and Far Eastern countries led to many allegations, primarily from the United States. There were even allegations that Leybold and its subsidiaries were untrustworthy and that companies that intended to continue to sell to the U.S. Department of Defense should refrain from doing business with Leybold.

The allegations led to investigations, not only in the United States but also in Germany. A Special Nuclear Task Force was established, and it took years before the charges were dropped and the files closed.

Soon after the first oil diffusion pumps were discovered by UN inspectors in Iraq, the IAEA sent official letters to Leybold asking what else had been supplied to the country, and where it might be hidden.

The then-new executive board of the company decided to fully support the efforts and open the books for the IAEA. All available

Figure 9.4 A, EMIS vacuum chamber in Iraqi desert (1991); B, vacuum pump (oil diffusion pump) as found in Iraq in the EMIS project. Used with permission from Oerlikon Leybold Vacuum.

B

information was forwarded to the IAEA immediately, and a dialogue began.

The "Leybold Charter"

With the new CEO coming on board in 1990, Leybold initiated a variety of new programs, from the introduction of total quality management over kanban production steering to a voluntary self-restraint program in export matters.

A look at the dual-use section of today's export control lists reveals that the majority of controlled vacuum-related goods and technologies are controlled for "nuclear nonproliferation" reasons, be it the oil diffusion pumps listed under 2B231 (entries from 201 to 299 are Nuclear Suppliers Group (NSG) entries), certain valves, frequency converters, mass spectrometers, vacuum gauges (in the language of the export control list called "pressure transducers"), and many other items.

In 1990, the German government introduced a rule according to which every company that exported controlled goods to a large group of countries had to nominate a top management official, a member of the executive body of the company. In the absence of a suitable English term, we call that person the "chief export control officer" (CECO), who is not to be confused with the export control manager of the company. The latter has the operational responsibility for the company's compliance with all export control regulations, but the CECO bears responsibility for all consequences of a violation, if it is the result of a systemic failure.

The German Federal Office of Economics and Export Control (BAFA) reserves the right to have exporters audited and to demand that the CECO resign from his or her post, if after the audit there remain concerns regarding the trustworthiness of the company and the efficiency of its internal export controls.

Due to the background (the threat of blacklisting Leybold in the United States, a high-level investigation in both the United States and Germany, embarrassing letters from the IAEA, and the risk for the CECO), it was a logical consequence that the new CECO felt the need to "clean up" thoroughly.

The executive board issued "Corporate Guidelines Governing Nuclear Export Controls" (figure 9.5), which, in some aspects, were ahead of their time. In addition to an unconditional commitment to strictly abide by all laws, the document, which soon became known as the "Leybold Charter," demanded voluntary self-restraint, meaning that if after consultation with authorities there remained concerns regarding the end use of the equipment, the business would be refused.

Moreover, the CECO established a centralized Export Control Office, equipped with engineers who not only had to study the

Corporate Principles Governing Internal Export Controls on Nuclear Non-Proliferation

As a result of global political developments which have occurred since the late 1980s, exports of certain goods—especially those of a highly technical or military nature—have acquired a special significance. Further, because of the possible misuse of some of those products—in particular, so-called "dual-use" items—the relevant export control regulations have been expanded and strengthened. This development has had an especially strong impact on Germany's export-oriented industry.

Leybold AG is primarily active in the area of vacuum technology, vacuum metallurgy and vacuum coating. The company neither manufactures weapons nor any other category of military equipment. Nonetheless, the company has developed and does produce certain types of state-of-the-art equipment and advanced technology, which, in today's complex, industrialized world, could be regarded as so-called "dual-use" items.

With the benefit of the experience gained in the last few years—particularly as a result of the Gulf War—and in recognition of its responsibility, the Executive Board of Leybold AG has resolved as follows:

1. Leybold AG´s Executive Board affirms its unequivocal and emphatic support for the policies regarding the non-proliferation of nuclear weapons and nuclear capable delivery systems.

2. Leybold AG and its worldwide subsidiaries endorse and adhere to the export controls established by the Federal Republic of Germany and its allies—in particular, the United States of America—for the purpose of achieving the goal of an effective nuclear non-proliferation policy.

3. All Leybold employees will actively assist in the achievement of this corporate goal.

   In particular, Leybold employees involved in the export of the company's commodities, technology or services will be familiar with, and strictly abide by, all applicable provisions of national and foreign export control laws and regulations.

4. Leybold attaches clear-cut and unambiguous priority to the goal of non-proliferation of nuclear weapons and their delivery systems over commercial interests. In practice, this means that even if a particular export transaction is legal, Leybold—in accordance with its corporate policy of voluntary self-restraint in export matters—will neither directly nor indirectly supply commodities, technology or services if the company knows or has reason to believe that such items will be used by its customer or end-user for the development or production of nuclear weapons or nuclear capable delivery systems. This policy applies to customers and end-users from non-nuclear weapons countries, as set forth in the Treaty of the Non-Proliferation of Nuclear Weapons, if these countries:
   - Are not signatories to the Treaty on the Non-Proliferation of Nuclear Weapons, or
   - Have not renounced the possession, acquisition and production of nuclear weapons by other acts binding under international law, or
   - Do not have in place full-scope safeguards in accordance with International Atomic Energy Agency (IAEA) requirements, or if there is any doubt about their implementation, or if these countries are classified as "sensitive" for other reasons.

Figure 9.5 Corporate Principles Governing Internal Export Controls on Nuclear Non-Proliferation.

5. This policy applies to domestic transactions as well, if Leybold knows or has reason to believe that its products are to be diverted to such countries for sensitive projects.

6. In order to ascertain which countries should be regarded as sensitive for the purpose of this policy, Leybold will establish and maintain contact with all responsible federal agencies, i.e., the Foreign Office (Auswärtiges Amt), the Ministry of Economics (Bundesministerium für Wirtschaft) and the Federal Export Control Authority (Bundesamt für Wirtschaft).

7. In the event of any doubt, the responsible federal agencies will immediately be asked for information and advice. Likewise, if an item is subject to U.S. jurisdiction due to its specific nature (e.g., intermediate products or components from an U.S. source) the U.S. Department of Commerce will be approached for information and counsel.

   In the event of any continuing concern regarding the end-use of items to be exported, Leybold AG will not conclude the transaction.

8. This policy applies to all divisions and subsidiaries of Leybold AG worldwide. The principles incorporated herein are to be immediately implemented within the framework of Leybold's existing internal export compliance program. This policy will continuously be reviewed and audited. The Executive Board will ensure that the management of all German and foreign subsidiaries will implement this policy by adopting appropriate export control procedures.

March 17, 1992

Figure 9.5 *(continued)* Corporate Principles Governing Internal Export Controls on Nuclear Non-Proliferation.

continuously expanding export control rules, but also were knowledgeable about the company's products and their possible applications.

These stringent internal controls yielded very positive results, but it should also be noted that soon international competitors stepped in and "helped" the rejected customers get what they wanted.

To this day, Oerlikon Leybold Vacuum has its "Charter" and applies it on a daily basis (figure 9.6). It has not been modified much from the original version.

The World's Second Oldest Business: Trade

It did not take long for Leybold's changed practices to be noticed and acknowledged by the authorities, primarily in the United States and Germany. The company had in the meantime established a centralized compliance organization (in which I had the responsibility for the

œrlikon

Corporate Guidelines Governing Export Compliance

Europe, several states in Asia and the USA, in particular, have been engaged in introducing widely harmonized and continuously intensified export control regulations to counteract the efforts of various countries, on the rise since the eighties, to realize acquisition programs for weapons of mass destruction.

As a globally active supplier of vacuum, coating and space components, solutions and services, Oerlikon wants to be the source address for clients in market segments with a promising future.

We do not produce weapons, but experience shows that especially vacuum technology is an indispensable medium for very many state-of-the-art production processes, and consequently, its use also extends into the field of mass destruction weapons. Based on the findings resulting from the second Gulf War, the necessity to work out a much more efficient non-proliferation policy became clear far more than a decade ago.

As a globally acting enterprise, we therefore need guidelines for all our sales activities that are applicable throughout the corporation. Based on the aforesaid, and in recognition of its own highest due responsibility before the law, management has resolved as follows:

1. Oerlikon pledges its unequivocal and emphatic support for a policy of non-proliferation.

2. All employees are obligated to actively participate towards achieving this corporate goal in their field of work. It is the duty of managing staff to ensure that employees have adequate knowledge of all relevant regulations, by means of trainings and access to regulations.

3. Our corporate goal of actively supporting a policy of non-proliferation has priority over commercial interest. Without prejudice to the legal permissibility of a specific transaction—we shall neither directly, nor indirectly—even in the case of domestic business—supply products, documents, technologies or services, if we know or have reason to believe that such items may ultimately be used in sensitive countries for weapons of mass destruction or for missile systems deployed to this end.

4. In order to ascertain which countries and entities should be regarded as sensitive for the purpose of this policy, we will also maintain contact with the responsible agencies. In the event of any continued concern regarding the end use, the transaction shall be immediately terminated.

5. This policy applies worldwide. It is to be immediately implemented within the framework of the existing internal compliance program, and must be monitored continuously. The undersigned will ensure that all managers implement the aforementioned guidelines by means of appropriate measures.

Pfäffikon SZ, August 23, 2006

Chief Executive Officer	Chief Financial Officer
Thomas Limberger	Rainer Mück

Figure 9.6 Corporate Guidelines Governing Export Compliance.

Cologne-based component business), visited all major subsidiaries in Germany and the United States to introduce the new policy, trained hundreds of employees, screened all products against the export control lists, and carefully monitored the relevant federal publications daily for new or amended regulations, etc.

In 1990, Germany issued guidelines for how companies should implement internal export controls, and Leybold followed its recommendations. Later, one could find very similar recommendations on the U.S. Department of Commerce Web site, encouraging companies to develop and introduce "export management systems." Several Asian countries—possibly motivated by U.S. or EU outreach activities—also published recommendations for so-called internal control programs or internal compliance programs (ICPs).

However, one element was obviously not given enough emphasis in Leybold's ICP. In autumn 1992, the CEO received a letter from Leybold's lawyers in the United States, stating that the law firm had received a warning from a U.S. national security agency for Leybold, and asking that it be passed on to headquarters in Germany.

The message was clear: although the company's compliance efforts and, in particular, its voluntary self-restraint were praised, the management's attention needed to be drawn to the risk of doing business with companies that were not themselves the end users of the equipment that Leybold sold.

Since a direct contact with the friendly U.S. agency was not possible, it was left to Leybold's export control department to find out if this was a well-targeted hint or a general warning. We diligently analyzed our business with trading companies and shortly discovered that a company employee had established a trading company, with his wife as managing director. That company was placing orders with Leybold in Cologne for many components, which, as was discovered during the subsequent investigation, were shipped by the trading company to "fronts" in Pakistan, which were well-known to the U.S. enforcement agency, presumably for end use in the nuclear program.

This was a life-changing experience with two lessons to learn:

- Careless business with traders is risky for manufacturers of dual-use goods.

- A company has little or no ability to protect itself against criminal impulses.

As immediate corrective action, internal procedures dealing with "end-use examination" were enhanced considerably, and the following procedures were added:

- It was immediately prohibited to sell to traders if there was any uncertainty about who was the end user.
- A "criteria list" was developed to help sales people identify sensitive inquiries from traders.

We do still business with trading companies, but on a different level:

- All purchase orders from traders go to the Central Export Control Office.
- Only there can it be decided if the item has already been identified as destined for an illicit end use.
- Price quotations include a proviso that, prior to a delivery, Oerlikon Leybold Vacuum will demand doubt free end-user evidence and—if deemed necessary—will seek clarification with the authorities.
- The trading company will—if possible—get a written confirmation ensuring it project protection, thus making clear that the supplier is not trying to cut the trader out of the deal to increase its profit margin.

It has to do with the nature of the business model that traders are reluctant to disclose their end users; when they refuse, we refrain from the transaction. However, it should be noted that most traders, following discussion with somebody in the order management group or, if they continue to argue, with the export control officer, do ultimately change their attitude and appreciate or at least tolerate the procedure.

Oerlikon Leybold Vacuum's experience with the harder cases is described in the next section.

Typical Procurement Patterns

The term *procurement patterns* refers here to the well-organized, often intelligence-directed and "state-driven" procurement activities aimed at bypassing the export regulations in the country of shipment, and at hiding the true end user and the intended end use. The "actors" in such transactions can be state as well as nonstate actors.

The following examples are procurement patterns that we have identified in more than 16 years of experience:

Change of Suppliers

- Many rejected entities have switched to European competitors.
- More deliveries are from newly emerging competitors in Asian countries (the products may not have the same quality, but are considerably cheaper).
- As a consequence of globalization, producing Asian entities of U.S. and European suppliers are regularly approached for deliveries.

Approaching (Foreign) Subsidiaries through Domestic Customers

- There is a trend to avoid "export related concerns" by targeting suitable companies domestically where no export controls seem to apply.
- This exploits the business model of many companies, where foreign subsidiaries are in charge of the domestic market in which they reside and they need not align with their headquarters.

Avoiding Countries with Stringent Export Controls/Enforcement

- We have noticed over the past years that former customers avoid contacting us in Germany where the export control headquarters is based and laws are more stringent than elsewhere.
- There seems to be a trend to "sourcing in Asia," but we believe this has less to do with the expected lower price level. Rather, it seems to have more to do with the underdeveloped export

control legislation in some countries and/or their less aggressive enforcement.

Company Web Sites, E-mail, and E-commerce

- As recent examples show, procurement agents have more than one contact in a supplier's global organization; they often e-mail their requirements to some or all subsidiaries or sales agents that they find on the manufacturer's Web site.
- Only trained employees and sales agents know how to react (i.e., in Leybold's case, to send the inquiry to the export control department in the headquarters for approval or denial).
- Geographic distance, time differences, and the expected short response times are a great challenge for the decision maker in the headquarters.
- Export control authorities are not prepared to answer requests for information about a recipient on short notice; and if the answer comes after weeks, the content may be outdated (no update obtained from intelligence) or so general that it does not help much.
- Export control authorities do not like requests for information about potential business partners; their system is primarily designed to respond to license applications. Any reply to a request for information about a recipient does not have the legal nature/character of a license and is thus not "watertight." Still, it is a tool for risk management, but the quality is vague and varies from case to case.

Splitting Larger Inquiries

- A not-too-recent procurement effort from Iran suggests that the end user split the original inquiry and sent the various parts to various potential suppliers in order not to let any one supplier see the entire volume of what would be procured. This became evident only after we were approached by a European security agency, showing us what they had intercepted. They were surprised to see that we had obviously received another part of the entire specification, and putting two and two together they began to see the larger picture.

- Another reason to source from different suppliers with comparable technology is that—as a general rule—"sole source supplier strategies" are not very common. If one goes bankrupt or is merged with a company in a less export-friendly country, or introduces stringent internal controls, the entire project can be at risk and may have to be suspended for years until a new supplier is qualified.
- In the mid-1980s, we attended tender openings in one country by sending our representative to these official meetings and could learn from the reports what our competitors had offered, and at what rates. The orders were later shared equally between the main competitor and ourselves.

Using Vague End-User Declarations (More Plausible Than Not)

- Trading companies, when asked to present end-user evidence written and signed by the ultimate user, often try to escape by presenting End-User Undertakings according to which they are themselves are "the customer" (which is correct, but not sufficient and hence not acceptable).
- End users are equally reluctant to admit what they really intend to do, and the end user declarations are often very vague. We send—together with the end-user declaration specimen copy— a standard explanation that we will not accept general wording such as "use in our vacuum laboratory"; and if the customer needs a pump as replacement for a defective one, we will not accept a simple statement such as "replacement for use in our vacuum furnace." The customer would have to explain what is produced by means of the vacuum furnace.
- In principle, the value of end-user declarations is low. Customers who turn out to be good guys feel discriminated against by having to certify that they do not produce or develop WMD or missiles. The bad guys will not tell you the truth anyway.

- The only real value of an EUD is that a licensing and/or security agency can check what is known about the entity or organization, such as the proprietors, names of individuals, fax, phone numbers, P.O. box, and whether one of the communication channels is shared with another known (sensitive) entity.

"Lower Than the List"

- As stated, only a very few products in Oerlikon Leybold Vacuum's product portfolio are controlled by the international non-proliferation regimes.
- Leading uranium enrichment experts, who may have their state-of-the-art enrichment plants of the newest generation in mind, will tell you that "simple," standard vacuum components cannot be used for enrichment purposes.
- Going through files described under "Jurassic business," we failed to find any delivery that would have required an export license. Old invoice copies evidencing deliveries to well-known addresses in Pakistan make very clear that simple, standard vacuum components do as good a job as much more sophisticated ones, at least until the next earthquake smashes a dozen centrifuges and new peripheral equipment such as aluminum valves, fittings, and gauge heads are needed.
- As long as it has to be assumed that old P1 and P2 drawings and all the required technology, shopping lists, and recommended supplier names are available on a nuclear black market for anybody who has sufficient financial means, it must be considered as almost certain that countries with clandestine or not fully safeguarded nuclear programs will buy "lower than the list" products—products that meet the requirements but are not controlled by the international export control lists.

Buying through "Legitimate" End Users

Two recent cases suggest that Iran may have decided in favor of a new, probably additional procurement pattern.

Following tips from a European intelligence agency, we discovered a new strategy used by Iran to circumvent export controls, in this case a clever scheme to obtain vacuum pump systems for its centrifuge program. The elaborate ruse involved a legitimate Chinese manufacturing company with an established relationship with Oerlikon Leybold Vacuum. In early 2006, we received a tip from a friendly European government to be on guard for orders from Saudi Arabian companies for certain types of pumping systems that would be diverted to Iran. We did not receive such an order, but our South Korean daughter company did receive a similar inquiry from an entity wanting to ship such items to Iran. The daughter company consulted the central export control office, which decided to refuse this order and inform the Korean authorities.

Several months later, the European intelligence agency asked again to look into a recent order placed by a Chinese company. After reviewing inquiries and contracts, we soon found that the Chinese company had ordered 15 such pump systems, seven of which had already been delivered to the Chinese company. The Chinese company, which is an established manufacturing company, called an original equipment manufacturer (OEM), had ordered the pumps as part of a larger order it had received to build oil purification equipment for electrical power plants. We did not need a government approval to supply the pumps; the sale did not require a license and was not at all suspicious. The Chinese company had not previously been associated with illicit activities.

After the discovery, our company officials immediately contacted the Chinese company and asked for the end user of the equipment. The Chinese customer was vague. He said that its equipment, including the pump systems, were for an overseas customer, and in fact the firm had already exported the seven pump systems, but it refused to reveal the customer. We stopped any further shipments of pumps to this company. The Chinese company officials demanded the rest of the pumps or all their money back. Then, the company cancelled the order, perhaps to prevent having to admit at some stage that its customer was Iran. European government authorities were notified, one of which learned from the Chinese government that the pumps did indeed go to Iran. Although they did not learn the exact end user, they believed Iran's centrifuge program was the likely customer. No prosecution was launched against Oerlikon Leybold Vacuum in Germany or the Chinese daughter company for the pump transactions. Instead, the intelligence services applauded our action to stop further exports and uncover this dangerous new Iranian scheme.

Status Quo: Daily Operations and Observations

Prone to Failure—Actual "Catch-all" Controls

The core of the "awareness" related export control regulations is the "positive knowledge" of the exporter about a WMD or missile end use. Only a very few countries go a bit beyond that to impose a license requirement if the exporter has "reason to believe" or "grounds for suspecting" that the goods intended for export are for any such end use.

When countries initiate a WMD program, they do not do so openly, with the international press being present, a nice Internet presence, and glossy brochures. We cannot expect TV spots and newspaper ads making the name of any new WMD organization known worldwide in the future.

Rather, the country will do everything it can to make sure that the program is camouflaged, most of the operations are run by intelligence services, and nothing leaks out.

Although Leybold was probably a preferred supplier for a variety of countries that had a nuclear program and also missile programs, I was never approached by any of the customers' representatives to explain that there was a military end use, nor was I ever shown any drawings or other documents that would have enabled me to file a license application owing to the "positive knowledge" that I had.

With a view to covert procurement attempts, it is unlikely that an exporter will have "reason to believe" or "grounds for suspecting" that his export sales could be for a WMD or missile end use.

Imagine you are in the export control manager's shoes: Would you be willing to put a nice deal with excellent profit margins at risk, knowing your competitor is ready to deliver? What will you be told when you inform your government about your suspicion? Will you be asked if you had a bad dream, or, worse, will you be questioned about your business relations with other customers in the country, or will you be sent an audit team to examine other shipments to typical diversion countries, middlemen, and front companies? Will the authorities be monitoring your visitors in future, reading your e-mail, and monitoring all your exports? Why should you—who don't "know" anything—make your life harder than it already is? Isn't it sufficient to abide by the existing laws and regulations? An argument that one often hears from industry representatives is that governments should change the laws if they see a need for certain additional controls.

Finally, a typical consequence of presenting "suspicious" cases to licensing authorities is that they approve the case. The exporter is hounded by an angry customer with reminders for a quick delivery, and the exporter swears he will not go through this "quasi" licensing procedure a second time unless forced to do so by law.

Ongoing Procurement Efforts

Contrary to the assumption that the arrests and trials of the recent past (German and Swiss nationals Gerhard Wisser and Daniel Geiges in South Africa; the German national Gotthard Lerch in Switzerland; and members of the Tinner family in Switzerland) destroyed the nuclear network of Pakistan's chief bomb scientist Dr. A. Q. Khan, the procurement attempts as described earlier continue. A look into the daily newspaper makes clear that the efforts are still successful; there is little about arrests and indictment of businessmen who wanted to make quick money, but much about the Iranian centrifuge program and often also scary articles speculating that terrorists or rogue countries may have gotten access to nuclear technology and warhead designs.

At Oerlikon Leybold Vacuum, we still see many inquiries coming through the same channels and from the same front companies from where they came before, prior to the arrests. Neither have the patterns been changed much, nor are there many new names, nor different products. It is still the vacuum components and spares business that were always on the shopping lists.

The fact that there is still large-scale "procurement" out there for illicit purposes reveals a very simple fact: The countries that have to procure high-technology for their illicit programs do not have the resources and capabilities to produce these technologies indigenously. In a technological sense, these countries are far from being "autonomous"; hence, they depend on a limited number of companies which are able to supply what is required.

What if *all* potential suppliers would refuse to deliver?

Voluntary Self-Restraint—More Important Than Ever

While we cannot take decisions for other companies, we can abide by our own philosophy: strictly adhere to the laws and regulations in countries where we are active, and, if necessary (e.g., in cases where we have continued concerns regarding the end use), go beyond the letter of the law and refrain from a sale. Proactively avoiding problems for our company has another positive effect: The procurement attempt fails, and the country's nuclear efforts are hindered and delayed. The fact that we see the same inquiries floating around for many years is evidence that we sometimes delay the work for a long period of time.

Information Sharing

In all the countries where we are active, but primarily in Germany and surrounding EU countries, we try to establish and maintain a good relationship with export control, enforcement, and security authorities. Again, the reasons are rather simple:

- If the company's own export control system is "per se" unable to protect the company against criminal impulses of individuals and entire procurement networks, an alliance with authorities will help.
- We explained our internal control procedures and pointed out the big problem of diversion and illicit procurement attempts. We made clear that we needed to protect ourselves, in order to avoid new investigation, and that we did not want to find our name in the media again. Soon, there came the first very useful hints from a German authority, informing us that we would soon

receive a certain order that we should not accept, and asking that we report a few details that the officials may not have known or which they wanted to have confirmed.

As noted, we made efforts to centralize our export and end-use controls. Owing to this strategy, we were able to discover that the same inquiries were sent to different subsidiaries, directly from the original customer who sent his inquiry to our HQ in Cologne. Procurement attempts included other EU countries, and we began to establish contacts with security agencies in those countries as well, with the intention of asking if they wanted to be informed of these inquiries. They did, and still do, want to be informed.

We never had the intention of "trading" information; rather, we wanted to prove that we made serious efforts to support the country's export controls. We never asked what happened to the companies which had tried to procure from us, nor did we ever ask if the information we provided was useful. After awhile, when there was mutual trust, officials of the respective security agencies contacted us by phone or e-mail to ask when we were available in the country for a meeting, and when we met they indicated that the information we provided was helping them a lot. We were encouraged to provide whatever we thought would help them to fulfill their responsibilities in their respective countries.

Soon after the first meeting, they began giving us tips, asking if we knew a certain customer in a country far away, and suggesting that we be cautious. It turned out that one of our sales agents was on their watch list, because he had business with an embargoed country, outside his own territory. Needless to say, we were not happy about this fact but appreciated the information, and we terminated the agent's contract immediately.

Time after time—recognizing that our authorities had no access to the information that we could gather, and seeing how much they were missing—we asked if they wanted information about sensitive procurement on a regular basis, and if there was an e-mail address to which we could forward what we thought was worth forwarding. It did not take long before an e-mail address was established, and we began to feed identical information into the pipelines of different authorities, to make sure that everybody involved was on the same page.

The answer to the question of whether we are doing somebody else's job, and whether we are spending too much time on this is a firm "no." When we see that an illicit procurement attempt is about to occur, we have an obligation to stop it by informing the authorities or, if we cannot anticipate that the attempt will be successful, to at least provide the names of the implicated companies to the authorities, so that they have them in their database and can do whatever they think needs to be done.

We receive the majority of sales inquiries by e-mail, and to forward these to an e-mail address that we have been given by an authority is not really time-consuming; it is as quick as clicking the "forward" button in your e-mail program and entering an e-mail address.

This takes just seconds, but it can be an important contribution to successfully fighting proliferation and making our planet a little bit safer.

How can we demand that our governments do something, if we retain precious information that we could have easily provided to them. Who is "the state"? In a democracy, it is not only the administration; it is the sum of all citizens, including the sum of all tangible and intangible assets, including our good will. How can we expect our police to do a better job if we—those who give the police their mandate—do not support them to the best of our ability?

In other words, nonproliferation is not only our government's job; it is also our duty to contribute whatever we can, and there is a lot that industry has to share.

Figure 9.7 presents a diagram describing how much information our authorities would miss unless industry is willing to share.

Global Industry-Government Cooperation: From Export Control to Counterproliferation

In the last ten years, many emerging countries—primarily in Asia— have introduced export control legislation, often with the help of the United States and the EU. For globally operating companies, many of which have shifted a part of their production to low-cost countries, this resulted in another challenge: understanding and abiding by the relevant national export control laws and regulations.

While there is, unfortunately, no real harmonization of export control laws, one thing has become very clear: Proliferation went global

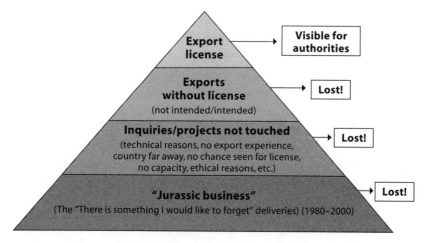

Figure 9.7 Information that is lost unless industry is willing to share.

long ago, and nonproliferation efforts had to follow as soon as possible, if we were to stay ahead of proliferation activities!

For a globally acting enterprise with subsidiaries in almost all Asian countries and permanently expanding production in China, the consequences include the following:

- One needs to be aware of sensitive procurement efforts in Asia.
- The vulnerability of Asia to proliferation activity makes it necessary to cooperate with authorities in Asia.
- A certain part of the Asia business should be controlled by the company headquarters.
- Sensitive inquiries received in Asia need to be shared with governmental authorities as well, owing to the support that Asian countries receive from the European Union and the United States.

Outlook: Where Do We Go?

Prerequisites

A good internal compliance program is not "heaven sent"; rather, it is the result of a deliberate effort. In high-tech companies—and these are the ones that are in constant danger of committing violations—a few rules should be followed:

1. There must be a clear management commitment to nonproliferation and compliance with regulations.
2. Sufficient time and resources must be provided to the compliance personnel.
3. The post of the export control manager must be assigned to a senior person with a strong technical background, applied knowledge, and a direct reporting line to the CEO.
4. The compliance organization must be both global and centralized.
5. There should be proactive cooperation with governmental authorities, including mutual information sharing.

Information Sharing in Selected EU Countries

The German and British governments started to bolster cooperation with their companies following a series of embarrassing revelations about equipment sent from these companies in the 1970s and 1980s to illicit nuclear programs in Pakistan, Iraq, Iran, and North Korea. German companies in particular faced the threat of trade bans imposed by other countries, despite the fact that they were renowned worldwide for the quality of their products. In the late 1980s and early 1990s, the British and German governments began to institute the reforms that were the predecessor to more advanced and efficient export control systems.

The British system authorizes a government "Acquisition Team," situated in the domestic intelligence service, to maintain contact with about 2,500 British companies, trade associations, and academic institutions. This program is voluntary; it has no power to compel cooperation. From companies, trade associations, and academia, the team receives technical advice and information about inquiries and orders from entities of concern, and suspicious inquiries from unknown entities. Team members provide confidential tips and lists of suspicious companies related to sensitive WMD programs.

Each year, the team meets face-to-face with over a hundred companies or contacts. As a result of these visits, the government in the vast majority of cases obtains operational intelligence. In a large number of cases, follow-up actions result in disruptions or improved compliance.

The German system also operates successfully on the basis of mutual trust. The government provides German companies confidential "early warning" letters that include lists of suspicious entities and strategies used by proliferant states. Companies forward suspicious inquiries to authorities on a voluntary basis. In the nuclear area, government officials meet periodically with key company officials to provide tips to be on the lookout for specific illicit procurement trading companies, technical specifications, and end users. In turn, they receive important information from the companies. Upon receiving these tips, a company's export control office may also review its recent inquiry data from all sales offices and report back to the authorities about any contact with these entities.

Common to the British and German systems is the notion that government and industry will prevent more illicit trade by working together because they both have limited access to each other's information about illicit procurement attempts and suspicious inquiries. Companies have intimate knowledge about the underlying technologies of their products and their potential misuse, usually far better than the government's knowledge. Governments have greater access to knowledge about illicit trading networks and suspicious entities. By working together, companies face less risk of inadvertent illegal exports and governments gain access to a range of invaluable information useful in stopping illicit trade domestically and internationally. As trust has been built in Britain and Germany, these relationships have become critical to both countries' efforts to thwart illicit nuclear trade to Iran and other sensitive countries.

Creating "Win-Win" Situations on a Broader Front

I have no doubt that the model of industry-government cooperation is transferable to more companies and could also be applied in more countries. There will be hurdles, such as the fear of company officials that giving too much information to authorities may result in prosecution of the company. This problem can be solved by assigning the industry liaison task to an authority with no obligation to automatically prosecute when it hears about a possible violation.

There can, however, also be no doubt that the initial discussions about possible cooperation must be held between experienced security officials and the company's top management; otherwise, the cooperation would not be authorized, and the export control manager might not know when and to what extent he could be violating the confidentiality agreement in his or her employment contract.

The authority, in return, could give assurances that the data the company provides will be kept in a secure area or work space with a strict access procedure, and will not be shared with other authorities; that any source information would be classified, and, most important, that nothing would leak through to the public.

Once the rules are agreed on, there will be only winners, on both sides. The authorities will gain invaluable information, while the enterprise gains trust and the occasional tip provided to protect it against illicit procurement efforts.

There would, no doubt, also be losers (the front companies and the illicit programs), which is the real goal of the activity and the most important part of the success story.

Is the "information-sharing" model worth a global roll-out, and, if so, who should participate? In an interview with the investigative German journalist Egmont R. Koch, the Dutch businessman Henk Slebos and (as he admitted) a close friend of Pakistani nuclear scientist Dr. A. Q. Kahn said Pakistan had had approximately 1,000 suppliers for its nuclear program. Assuming that this figure includes the suppliers of infrastructure and peripheral accessories, the number of "core technology" suppliers must be considerably lower.

While every enrichment method may have its own indispensable core technology, gas centrifuge enrichment is impossible without vacuums. Other indispensable parts are the balancing machines, frequency converters, mass spectrometers, and, assuming a country does not have the latest carbon fiber centrifuge designs, special grade aluminum or maraging steel.

Working with the IAEA

For several years, Oerlikon Leybold Vacuum has been cooperating with the IAEA. A new unit in the Department of Safeguards analyzes data obtained from member states that agree to share information with the IAEA, in full accordance with UN Resolution 1540.

It is with the full knowledge, support, and participation of the member states that a few companies already contribute to the state evaluation process and to the institutional memory of the IAEA. It is desirable that many more company CEOs commit to support fully the IAEA and comply with its request to share potentially sensitive inquiries. The inquiries are encrypted when passed on, and the data are stored and evaluated by a few authorized staff members only. The offices are in secure areas, with keypad-activated alarms, and the unit's computer network itself is strictly separated from the normal computer network that the IAEA maintains, including its e-mail system. The fact that the "Trade & Technology Analysis" unit is part of the much larger IT division within the Department of Safeguards guarantees the highest level of confidentiality and professionalism.

Consideration should be given to establishing similar analysis units for non-nuclear weapons and missiles, in other organizations under the umbrella of the UN or other nonproliferation regimes such as the Australia Group and the Missile Technology Control Regime.

International Outreach Activities

In the context of existing outreach activities of both the United States and the European Union, the participants from both sides—government and industry—should consider the previously mentioned idea. It should be made clear from the beginning that it is not enough just to refrain from that which is expressly forbidden. To change this mind set is not a goal that will be accomplished quickly; as with other educational endeavors, it is the reiteration of the concept, not the length of the talk, that finally makes change possible. Morality is something we are still able to learn.

Business Ethics and More Controls

What have the recent years brought to industry? Export control regulations have become more extensive and complex as more exemptions and exemptions from the exemptions were formulated. It is because of the overnuanced rules, the many unnecessary requirements, and the cost they generate, while being basically ineffective, that export controls have little acceptance in industry circles.

A voluntary self-restraint system in certain industries can help make life easier for all. If the controls become more effective through industry information, the authorities can focus on the cases where controls are really needed, since they would receive up-to-date information without delay (another advantage of the "forwarding information by mouse click").

There is not much time to lose: enrichment programs are in vogue, Iran may—contrary to its public statements—decide to enrich its low-enriched uranium to high-enriched uranium, and who knows which other countries came into the possession of the enrichment technology offered by Dr. Khan's network. Look at the opportunities that such a voluntary self-restraint initiative holds:

- With effective and relevant information, the quality of analysis improves considerably.
- All involved would focus on the critical cases, saving time and money.
- Proliferation projects and illicit weapons projects would be massively disrupted
- The exporting country and the company would both be protected.
- The model—once successful in a country—could be quickly transferred to other countries.
- Voluntary self-restraint would be motivated by moral values that are greater than pure economic interest.

If we fail to make the very best use of this opportunity for self-restraint, the export control regulations will be intensified further, and the administrative burden and, along with it, the cost for companies will grow. And there will be hardly any positive impact on covert procurement. The shopping will continue and the clandestine projects will succeed.

Appendix A. *Wall Street Journal* Op-eds

A World Free of Nuclear Weapons[1]

By George P. Shultz, William J. Perry, Henry A. Kissinger, and Sam Nunn

Nuclear weapons today present tremendous dangers, but also an historic opportunity. U.S. leadership will be required to take the world to the next stage—to a solid consensus for reversing reliance on nuclear weapons globally as a vital contribution to preventing their proliferation into potentially dangerous hands, and ultimately ending them as a threat to the world.

Nuclear weapons were essential to maintaining international security during the Cold War because they were a means of deterrence. The end of the Cold War made the doctrine of mutual Soviet-American deterrence obsolete. Deterrence continues to be a relevant consideration for many states with regard to threats from other states. But reliance on nuclear weapons for this purpose is becoming increasingly hazardous and decreasingly effective.

North Korea's recent nuclear test and Iran's refusal to stop its program to enrich uranium—potentially to weapons grade—highlight the fact that the world is now on the precipice of a new and dangerous nuclear era.

Most alarmingly, the likelihood that non-state terrorists will get their hands on nuclear weaponry is increasing. In today's war waged on world order by terrorists, nuclear weapons are the ultimate means of mass devastation. And non-state terrorist groups with nuclear weapons are conceptually outside the bounds of a deterrent strategy and present difficult new security challenges.

Apart from the terrorist threat, unless urgent new actions are taken, the United States soon will be compelled to enter a new nuclear era that will be more precarious, psychologically disorienting, and economically even more costly than was Cold War deterrence. It is far from certain that we can successfully replicate the old Soviet-American "mutually assured destruction" with an increasing number of potential nuclear enemies worldwide without dramatically increasing the risk that nuclear weapons will be used. New nuclear states do not have the benefit of years of step-by-step safeguards put in effect during the Cold War to prevent nuclear accidents, misjudgments, or unauthorized launches. The United States and the Soviet Union learned from mistakes that were less than fatal. Both countries were diligent to ensure that no nuclear weapon was used during the Cold War by design or by accident. Will new nuclear nations and the world be as fortunate in the next 50 years as we were during the Cold War?

Leaders addressed this issue in earlier times. In his "Atoms for Peace" address to the United Nations in 1953, Dwight D. Eisenhower pledged America's "determination to help solve the fearful atomic dilemma—to devote its entire heart and mind to find the way by which the miraculous inventiveness of man shall not be dedicated to his death, but consecrated to his life." John F. Kennedy, seeking to break the logjam on nuclear disarmament, said, "The world was not meant to be a prison in which man awaits his execution."

Rajiv Gandhi, addressing the U.N. General Assembly on June 9, 1988, appealed, "Nuclear war will not mean the death of a hundred million people. Or even a thousand million. It will mean the extinction of four thousand million: the end of life as we know it on our planet earth. We come to the United Nations to seek your support. We seek your support to put a stop to this madness."

Ronald Reagan called for the abolishment of "all nuclear weapons," which he considered to be "totally irrational, totally inhumane, good for nothing but killing, possibly destructive of life on earth and civilization." Mikhail Gorbachev shared this vision, which had also been expressed by previous American presidents.

Although Reagan and Gorbachev failed at Reykjavik to achieve the goal of an agreement to get rid of all nuclear weapons, they did succeed in turning the arms race on its head. They initiated steps leading to significant reductions in deployed long- and intermediate-range nuclear forces, including the elimination of an entire class of threatening missiles.

What will it take to rekindle the vision shared by Reagan and Gorbachev? Can a world-wide consensus be forged that defines a series of practical steps leading to major reductions in the nuclear danger? There is an urgent need to address the challenge posed by these two questions.

The Non-Proliferation Treaty (NPT) envisioned the end of all nuclear weapons. It provides (a) that states that did not possess nuclear weapons as of 1967 agree not to obtain them, and (b) that states that do possess them agree to divest themselves of these weapons over time. Every president of both parties since Richard Nixon has reaffirmed these treaty obligations, but non-nuclear weapon states have grown increasingly skeptical of the sincerity of the nuclear powers.

Strong non-proliferation efforts are under way. The Cooperative Threat Reduction program, the Global Threat Reduction Initiative, the Proliferation Security Initiative and the Additional Protocols are innovative approaches that provide powerful new tools for detecting activities that violate the NPT and endanger world security. They deserve full implementation. The negotiations on proliferation of nuclear weapons by North Korea and Iran, involving all the permanent members of the Security Council plus Germany and Japan, are crucially important. They must be energetically pursued.

But by themselves, none of these steps are adequate to the danger. Reagan and Gorbachev aspired to accomplish more at their meeting in Reykjavik 20 years ago—the elimination of nuclear weapons altogether. Their vision shocked experts in the doctrine of nuclear deterrence, but galvanized the hopes of people around the world. The leaders of the two countries with the largest arsenals of nuclear weapons discussed the abolition of their most powerful weapons.

What should be done? Can the promise of the NPT and the possibilities envisioned at Reykjavik be brought to fruition? We believe that a major effort should be launched by the United States to produce a positive answer through concrete stages.

First and foremost is intensive work with leaders of the countries in possession of nuclear weapons to turn the goal of a world without nuclear weapons into a joint enterprise. Such a joint enterprise, by involving changes in the disposition of the states possessing nuclear weapons, would lend additional weight to efforts already under way to avoid the emergence of a nuclear-armed North Korea and Iran.

The program on which agreements should be sought would constitute a series of agreed and urgent steps that would lay the groundwork for a world free of the nuclear threat. Steps would include:

- Changing the Cold War posture of deployed nuclear weapons to increase warning time and thereby reduce the danger of an accidental or unauthorized use of a nuclear weapon.
- Continuing to reduce substantially the size of nuclear forces in all states that possess them.
- Eliminating short-range nuclear weapons designed to be forward-deployed.
- Initiating a bipartisan process with the Senate, including understandings to increase confidence and provide for periodic review, to achieve ratification of the Comprehensive Test Ban Treaty, taking advantage of recent technical advances, and working to secure ratification by other key states.
- Providing the highest possible standards of security for all stocks of weapons, weapons-usable plutonium, and highly enriched uranium everywhere in the world.
- Getting control of the uranium enrichment process, combined with the guarantee that uranium for nuclear power reactors could be obtained at a reasonable price, first from the Nuclear Suppliers Group and then from the International Atomic Energy Agency or other controlled international reserves. It will also be necessary to deal with proliferation issues presented by spent fuel from reactors producing electricity.
- Halting the production of fissile material for weapons globally; phasing out the use of highly enriched uranium in civil commerce

and removing weapons-usable uranium from research facilities around the world and rendering the materials safe.

- Redoubling our efforts to resolve regional confrontations and conflicts that give rise to new nuclear powers.

Achieving the goal of a world free of nuclear weapons will also require effective measures to impede or counter any nuclear-related conduct that is potentially threatening to the security of any state or peoples.

Reassertion of the vision of a world free of nuclear weapons and practical measures toward achieving that goal would be, and would be perceived as, a bold initiative consistent with America's moral heritage. The effort could have a profoundly positive impact on the security of future generations. Without the bold vision, the actions will not be perceived as fair or urgent. Without the actions, the vision will not be perceived as realistic or possible.

We endorse setting the goal of a world free of nuclear weapons and working energetically on the actions required to achieve that goal, beginning with the measures outlined above.

Mr. Shultz, a distinguished fellow at the Hoover Institution at Stanford, was secretary of state from 1982 to 1989. Mr. Perry was secretary of defense from 1994 to 1997. Mr. Kissinger, chairman of Kissinger Associates, was secretary of state from 1973 to 1977. Mr. Nunn is former chairman of the Senate Armed Services Committee.

A conference organized by Mr. Shultz and Sidney D. Drell was held at Hoover to reconsider the vision that Reagan and Gorbachev brought to Reykjavik. In addition to Messrs. Shultz and Drell, the following participants also endorse the view in this statement: Martin Anderson, Steve Andreasen, Michael Armacost, William Crowe, James Goodby, Thomas Graham Jr., Thomas Henriksen, David Holloway, Max Kampelman, Jack Matlock, John McLaughlin, Don Oberdorfer, Rozanne Ridgway, Henry Rowen, Roald Sagdeev, and Abraham Sofaer.

Toward a Nuclear-Free World[2]

By George P. Shultz, William J. Perry, Henry A. Kissinger, and Sam Nunn

The accelerating spread of nuclear weapons, nuclear know-how and nuclear material has brought us to a nuclear tipping point. We face a very real possibility that the deadliest weapons ever invented could fall into dangerous hands.

The steps we are taking now to address these threats are not adequate to the danger. With nuclear weapons more widely available, deterrence is decreasingly effective and increasingly hazardous.

One year ago, in an essay in this paper, we called for a global effort to reduce reliance on nuclear weapons, to prevent their spread into potentially dangerous hands, and ultimately to end them as a threat to the world. The interest, momentum and growing political space that has been created to address these issues over the past year has been extraordinary, with strong positive responses from people all over the world.

Mikhail Gorbachev wrote in January 2007 that, as someone who signed the first treaties on real reductions in nuclear weapons, he thought it his duty to support our call for urgent action: "It is becoming clearer that nuclear weapons are no longer a means of achieving security; in fact, with every passing year they make our security more precarious."

In June, the United Kingdom's foreign secretary, Margaret Beckett, signaled her government's support, stating: "What we need is both a vision—a scenario for a world free of nuclear weapons—and action—progressive steps to reduce warhead numbers and to limit the role of nuclear weapons in security policy. These two strands are separate but they are mutually reinforcing. Both are necessary, but at the moment too weak."

We have also been encouraged by additional indications of general support for this project from other former U.S. officials with extensive experience as secretaries of state and defense and national security advisors. These include: Madeleine Albright, Richard V. Allen, James A. Baker III, Samuel R. Berger, Zbigniew Brzezinski, Frank Carlucci, Warren Christopher, William Cohen, Lawrence Eagleburger, Melvin Laird, Anthony Lake, Robert McFarlane, Robert McNamara, and Colin Powell.

Inspired by this reaction, in October 2007, we convened veterans of the past six administrations, along with a number of other experts on nuclear issues, for a conference at Stanford University's Hoover Institution. There was general agreement about the importance of the vision of a world free of nuclear weapons as a guide to our thinking about nuclear policies, and about the importance of a series of steps that will pull us back from the nuclear precipice.

The United States and Russia, which possess close to 95 percent of the world's nuclear warheads, have a special responsibility, obligation and experience to demonstrate leadership, but other nations must join.

Some steps are already in progress, such as the ongoing reductions in the number of nuclear warheads deployed on long-range, or strategic, bombers and missiles. Other near-term steps that the United States and Russia could take, beginning in 2008, can in and of themselves dramatically reduce nuclear dangers. They include:

- *Extend key provisions of the Strategic Arms Reduction Treaty of 1991.* Much has been learned about the vital task of verification from the application of these provisions. The treaty is scheduled to expire on Dec. 5, 2009. The key provisions of this treaty, including their essential monitoring and verification requirements, should be extended, and the further reductions agreed upon in the 2002 Moscow Treaty on Strategic Offensive Reductions should be completed as soon as possible.
- *Take steps to increase the warning and decision times for the launch of all nuclear-armed ballistic missiles, thereby reducing risks of accidental or unauthorized attacks.* Reliance on launch procedures that deny command authorities sufficient time to

make careful and prudent decisions is unnecessary and dangerous in today's environment. Furthermore, developments in cyber-warfare pose new threats that could have disastrous consequences if the command-and-control systems of any nuclear-weapons state were compromised by mischievous or hostile hackers. Further steps could be implemented in time, as trust grows in the U.S.-Russian relationship, by introducing mutually agreed and verified physical barriers in the command-and-control sequence.

- *Discard any existing operational plans for massive attacks that still remain from the Cold War days.* Interpreting deterrence as requiring mutual assured destruction (MAD) is an obsolete policy in today's world, with the United States and Russia formally having declared that they are allied against terrorism and no longer perceive each other as enemies.

- *Undertake negotiations toward developing cooperative multilateral ballistic-missile defense and early warning systems, as proposed by Presidents Bush and Putin at their 2002 Moscow summit meeting.* This should include agreement on plans for countering missile threats to Europe, Russia and the United States from the Middle East, along with completion of work to establish the Joint Data Exchange Center in Moscow. Reducing tensions over missile defense will enhance the possibility of progress on the broader range of nuclear issues so essential to our security. Failure to do so will make broader nuclear cooperation much more difficult.

- *Dramatically accelerate work to provide the highest possible standards of security for nuclear weapons, as well as for nuclear materials everywhere in the world, to prevent terrorists from acquiring a nuclear bomb.* There are nuclear weapons materials in more than 40 countries around the world, and there are recent reports of alleged attempts to smuggle nuclear material in Eastern Europe and the Caucasus. The United States, Russia and other nations that have worked with the Nunn-Lugar programs, in cooperation with the International Atomic Energy Agency (IAEA), should play a key role in helping to implement

United Nations Security Council Resolution 1540 relating to improving nuclear security—by offering teams to assist jointly any nation in meeting its obligations under this resolution to provide for appropriate, effective security of these materials.

As Gov. Arnold Schwarzenegger put it in his address at our October conference, "Mistakes are made in every other human endeavor. Why should nuclear weapons be exempt?" To underline the governor's point, on August 29–30, 2007, six cruise missiles armed with nuclear warheads were loaded on a U.S. Air Force plane, flown across the country and unloaded. For 36 hours, no one knew where the warheads were, or even that they were missing.

- *Start a dialogue, including within NATO and with Russia, on consolidating the nuclear weapons designed for forward deployment to enhance their security, and as a first step toward careful accounting for them and their eventual elimination.* These smaller and more portable nuclear weapons are, given their characteristics, inviting acquisition targets for terrorist groups.

- *Strengthen the means of monitoring compliance with the nuclear Non-Proliferation Treaty (NPT) as a counter to the global spread of advanced technologies.* More progress in this direction is urgent, and could be achieved through requiring the application of monitoring provisions (Additional Protocols) designed by the IAEA to all signatories of the NPT.

- *Adopt a process for bringing the Comprehensive Test Ban Treaty (CTBT) into effect, which would strengthen the NPT and aid international monitoring of nuclear activities.* This calls for a bipartisan review, first, to examine improvements over the past decade of the international monitoring system to identify and locate explosive underground nuclear tests in violation of the CTBT; and, second, to assess the technical progress made over the past decade in maintaining high confidence in the reliability, safety and effectiveness of the nation's nuclear arsenal under a test ban. The Comprehensive Test Ban Treaty Organization is putting in place new monitoring stations to detect nuclear tests—an effort the United States should urgently support even prior to ratification.

In parallel with these steps by the United States and Russia, the dialogue must broaden on an international scale, including non-nuclear as well as nuclear nations.

Key subjects include turning the goal of a world without nuclear weapons into a practical enterprise among nations, by applying the necessary political will to build an international consensus on priorities. The government of Norway will sponsor a conference in February that will contribute to this process.

Another subject: Developing an international system to manage the risks of the nuclear fuel cycle. With the growing global interest in developing nuclear energy and the potential proliferation of nuclear enrichment capabilities, an international program should be created by advanced nuclear countries and a strengthened IAEA. The purpose should be to provide for reliable supplies of nuclear fuel, reserves of enriched uranium, infrastructure assistance, financing, and spent fuel management—to ensure that the means to make nuclear weapons materials isn't spread around the globe.

There should also be an agreement to undertake further substantial reductions in United States and Russian nuclear forces beyond those recorded in the U.S.-Russia Strategic Offensive Reductions Treaty. As the reductions proceed, other nuclear nations would become involved.

President Reagan's maxim of "trust but verify" should be reaffirmed. Completing a verifiable treaty to prevent nations from producing nuclear materials for weapons would contribute to a more rigorous system of accounting and security for nuclear materials.

We should also build an international consensus on ways to deter or, when required, to respond to, secret attempts by countries to break out of agreements.

Progress must be facilitated by a clear statement of our ultimate goal. Indeed, this is the only way to build the kind of international trust and broad cooperation that will be required to effectively address today's threats. Without the vision of moving toward zero, we will not find the essential cooperation required to stop our downward spiral.

In some respects, the goal of a world free of nuclear weapons is like the top of a very tall mountain. From the vantage point of our troubled world today, we can't even see the top of the mountain, and it is tempting and easy to say we can't get there from here. But the risks from continuing to go down the mountain or standing pat are too real to ignore. We must chart a course to higher ground where the mountaintop becomes more visible.

Mr. Shultz was secretary of state from 1982 to 1989. Mr. Perry was secretary of defense from 1994 to 1997. Mr. Kissinger was secretary of state from 1973 to 1977. Mr. Nunn is former chairman of the Senate Armed Services Committee.

The following participants in the Hoover-NTI conference also endorse the view in this statement: General John Abizaid, Graham Allison, Brooke Anderson, Martin Anderson, Steve Andreasen, Mike Armacost, Bruce Blair, Matt Bunn, Ashton Carter, Sidney Drell, General Vladimir Dvorkin, Bob Einhorn, Mark Fitzpatrick, James Goodby, Rose Gottemoeller, Tom Graham, David Hamburg, Siegfried Hecker, Tom Henriksen, David Holloway, Raymond Jeanloz, Ray Juzaitis, Max Kampelman, Jack Matlock, Michael McFaul, John McLaughlin, Don Oberdorfer, Pavel Podvig, William Potter, Richard Rhodes, Joan Rohlfing, Scott Sagan, Roald Sagdeev, Abe Sofaer, Richard Solomon, and Philip Zelikow.

Appendix B. Workshop Attendees

The following individuals were confirmed participants at the expert meeting, Verification, Monitoring, and Enforcement for a World Free of Nuclear Weapons, held January 14–January 15, 2009. Affiliations are for identification purposes only.

David Albright, Institute for Science and International Security
Steven P. Andreasen, Consultant
Everet H. Beckner, Consultant
Joe Cirincione, Ploughshares Fund
Steve Fetter, University of Maryland
Trevor Findlay, Canadian Centre for Treaty Compliance
Jim Fuller, Consultant
Mark Goodman, NNSA, U.S. Department of Energy
Rose Gottemoeller, Carnegie Endowment for International Peace
Corey Hinderstein, Nuclear Threat Initiative
Steinar Høibråten, Norwegian Defense Research Establishment
Laura Holgate, Nuclear Threat Initiative
Richard Hooper, Consultant
Sally Horn, Consultant
Edward Ifft, Georgetown University
Ray Juzaitis, Texas A&M University
Susan Koch, Consultant
Roger Molander, RAND
George Perkovich, Carnegie Endowment for International Peace
Arian Pregenzer, Sandia National Laboratories

Joan Rohlfing, Nuclear Threat Initiative
Scott Sagan, Stanford University
Peter Sawczak, Embassy of Australia
Larry Scheinman, Monterey Institute of International Studies
Matthew Sharp, Harvard University
Thomas E. Shea, Pacific Northwest National Laboratory
Jim Tape, Consultant
Isabelle Williams, Nuclear Threat Initiative
Ralf Wirtz, OC Oerlikon Management AG

About the Contributors

Steven P. Andreasen

Steven P. Andreasen is a national security consultant with the Nuclear Threat Initiative (NTI) in Washington, DC, and teaches courses on national security policy and crisis management in foreign affairs at the Hubert H. Humphrey Institute of Public Affairs, University of Minnesota. He served as Director for Defense Policy and Arms Control on the National Security Council at the White House from February 1993 to January 2001. He was the principal advisor on strategic policy, nuclear arms control, and missile defense to the national security advisor and the president. During the George H. W. Bush and Reagan administrations, Andreasen served in the State Department's Bureau of Politico-Military Affairs and the Bureau of Intelligence and Research, dealing with a wide range of defense policy, arms control, nuclear weapons, and intelligence issues. As a Presidential Management Fellow, he served as a Special Assistant to Ambassador Paul H. Nitze in the State Department focusing on the Strategic Arms Reduction Talks, and as a Foreign Policy and Defense Legislative Assistant in the office of Senator Albert Gore, Jr. Andreasen received his BA from Gustavus Adolphus College in 1984 and graduated with an MA from the Hubert H. Humphrey Institute of Public Affairs at the University of Minnesota in 1986.

Everet H. Beckner

Everet H. Beckner received his PhD in physics from Rice University in 1961. He joined the research staff at Sandia National Laboratories, Albuquerque, New Mexico, to conduct research in plasma physics. He later became Manager of the Inertial Confinement Fusion program, then Director of the Waste Management Program before being named Vice President of Energy Programs in 1983. In 1986, he became Vice President of Defense Programs. He left Sandia in 1991 to become Principal Deputy Assistant Secretary for Defense Programs for the U.S. Department of Energy. In 1996, he joined the Energy and Environment Sector of Lockheed Martin Corporation as VP for Technical Operations and subsequently became Deputy General Manager of the United Kingdom Atomic Weapons Establishment at Aldermaston. In 2001, he returned to the United States to become Deputy Administrator for Defense Programs of the National Nuclear Security Administration (NNSA). He retired from NNSA in 2005 and presently consults for several companies as well as the U.S. government. Beckner is a fellow of the American Physical Society

James Fuller

James Fuller is an affiliate professor in the Henry M. Jackson School of International Studies at the University of Washington and also serves as a member of its Visiting Committee. For many years, until his retirement in 2003, he was Director of Defense Nuclear Nonproliferation Programs at the Pacific Northwest National Laboratory in Richland, Washington. He holds a PhD in nuclear science, specializing in plasma physics, from the University of Florida. He is credited as a team member with developing and demonstrating the first nuclear driven laser. He served in the U.S. government as a national lab scientist in many capacities in his career, most recently on work related to nuclear weapons material control and nuclear warhead dismantlement monitoring. Some relevant examples of this service include: Executive Secretary in the first Bush administration of the President's Committee on Fissile Material Control and Nuclear Warhead Monitoring, Scientific Peer Review Group Chairman of the NNSA Warhead Radiation Signatures Campaign, and Chair of the NNSA Information Barrier Advisory Group—a group whose task it was to develop equipment to monitor nuclear warhead dismantlement on a bilateral or multilateral basis with other nuclear states. He was heavily involved in the U.S.-Russian Warhead Safety and Security Exchange (WSSX) Agreement. Recently he was a member of a United States National Academy of Sciences group working in cooperation with the Russian Federation Academy of Sciences to study the future of the U.S.-Russian nuclear security relationship.

Corey Hinderstein

Corey Hinderstein is Vice President for International Programs of the Nuclear Threat Initiative (NTI). At NTI, Hinderstein leads projects related to the improvement of nuclear material security worldwide, new and emerging proliferations challenges, the minimization of commercial uses of highly enriched uranium, and other international nuclear risk reduction efforts. She also led NTI's work in developing and launching the new World Institute for Nuclear Security (WINS), an international organization based in Vienna. Previously, Hinderstein was Deputy Director and Senior Analyst at the Institute for Science and International Security (ISIS). She is a Term Member of the Council on Foreign Relations, member-at-large on the international Executive Committee for the Institute of Nuclear Materials Management (INMM), member-at-large on the Board of Directors of ISIS, and a member of Women in International Security. She graduated cum laude from Clark University in Worcester, Massachusetts, where she was elected to Phi Beta Kappa.

Steinar Høibråten

Steinar Høibråten is a Chief Scientist at the Norwegian Defence Research Establishment (FFI). He holds a PhD in experimental nuclear physics from MIT and a M.Sc. in engineering physics from the Norwegian Institute of Technology at the University of Trondheim. Before joining FFI in 1994, he did postdoctoral work in basic nuclear physics at the University of Colorado and the University of Virginia. At FFI, he has worked on many aspects of "defense-related nuclear physics," including nuclear weapons, nuclear submarines, and related environmental and waste-handling issues. In 2003, Høibråten served as a nuclear weapons inspector in Iraq for the International Atomic Energy Agency (IAEA) and the United Nations.

Edward Ifft

Edward Ifft, a retired member of the Senior Executive Service, has been involved in negotiating and implementing many of the key arms control agreements of the past 40 years. He has a PhD in physics from Ohio State University and is a graduate of the Senior Managers in Government program at Harvard University. Ifft's career has been primarily in the State Department, with assignments in the United States Arms Control and Disarmament Agency, NASA, and the Department of Defense. He served on the U.S. delegations to the negotiations on SALT, TTBT, START, and the CTBT. He served as Senior Policy Advisor and then Senior State Department Representative to the START negotiations in Geneva and was also Deputy Chief United States Negotiator during 1988. After START concluded, he became Deputy Director of the On-Site Inspection Agency (OSIA). When OSIA was incorporated into the new Defense Threat Reduction Agency (DTRA) in 1998, he became Senior Advisor and State Department liaison to DTRA. As a U.S. START Inspector, he has participated in inspections of many sensitive military installations in the former Soviet Union. He also served as the last United States Commissioner (Acting) for the ABM Treaty until the United States withdrew from the treaty in 2002. Ifft is the author of many articles in scholarly journals published in the United States, Europe, and Russia, as well as of chapters in two books published by the United Nations. He continues to work part-time at the U.S. State Department and is an adjunct professor in the Security Studies Program of the Walsh School of Foreign Service at Georgetown University.

Halvor Kippe

Halvor Kippe is a Senior Scientist at the Norwegian Defence Research Establishment (FFI), specializing in nuclear nonproliferation and disarmament studies. Kippe is particularly interested in emerging (potential) nuclear weapons states, such as North Korea and Iran. Radiological terrorism has also been a field of interest, and he has, together with Høibråten, taken part in the cooperation between the United Kingdom and Norway exploring non–nuclear weapon states' verification of nuclear disarmament. He holds an M.Sc. in particle physics from the University of Oslo.

Harald Müller

Harald Müller is Director of the Peace Research Institute Frankfurt (PRIF) and a professor of international relations at Goethe University

Frankfurt, Germany. He is a visiting professor at the Johns Hopkins University Center for International Relations in Bologna, Italy. Müller was a member of the Advisory Board on Disarmament Matters of the United Nations Secretary General from 1999 to 2005 (chair in 2004); of the German delegations to the NPT Review Conferences in 1995, 2000, and 2005; and of the IAEA Expert Group on Multinational Nuclear Arrangements in 2004–2005. He has written intensely on matters of international security, arms control, disarmament, and nonproliferation as well as on international relations theory. His latest book is *Building a New World Order: Sustainable Policies for the Future* (2009).

Annette Schaper

Annette Schaper is senior research associate at the Peace Research Institute Frankfurt (PRIF). Her research covers nuclear arms control and its technical aspects, including the test ban, a fissile material cutoff, verification of nuclear disarmament, fissile materials disposition, and nonproliferation problems arising from the civilian-military ambivalence of science and technology. She was a part-time member of the German delegation to the Conference on Disarmament in Geneva in the CTBT negotiations and member of the German delegation at the NPT Review and Extension Conference. Schaper holds a PhD in physics from Düsseldorf University.

Thomas E. Shea

Thomas E. Shea is a senior staff member at the Pacific Northwest National Laboratory Center for Global Security and adjunct professor at Washington State University. He is an expert in international nuclear security, including policy analysis and technological and institutional mechanisms addressing nonproliferation, arms control and disarmament, the global expansion of nuclear power, and nuclear safeguards. Prior to joining PNNL in 2004, Shea served for 24 years in the IAEA Safeguards Department where, in addition to safeguards assignments, he headed the Trilateral Initiative Office and led IAEA studies in a fissile material cutoff treaty. He is the recipient of the 2007 Institute of Nuclear Materials Management Distinguished Service Award, a member of the International Nuclear Energy Academy, and a member of the

Scientific Board, Landau Network–Centro Volta in Como, Italy. Shea holds a PhD in nuclear science from Rensselaer Polytechnic Institute.

Ralf Wirtz

Ralf Wirtz is currently Head of Global Trade Control with Swiss Oerlikon group of companies, in charge of implementing, maintaining, and improving trade compliance for all segments of the company. The company actively supports the European Union and the United States Export Control Outreach to a variety of countries. In this role, Wirtz identifies and repels clandestine procurement activities of nuclear programs and helps establish industry-government information sharing. Oerlikon Leybold Vacuum was one of the first companies to contribute to the International Atomic Energy Agency's Procurement Outreach Program. Previously, Wirtz held positions with Leybold Heraeus and Leybold AG as export control manager of the Leybold vacuum pump and component business and international sales.

Index